Visit us at

www.syngress.com

Syngress is committed to publishing high-quality books for IT Professionals and delivering those books in media and formats that fit the demands of our customers. We are also committed to extending the utility of the book you purchase via additional materials available from our Web site.

SOLUTIONS WEB SITE

To register your book, visit www.syngress.com/solutions. Once registered, you can access our solutions@syngress.com Web pages. There you may find an assortment of valueadded features such as free e-books related to the topic of this book, URLs of related Web sites, FAQs from the book, corrections, and any updates from the author(s).

ULTIMATE CDs

Our Ultimate CD product line offers our readers budget-conscious compilations of some of our best-selling backlist titles in Adobe PDF form. These CDs are the perfect way to extend your reference library on key topics pertaining to your area of expertise, including Cisco Engineering, Microsoft Windows System Administration, CyberCrime Investigation, Open Source Security, and Firewall Configuration, to name a few.

DOWNLOADABLE E-BOOKS

For readers who can't wait for hard copy, we offer most of our titles in downloadable Adobe PDF form. These e-books are often available weeks before hard copies, and are priced affordably.

SYNGRESS OUTLET

Our outlet store at syngress.com features overstocked, out-of-print, or slightly hurt books at significant savings.

SITE LICENSING

Syngress has a well-established program for site licensing our e-books onto servers in corporations, educational institutions, and large organizations. Contact us at sales@syngress.com for more information.

CUSTOM PUBLISHING

Many organizations welcome the ability to combine parts of multiple Syngress books, as well as their own content, into a single volume for their own internal use. Contact us at sales@syngress.com for more information.

OSSEC Host-Based Intrusion Detection Guide

Andrew Hay
Daniel Cid, Creator of OSSEC
Rory Bray

Foreword by
Stephen Northcutt, President
The SANS Technology Institute,
a post graduate security college
www.sans.edu

KEY	SERIAL NUMBER
001	HJIRTCV764
002	PO9873D5FG
003	829KM8NJH2
004	BAL923457U
005	CVPLQ6WQ23
006	VBP965T5T5
007	HJJJ863WD3E
008	2987GVTWMK
009	629MP5SDJT
010	IMWQ295T6T

PUBLISHED BY
Syngress Publishing, Inc.
Elsevier, Inc.
30 Corporate Drive
Burlington, MA 01803

OSSEC Host-Based Intrusion Detection Guide

Printed in the United States of America
1 2 3 4 5 6 7 8 9 0

ISBN 13: 978-1-59749-240-9

Page Layout and Art: SPi
Copy Editor: Beth Roberts

For information on rights, translations, and bulk sales, contact Matt Pedersen, Commercial Sales Director and Rights, at Syngress Publishing; email m.pedersen@elsevier.com.

Lead Authors

Andrew Hay leads a team of software developers at Q1 Labs Inc. integrating 3rd party event and vulnerability data into QRadar, their flagship network security management solution. Prior to joining Q1 Labs, Andrew was CEO and co-founder of Koteas Corporation, a leading provider of end to end security and privacy solutions for government and enterprise. His resume also includes such organizations as Nokia Enterprise Solutions, Nortel Networks, and Magma Communications, a division of Primus. Andrew is a strong advocate of security training, certification programs, and public awareness initiatives. He also holds several industry certifications including the CCNA, CCSA, CCSE, CCSE NGX, CCSE Plus, Security+, GCIA, GCIH, SSP-MPA, SSP-CNSA, NSA, RHCT, and RHCE.

Andrew would first like to thank his wife Keli for her support, guidance, and unlimited understanding when it comes to his interests. He would also like to thank George Hanna, Chris Cahill, Chris Fanjoy, Daniella Degrace, Shawn McPartlin, the Trusted Catalyst Community, and of course his parents, Michel and Ellen Hay (and no mom, this is nothing like Star Trek), for their continued support. He would also like to thank Daniel Cid for creating such a great product.

Daniel Cid is the creator and main developer of the OSSEC HIDS (Open Source Security Host Intrusion Detection System). Daniel has been working in the security area for many years, with a special interest in intrusion detection, log analysis and secure development. He is currently working at Q1 Labs Inc. as a software engineer. In the past, he worked at Sourcefire, NIH and Opensolutions. Daniel holds several industry certifications including the CCNP, GCIH, and CISSP.

Daniel would like to thank God for the gift of life, his wife Liliane for all the help and understanding, his son, Davi, for all the countless nights without sleep, and his family for all the support in life so far.

Rory Bray is senior software engineer at Q1 Labs Inc. with years of experience developing Internet and security related services. In addition to being a long-time advocate of Open Source software, Rory has developed a strong interest in network security and secure development practices. Rory has a diverse background which includes embedded development, web application design, software architecture, security consulting and technical editing. This broad range of experience provides a unique perspective on security solutions.

Rory would like to thank his lovely wife Rachel for putting up with the interruptions to normal life caused by work on this book. His career path has always been a hectic one, requiring a great deal of her patience and flexibility. He knows it has never been easy to live with a member of the "Nerd Herd".

The authors would like to thank Andrew Williams at Syngress for his help, support, and understanding as we worked together through our first book. We'd also like the thank Anton Chuvakin, Peter Giannoulis, Adam Winnington, and Michael Santarcangelo for their appendix contributions and Stephen Northcutt for taking the time out of his busy schedule to write the forward.

Contributors

Dr Anton Chuvakin, GCIA, GCIH, GCFA (http://www.chuvakin.org) is a recognized security expert and book author. In his current role as a Chief Logging Evangelist with LogLogic, a log management and intelligence company, he is involved with projecting LogLogic's product vision and strategy to the outside world, conducting logging research as well as influencing company vision and roadmap.

A frequent conference speaker, he also represents the company at various security meetings and standards organizations. He is an author of a book "Security Warrior" and a contributor to "Know Your Enemy II", "Information Security Management Handbook", "Hacker's Challenge 3", "PCI Compliance" and the upcoming book on logs. Anton also published numerous papers on a broad range of security and logging subjects. In his spare time he maintains his security portal http://www.info-secure.org and several blogs such as one at http://www.securitywarrior.org". *Anton wrote Appendix A.*

Michael Santarcangelo is a human catalyst. As an expert who speaks on information protection, including compliance, privacy, and awareness, Michael energizes and inspires his audiences to change how they protect information. His passion and approach gets results that change behaviors.

As a full member of the National Speakers Association, Michael is known for delivering substantial content in a way that is energetic and entertaining. Michael connects with those he works with, and helps them engage in natural and comfortable ways. He literally makes security relevant and simple to understand!

His unique insights, innovative concepts, and effective strategies are informed by extensive experience and continued research. His first book, *Into the Breach* (early 2008; www.intothebreach.com), is the answer business executives have been looking for to defend their organization against breaches, while discovering how to increase revenue, protect the bottom line, and manage people, information, and risk efficiently. *Michael wrote Appendix B.*

Peter Giannoulis is an information security consultant in Toronto, Ontario. Over the last 9 years Peter has been involved in the design and implementation of client defenses using many different security technologies. He is also skilled in vulnerability and penetration testing having taken part in hundreds of assessments. Peter has been involved with SANS and GIAC for quite some time as an Authorized Grader for the GSEC certification, courseware author, exam developer, Advisory Board member, Stay Sharp instructor and is currently a Technical Director for the GIAC family of certifications. In the near future he will be pursuing the SANS Masters of Science Degree in Information Security Engineering. Peter's current certifications include: GSEC, GCIH, GCIA, GCFA, GCFW, GREM, CISSP, CCSI, INFOSEC, CCSP, & MCSE. *Peter contributed to Appendix C.*

Adam Winnington is a Network Security Professional in Toronto, Ontario. He helps his clients implement secure solutions that the solve problems they have in their environments. He has worked with computer networking and security for the last 15 years in large and small environments helping clients manage their infrastructure and their problems. Adam received his Masters of Science in Information Technology from the University of Liverpool; he is an instructor for Check Point, Iron Port, and Nokia. Adam has trained hundreds of individuals in the last 8 years and has developed courseware to replace or augment the documentation provided by vendors. *Adam contributed to Appendix C.*

Contents

About this Book

November 10th, 2007 – Computer consultant John Kenneth Schiefer plead guilty to four felony charges for his involvement in the compromise of as many as a quarter-million PCs. These compromised systems, or bots, were used to steal money and identities. Schiefer was able to control all of these systems, typically referred to as bot herding, from centralized servers to perform any nefarious task that he wished.

November 18th, 2007 – A MSN Trojan spreads throughout the Internet at an alarming rate. The Trojan, an IRC bot that may have been the first to include VNC server scanning capabilities, was transmitted via files disguised as photographs from people pretending to be an acquaintance.

November 9th, 2007 – Grammy award winning R&B singer Alicia Keyes has her MySpace page hacked. The attacker placed a rootkit so that unsuspecting fans who visited the site were infected with malware from an exploit site in China. If the system was patched against the exploit then the user was prompted to download and install a special codec.

These incidents are real world examples of malicious software that was installed without the consent of the end user. Unfortunately these examples are a small cross-section of one month in 2007. As scary as this might be - these were only ones that were reported. Not all websites, organizations, and users disclose that their machines were infected or compromised because, let's face it a compromise looks bad. An advertising firm may not want to let their customer know that a competitor may have stolen their fancy new advertising campaign because the firm's database was compromised. A social community website may not want to let their users know that a rootkit was somehow installed on some of their websites because it shows a weakness in their application.

"If the customer knew their campaign was stolen then we might lose the account! We won't tell them. I'm sure it will be fine."

"A rootkit? Let's clean that up before anyone notices and say that we had scheduled database maintenance during that time."

You might think that an organization would not be that reckless, but the unfortunate reality is that sometimes the risk of a cover-up is far less than the financial fallout from coming clean on a system breach. With the exception of certain regulated industries, such as the banking industry, the choice to publicize an intrusion or breach is at the discretion of the business decision makers. If you knew that the company that you were doing business with was not disclosing intrusions you would likely take your business elsewhere. However, if you were not aware of any security issues you would have no reason to leave, which is what these unscrupulous organizations are counting on.

NOTE

"Never awake me when you have good news to announce, because with good news nothing presses; but when you have bad news, arouse me immediately, for then there is not an instant to be lost."
- **Napoleon Bonaparte**

"Though it be honest, it is never good to bring bad news."
- **William Shakespeare**

"KHAAANNNN!!!!!!!!!" - **William Shatner as James T. Kirk, Star Trek III: The Wrath of Khan**

Who Should Read This Book?

This book was written for network, systems, and security administrators who are responsible for protecting assets in their infrastructure. This book is also for those involved in the incident handling process and forensic analysis of servers and workstations. Documentation on how to install and configure OSSEC has been freely available on the OSSEC website for some time, but a definitive guide has never been released. This has left very important and powerful features of the product undocumented... until now! Using this book you will be able to install and configure OSSEC, on the operating system of your choosing, and provide detailed examples to help you prevent and mitigate attacks on your systems.

Organization of the Book

Solutions In This Chapter

At the beginning of each chapter a bulleted list of the major topics is provided. This provides a high-level overview of the areas covered within the chapter.

Summary

This section summarizes the most important Solutions covered in the chapter. A brief recap of the information covered within the chapter is provided to give you a chance to go back and review any topic that you may not have found clear the first time around.

Solutions Fast Track

The Solutions Fast Track provides an outline of each topic covered within the chapter. You can use this section as a quick reference guide to quickly check which important facts are covered in each chapter.

Frequently Asked Questions

At the end of each chapter a Frequently Asked Questions, or FAQ, section lists the most common questions associated with the concepts covered in the chapter. These questions were derived from questions posed to the OSSEC mailing list, asked at conferences, or questions the authors felt might be asked in the future.

Chapter Descriptions

Here is a brief overview of the information covered in each chapter:

Chapter 1: Getting Started With OSSEC

This chapter provides an overview of the features of OSSEC including commonly used terminology, pre-install preparation, and deployment considerations.

Chapter 2: Installation

This chapter walks through the installation process for the "local", "agent", and "server" install types on some of the most popular operating systems available. Techniques to automate multiple agent installations are also covered in depth to ensure a smooth deployment across multiple systems in a large environment.

Chapter 3: Configuration

This chapter discusses the post-install configuration of OSSEC. Within this chapter you will learn the basic configuration options for your install type and learn how to monitor log files, receive remote messages, configure email notification, and configure alert levels.

Chapter 4: Working With Rules

This chapter shows you how to extract key information from logs using decoders and how you can leverage rules to alert you of strange occurrences on your network. It includes examples on how to parse atomic and composite rules, how to keep state between messages, how to remove false positives, and how to tune OSSEC appropriately for your network.

Chapter 5: System Integrity Check and Rootkit Detection

This chapter explains the system integrity check features of OSSEC, including monitoring binary executable files, system configuration files, and the Microsoft Windows registry.

Chapter 6: Active Response Configuration

Active response allows you to automatically execute "commands" or responses when a specific event, or a set of events, occur. On the OSSEC HIDS, active response is very scalable, allowing you to execute commands on the agent or on the server side. This chapter explains how to configure the active response actions you want and how to bind the actions to specific rules and sequence of events.

Chapter 7: Using the OSSEC Web User Interface

This chapter explains how to install, configure, and use the community-developed, open source web interface available for OSSEC.

Epilogue

This chapter concludes the story carried throughout the book and provides some final thoughts from the authors.

Appendix A: Log Data Mining

Dr. Anton Chuvakin, Chief Log Evangelist, LogLogic Inc.

This chapter is devoted to log mining or log knowledge discovery - a different type of log analysis, which does not rely on knowing what to look for. This takes the "high art" of log analysis to the next level by breaking the dependence on the lists of strings or patterns to look for in the logs.

Appendix B: Implementing a Successful OSSEC Policy

Michael J. Santarcangelo, II, Founder and Chief Security Catalyst, The Michaelangelo Group.

To be successful in implementing OSSEC in your organization, you need to have an effective policy to guide and support your actions. This appendix will explain the steps you need to take in order to quickly and successfully develop and implement your policy.

Appendix C: Rootkit Detection Using Host-Based IDS

By Peter Giannoulis and Adam Winnington, Information Security Consultants, Access 2 Networks

This appendix chapter provides a brief history of rootkits and how host-based IDS solutions can assist in their prevention and detection. The positives and negatives of HIDS technologies are also discussed.

Appendix D: Using the OSSEC VMware Environment

Included with the book is a DVD that contains a pre-configured Ubuntu 7.10 server running the OSSEC HIDS. The OSSEC HIDS VMware Guest image allows you to implement what you have learned in a sandbox-style environment. This appendix explains how the OSSEC HIDS VMware Guest image was create and explains how you can create a OSSEC HIDS VMware Guest image of your own.

About the DVD

The OSSEC HIDS Installation Video

Included on the DVD is an installation video that shows you how to perform a 'local' Windows, a 'local' Linux installation, and a 'server' installation on a Linux system. The Camtasia Studio video content presented here requires JavaScript to be enabled and the latest version of the Adobe Flash Player. If you are you using a browser with JavaScript disabled please enable it before launching the video. Otherwise, please update your version of the free Flash Player by downloading it from the Adobe site: http://www.adobe.com.

To launch the video, double-click on the 'OSSEC Installation.html' file in the 'OSSEC Installation' folder and the video presentation will begin in your default browser.

The OSSEC HIDS VMware Image

The included VMware image provides a complete 'local' installation of OSSEC HIDS on Ubuntu Server 7.10. The Web UI is also properly installed with SSL enabled. This image will work with VMware Server, Workstation, and Player products. For more information about VMware and to download VMware player, go to http://www.vmware.com

To use the OSSEC_HIDS image, copy it from the DVD disk to your hard drive. With VMware (Workstation or Server) choose the option to open an image from the File menu. VMware Player will prompt you to browse for an image as soon as you start it. Use the Open dialog to find the folder where you copied the VMware image and open the OSSEC_HIDS.vmx file. If you are using VMware player the image will boot immediately. With the other VMware products you will be presented with the settings window from which you can start the virtual machine.

NOTE

When you first start the image in VMware player you will be asked if you moved it or copied it. You must choose 'I moved it' otherwise there may be issues with network connectivity. Likewise, when you first start the image in VMware Workstation or VMware Server you will be asked if you would like to 'keep' the existing identifier or 'create' a new one. Always 'keep' the existing unique identifier.

The Ubuntu installation is configured to use DHCP on the eth0 interface. Once the image is booted, you will have to log in to discover the IP address assigned to it. The username for the image is from the stories in the book. The username is 'marty' and the password is 'ossec' (do not include the quotes).

To log in to the virtual machine, click on it (once it has fully booted) and press ENTER once to get a login prompt. You may then log in using the above username and password.

Some useful commands to start:

ifconfig eth0

The ifconfig command will show the network interface configuration from which you can see the IP address assignment. Use this address to connect to the virtual machine with your browser.

sudo -i

sudo will prompt for a password; use the same password as you did to log in (ossec). You will then become the root user on the virtual machine that is necessary to access the OSSEC HIDS configuration.

The OSSEC HIDS software is installed in the default location of /var/ossec. All configuration files, rules, and utilities can be found there as described throughout the book.

The Web UI for OSSEC HIDS is installed in the directory /var/www/osui and may be accessed with the following URLs where <IP_Address> is replaced with the IP address from ifconfig. The username and password are the same as for the system login ('marty' and 'ossec').

```
http://IP_Address/osui
https://IP_Address/osui
```

For example:

```
https://172.16.156.130/osui
```

We hope this virtual machine image will get you up and running with OSSEC HIDS quickly and will provide a useful reference as you make your way through the book.

– Rory Bray, Andrew Hay, and Daniel Cid

Foreword

If you have picked this book off the shelf and opened the cover, you probably already know what OSSEC is, but just in case you don't know, as it states on the OSSEC web page, "OSSEC HIDS is an Open Source Host-based Intrusion Detection System. It performs log analysis and correlation, file integrity checking, rootkit detection, time-based alerting and active response." Linuxworld, who rated OSSEC the number one of five tools used in production in an enterprise environment said, "The OSSEC HIDS project has been gaining widespread use and is quickly being deployed within organizations around the world as a method of protecting systems at the host level after attacks have made it past network defenses." OSSEC runs on most operating systems, including Linux, OpenBSD, FreeBSD, Solaris and Windows." Since its launch in October 2003, OSSEC has gained momentum to the tune of 10,000 downloads each month from all over the world.

People love it! One user wrote, "I do PCI (payment card industry) consulting, and every client needs to have a centralized log server and file integrity solution." Well-known security researcher Anton Chuvakin wrote, "that it was an awesome move for OSSEC to incorporate database log alerts for MySQL and PostreSQL. I think this will help bringing database logging into the mainstream much faster!" OSSEC is one of those rare open source tools that meets or exceeds the capabilities of its commercial counterparts, if indeed OSSEC really does have a commercial counterpart. Commercial host-based intrusion detection solutions range from $60 to as high as thousands of dollars. Because there is no free host-based intrusion detection solution that can match the functionality, scalability, and simplicity of OSSEC, it stands in a class by itself. "This is a piece of software that literally springs to life," Richard Bejtlich wrote on his blog. "Yesterday morning I installed OSSEC on the one system I expose to the Internet. OSSEC is really amazing in the sense that you can install it and immediately it starts parsing system logs for interesting activity."

Each chapter begins with a story to illustrate the important material in the chapter. The book starts with a fictional story about a hacker, Byung-Soon, an expert in the electronic theft of corporate information and asserts, that with the right technology and process, everything he tries to do can be detected and logged. His software even sends the information it collects to different servers to make detection harder. He then runs a script to collect the information from each of the servers and has it sent to him. The book compares Network Intrusion Detection, the technology that we have counted on for years, with Host Based Intrusion Detection, which might be the future. For instance, with OSSEC installed it would have been possible to track all of the bits of information being sent to the different servers in the story. The pervasive deployment of wireless, Bluetooth, and EVDO means that perimeter checkpoints are not as effective as they once were and puts a tremendous amount of pressure on the endpoint system for security. Perhaps the most promising assertion in the first part of the book is the discussion on rootkit detection. Rootkits are the biggest problem the security community has to face over the next couple of years.

This book is the definitive guide on the OSSEC Host-based Intrusion Detection system and frankly, to really use OSSEC you are going to need a definitive guide. Documentation has been available since the start of the OSSEC project but, due to time constraints, no formal book has been created to outline the various features and functions of the OSSEC product. This has left very important and powerful features of the product undocumented...until now! The book you are holding will show you how to install and configure OSSEC on the operating system of your choice and provide detailed examples to help prevent and mitigate attacks on your systems. Included with the book is a DVD containing the latest OSSEC software for Windows and Linux/Unix, a pre-configured Ubuntu VMware image with OSSEC already installed, and a step-by-step video detailing how to get OSSEC up-and-running on your system. In the story line of the book, the people involved decide to install OSSEC after they have been compromised with a rootkit and had their software stolen:

"What about that open source HIDS tool that we saw on that SANS Institute webinar a few weeks back?" said Marty. "Do you think that would do the trick?" Simran remembered that OSSEC sounded like a very capable and feature rich HIDS and jotted some notes down in her notebook to follow up on it at a later time. "Good idea Marty." said Simran, thinking to herself that this was the exact reason why you should always surround yourself with smart people.

Then the book takes you into the pragmatics of installation I have already described. When you pick up a book like this, you want to understand what the value add is. The author team, Bray, Cid, and Hay is quite experienced. The team brings a true security and analysis perspective to the pages of this book. Rory Bray is senior software engineer at Q1 Labs Inc. Daniel Cid is the creator and main developer of the OSSEC HIDS. Daniel has been working in the security area for many years, with a special interest in intrusion detection, log analysis, and secure development. He also works at Q1 Labs Inc. as a software engineer. Andrew Hay also works at Q1 Labs Inc., leading the team that Rory and Daniel are on. Together, they deal with security related issues day in and day out when integrating 3rd party event and vulnerability data into Q1 Labs' flagship product, QRadar. These guys have been working in the security industry for a long time. From helping people with OSSEC they have a great understanding into the questions people have about configuration, rule writing, and the management of a host based IDS system. This is where your real investment is made. Take a look at this fragment from the story the starts chapter 3 and see if it doesn't sound familiar:

"OK," said David "how does this OSSEC HIDS thing communicate between the agents and the server? I don't want to have to open up all kinds of special ports just so that these things can communicate." Marty did his best not to roll his eyes, sigh, or react negatively in any way. In dealing with David before he knew that his primary concern was always opening new ports between network segments to allow communication between client and server application deployments.

In the story, David is the department head of operations and he wants to support security, but he understands the true cost of added complexity in a perimeter environment. In the same way, the experience Bray, Cid, and Hay have earned supporting users is reflected in this book. They understand what it means to run OSSEC in the real world. If you have picked this book up, you have probably heard of OSSEC and are thinking about running it. Let me encourage you to give it a try, as it is a very promising software distribution. And take a few minutes to leaf through this book. Can you find the answers you need without this book? Probably! Is your installation and implementation likely to be more effective with this book? Almost certainly.

And to the authors, I am sure I speak for the security community when I say thank you, thanks for all the time creating and testing OSSEC, for your willingness to help us on the mailing lists and for the sacrifice of time to create this very useful book. You have done your part to make security a bit more attainable by those that seek greater assurance and we appreciate that.

Stephen Northcutt, President
The SANS Technology Institute,
a post graduate security college
www.sans.edu

Chapter 1

Getting Started with OSSEC

Solutions in this chapter:

- Introducing Intrusion Detection
- Introducing OSSEC
- Planning Your Deployment
- Identifying OSSEC Pre-installation Considerations

☑ Summary

☑ Solutions Fast Track

☑ Frequently Asked Questions

Introduction

It's 8:15 P.M. on a Friday night in a tiny apartment building in Seoul, South Korea. Byung-Soon, an expert in the electronic theft of corporate information, is exploiting a well-known Internet Information Services (IIS) vulnerability on an American Web server in San Francisco, California. After spending weeks of careful reconnaissance against servers in his target's DMZ, he has finally found a way in through a well-known Microsoft IIS 6.0 vulnerability that, left unpatched, has provided him full access to the server. The target is a medium-sized consultancy firm that is known to do business with a large defense contractor who designs, among other things, ballistic missiles for sale to the United States military.

Byung-Soon begins searching through the various Web directories on the server and notices that an intranet site has been set up so that consultants within the firm can log their hours for work performed at the defense contractor. He downloads the index page for the intranet site and includes some malicious JavaScript that, when run, connects to a previously exploited system in India and downloads his rootkit. The rootkit, invisible to the user and other system processes, acts as a key-logger to record user keystrokes and enables Byung-Soon to connect directly to the compromised host through an encrypted remote access connection. After modifying the index page, he uploads his modified copy, removes any log entries generated by his actions, and heads out for a late dinner. In four hours, when the consultants start their day, Byung-Soon's plan begins.

Bob, a senior consultant assigned to the defense contract, logs in to the company intranet to start his day. Although this is the most boring part of his day, he knows he must keep an accurate count of the hours spent on this project so that his company, and of course he, gets paid. The process goes like clockwork, as it does every day, and Bob, like several of his coworkers, unwittingly installs Byung-Soon's rootkit. When he finishes with the intranet page, he launches Eclipse, the development platform the defense contractor uses for development of software, and starts working. The rootkit records all of Bob's keystrokes, including usernames, passwords, and server information, as it is designed to do. At random intervals throughout the day, Byung-Soon's rootkit sends out snippets of logged information to a collection of previously exploited servers located all over the world.

On Monday, Byung-Soon wakes up in his tiny apartment in Seoul and decides to check on his progress. He logs in to an exploited box at a university in Italy and executes a script to pull all the pieces of collected information together. He then pulls the compiled information down to another server in Warsaw, Poland and starts parsing the information for keywords provided by his employer. Luckily, the developers provide extensive comments within their code so Byung-Soon's script is able to easily identify the target code. The code belongs to

Bob Johnson, one of the contractors whose system has a certain rootkit installed. Byung-Soon decides that it is time to connect to this system and finish the job he was hired to do.

This story, although fictional, is entirely possible and might be happening to your organization right now. By adding a host-based intrusion detection system (HIDS) to your servers and workstations, this embarrassing and potentially dangerous scenario, can be completely avoided. If an HIDS solution was installed on the compromised Web server, the remote access connection, file changes, and removal of the logs to cover Byung-Soon's tracks could have been logged, and potentially blocked, depending on the type of HIDS. If each client machine had an HIDS solution installed, the rootkit download, installation, and communications could have also been logged and blocked.

Introducing Intrusion Detection

Have you ever wondered what was happening on your network at any given time? What about the type of traffic trying to get to a server on your network? *Intrusion detection* is the act of detecting events that have been deemed inappropriate or unwelcome by the business, organizational unit, department, or group. This can be anything from the emailing of company secrets to a competitor, to malicious attacks from a host on the Internet, to the viewing of inappropriate Web content during your lunch break.

Intrusion detection can be performed manually, by inspecting network traffic and logs from access resources, or automatically, using tools. A tools used to automate the processing of intrusion-related information is typically classified as an intrusion detection system (IDS).

Before understanding how the Open Source Security (OSSEC) host intrusion detection system (HIDS) works, we should first review the differences between an HIDS and a network intrusion detection system (NIDS).

Network Intrusion Detection

When you hear the term "intrusion detection system," or "IDS," you probably think of an NIDS. Network intrusion detection systems have become widely used over the past decade because of the impressive capability to provide a granular view of what is happening on your network. The NIDS monitors network traffic using a network interface card (NIC) that is directly connected into your network. The monitoring can be implemented by connecting your NIC to a HUB (Figure 1.1), which allows you to monitor all traffic that crosses the hub; connecting to a SPAN port on a switch (Figure 1.2), which mirrors the traffic seen on another port of the switch; or connecting to a network tap (Figure 1.3), which is an inline device that sits between two interfaces and mirrors the traffic that passes between devices.

Figure 1.1 NIDS Monitoring Using a Hub

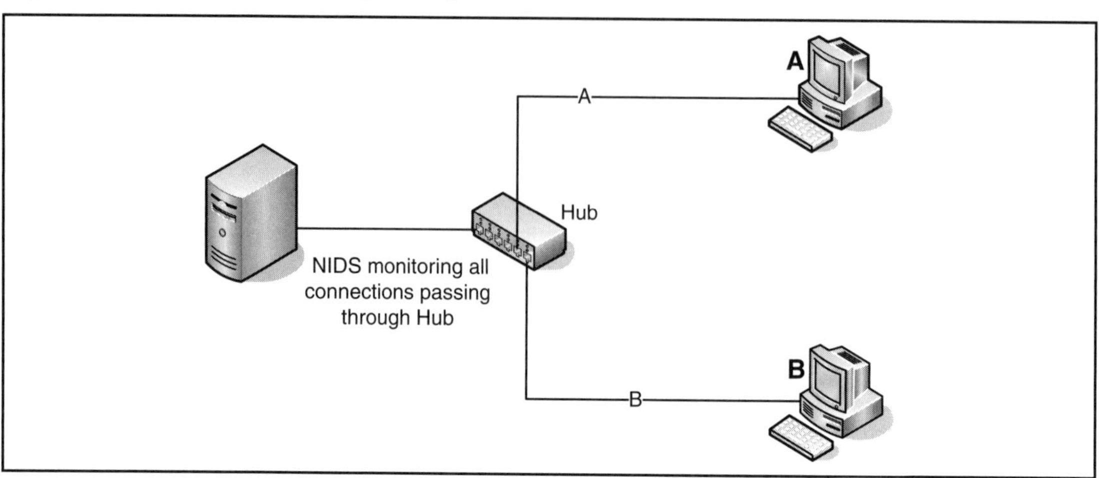

Figure 1.2 NIDS Monitoring Using a SPAN Port on a Switch

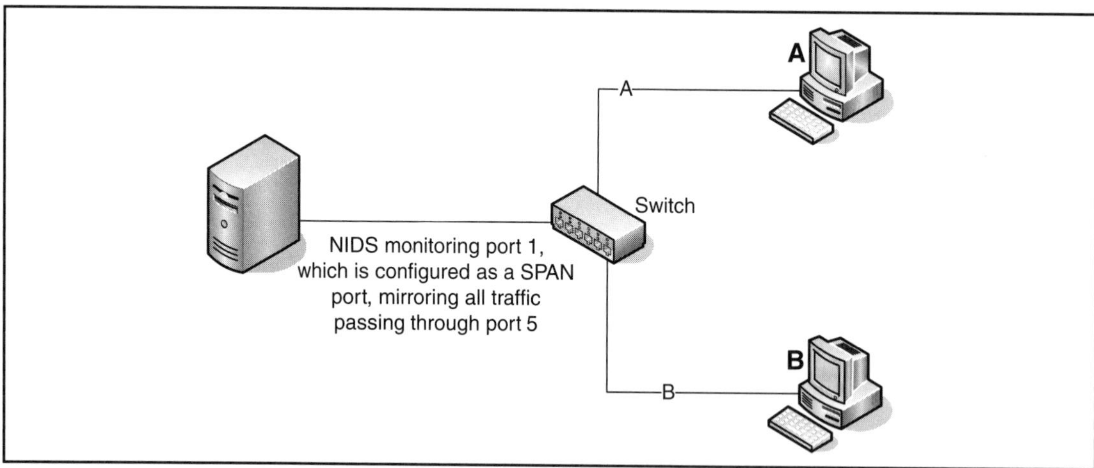

Figure 1.3 NIDS Monitoring Using a Network Tap Connected to a Switch

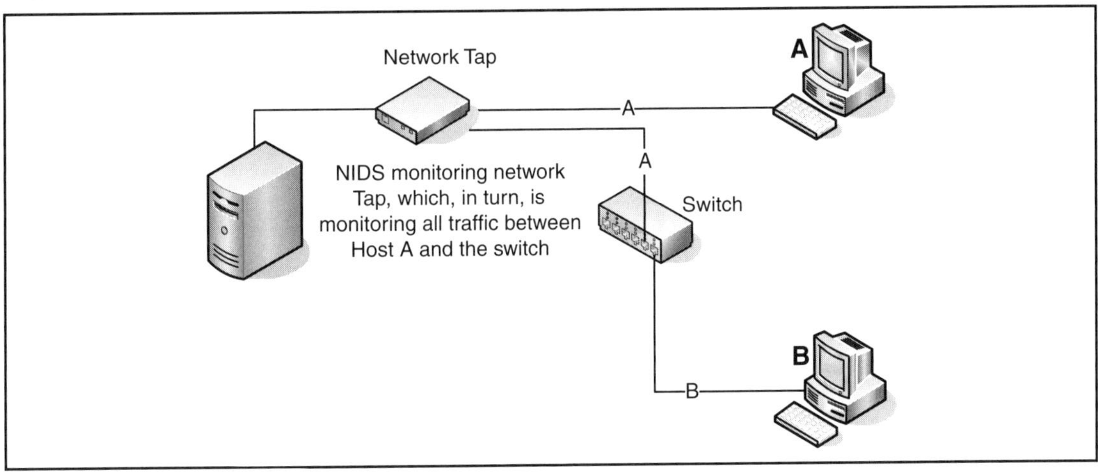

NIDS is typically deployed to passively monitor a sensitive segment of your network, such as a DMZ off the firewall where your corporate Web servers are located (Figure 1.4) or monitoring connections to an internal database that holds your customer credit card information (Figure 1.5). This monitoring allows you to passively watch all communications between your server and the systems attempting to access it.

Figure 1.4 NIDS Monitoring the DMZ

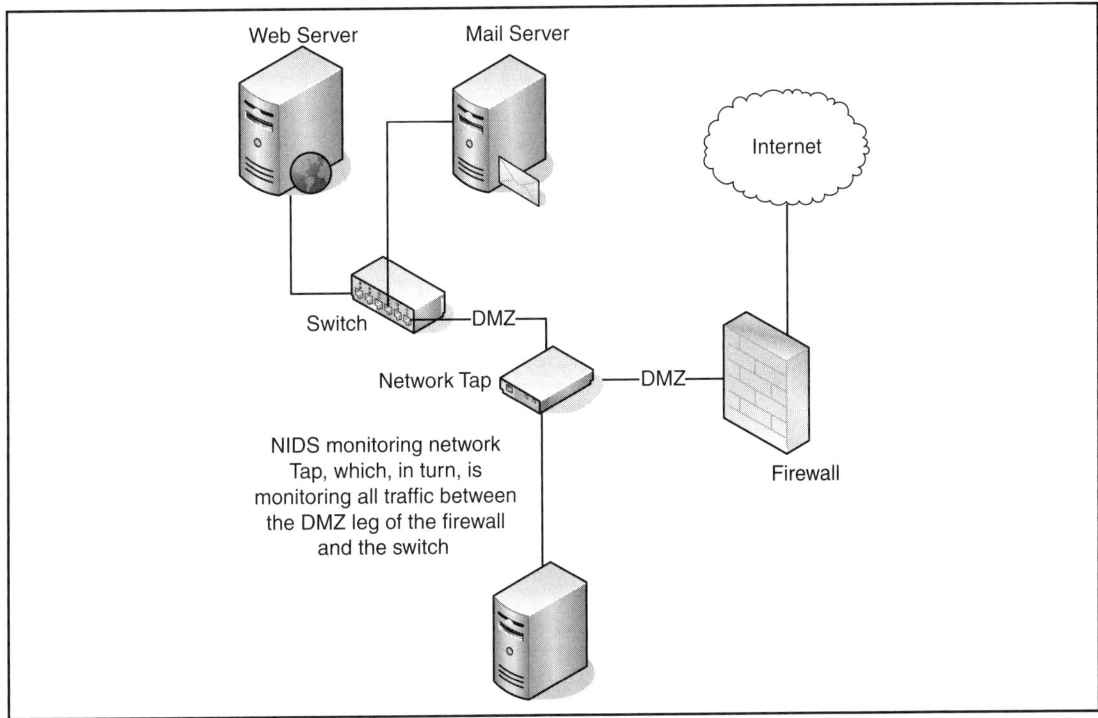

Figure 1.5 NIDS Deployment Monitoring Connections to an Internal Database

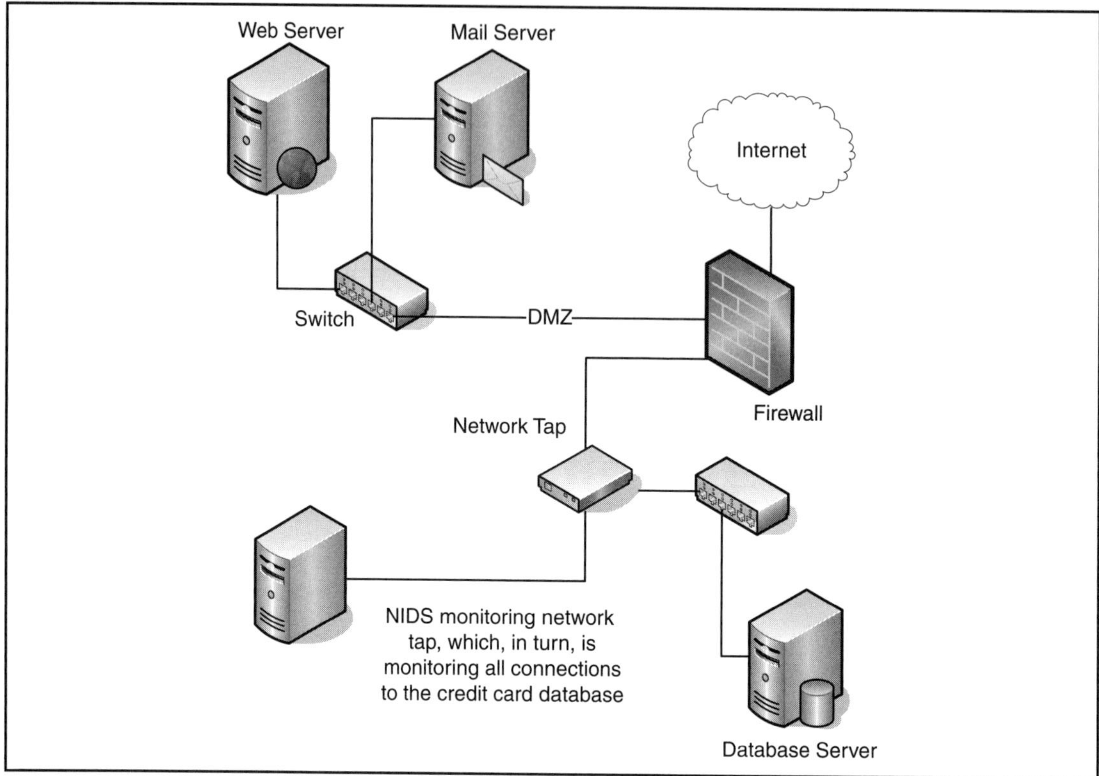

A signature or pattern is used to match specific events, such as an attack attempt, to traffic seen on your network. If the traffic seen on your network matches your defined IDS signature, an alert is generated. An alert can also trigger an action, such as logging the alert to a file, sending an email to someone with details of the alert, or following an action to address this alert, such as adding a firewall rule to block the traffic on another device.

NOTE

Not all network intrusion detection systems can perform an action as a result of a generated alert. These advanced features are sometimes the key differentiator between an NIDS and a network intrusion prevention system (NIPS).

An NIDS is a powerful monitoring system for your network traffic, but there are some things to remember before deploying one:

- What do you do if well-known NIDS evasion techniques are used to bypass your NIDS and signatures? Common NIDS evasion techniques such as fragmentation attacks, session splicing, and even denial-of-service (DoS) attacks can be used to bypass your NIDS, rendering it useless.
- What do you do if the communications between hosts are encrypted? With an NIDS you are passively monitoring traffic and do not have the ability to look into an encrypted packet.
- What do you do if an attack is used against your server, but it is encrypted? Your carefully designed signatures would be unable to catch the attacks that your NIDS is deployed to protect against.

Notes from the Underground...

Common NIDS Evasion Techniques

Several very popular evasion techniques exist to bypass, or sidestep, the watchful eyes of your NIDS solution. Most network intrusion detection systems today have some way to mitigate these techniques by reassembling the full traffic session in memory. As you would expect, this can prove dangerous on a busy network or on an NIDS that hasn't been properly tuned, because of the potential to exhaust all system resources.

- **String matching** weaknesses are the result of poorly created NIDS signatures. Most network intrusion detection systems are signature-based, so if the attacker knows that the publicly available signature, or your own custom signature, does not look for the correct attack information the attacker can change his attack to hide from your NIDS. For example, if you created a signature to watch for anyone accessing the OSSEC Web site using www.ossec.net, you would expect to have an alert generated for anyone who tried to access the site. What if someone types http://ossec.net/ into the browser? Is your signature going to match it properly?
- **Session splicing** allows you to send your data, or attack, across the network in pieces. If you are using TCP to send your data across the network, the stream will not be reassembled until it reaches its final destination. So, instead of trying to get to http://www.ossec.net, you could create three

Continued

packets that have the URL in pieces: http://ww, w.osse, and c.net, respectively. This splicing would also cause your signature not to alert because it does not match what you are looking for. Some network intrusion detection systems do, however, allow you to reassemble the TCP stream to check for these types of evasions, but the reassembling increases the processing duties on your NIDS.

- **Fragmentation attacks** are similar to session splicing attacks, but are a little more advanced. Fragmentation overlap attacks instruct the host to reassemble the packets and overlap or overwrite some of the previously received packets at certain offsets. Fragmentation time-out attacks rely on fragmentation timers on NIDS flushing the reassembly caches after waiting a certain amount of time.
- **Denial of service (DoS) attacks** allow you to evade the NIDS by blinding it. A DoS can be used to consume the NIDS' reassembly engine or exploit a known issue within the NIDS code causing it to crash.

Tuning your NIDS to detect or account for these types of attacks will go a long way to help you focus your time on actual incidents instead of chasing down false positives. Each NIDS must be tuned for the network segment it is monitoring. Remember that most NIDS solutions take a top-down approach to comparing traffic against your signature set. Reducing the number of rules in your deployed signature set reduces processor and memory usage on your NIDS solution. If the DMZ your NIDS is deployed on doesn't contain any Web servers, you probably do not need to include signatures to detect Web server attacks.

Attackers are becoming adept at sidestepping an NIDS, which is why an HIDS is now a necessary safeguard to supplement your current NIDS deployments. Detecting these attacks at the final destination allow you to mitigate the previously mentioned NIDS headaches.

Host-Based Intrusion Detection

An HIDS detects events on a server or workstation and can generate alerts similar to an NIDS. An HIDS, however, is able to inspect the full communications stream. NIDS evasion techniques, such as fragmentation attacks or session splicing, do not apply because the HIDS is able to inspect the fully recombined session as it is presented to the operating system. Encrypted communications can be monitored because your HIDS inspection can look at the traffic before it is encrypted. This means that HIDS signatures will still be able to match against common attacks and not be blinded by encryption.

An HIDS is also capable of performing additional system level checks that only IDS software installed on a host machine can do, such as file integrity checking, registry monitoring, log analysis, rootkit detection, and active response.

File Integrity Checking

Every file on an operating system generates a unique digital fingerprint, also known as a cryptographic hash. This fingerprint is generated based on the name and contents of the file (Figure 1.6). An HIDS can monitor important files to detect changes in this fingerprint when someone, or something, modifies the contents of the file or replaces the file with a completely different version of the file.

Figure 1.6 Example of a Cryptographic Hash Generated from Different Input

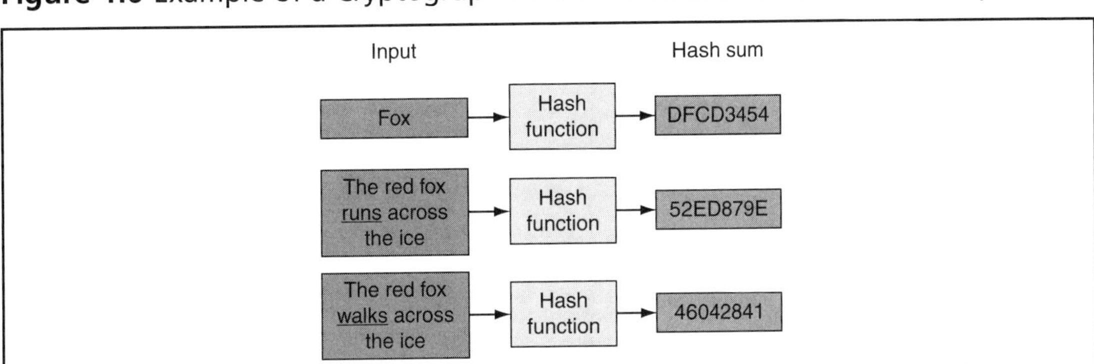

Registry Monitoring

The system registry is a directory listing of all hardware and software settings, operating system configurations, and users, groups, and preferences on a Microsoft Windows system. Changes made by users and administrators to the system are recorded in the system registry keys so that the changes are saved when the user logs out or the system is rebooted. The registry also allows you to look at how the system kernel interacts with hardware and software.

An HIDS can watch for these changes to important registry keys to ensure that a user or application isn't installing a new or modifying an existing program with malicious intent. For example, a password management utility can be replaced with a modified executable and the registry key changed to point to the malicious copy (Figure 1.7).

Figure 1.7 Windows 2000 Professional Registry

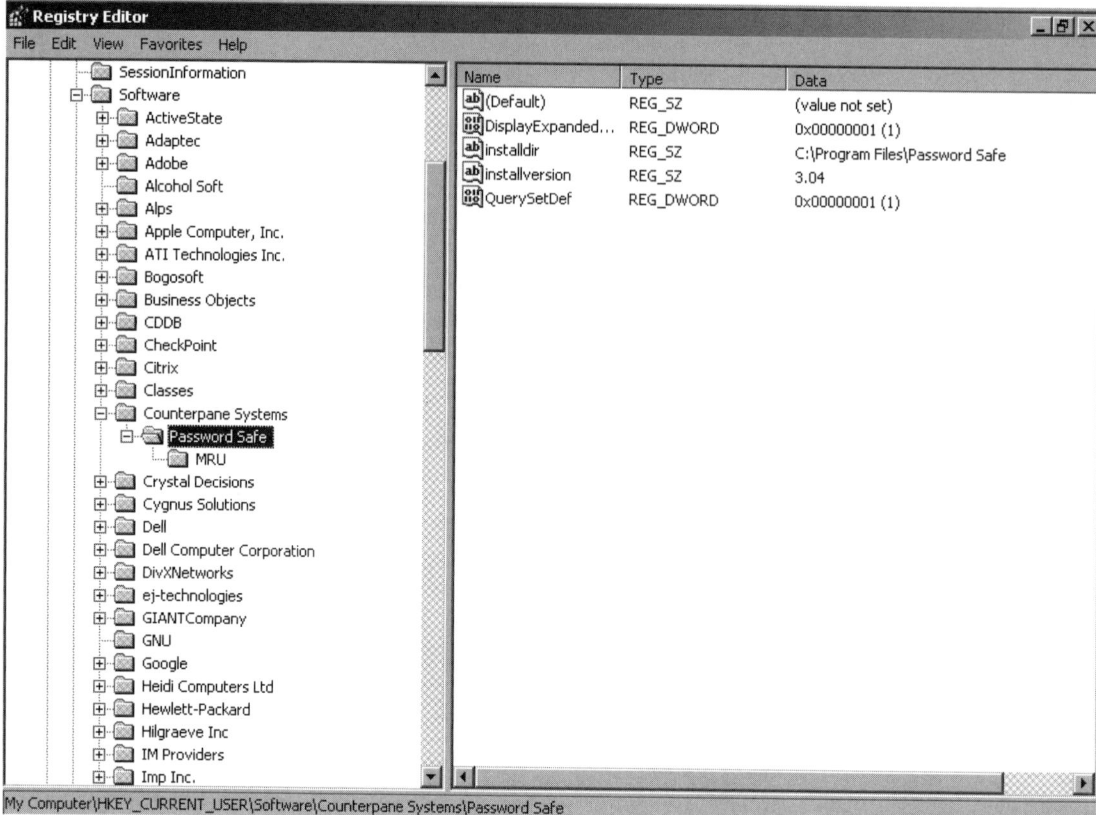

Rootkit Detection

A rootkit is a program developed to gain covert control over an operating system while hiding from and interacting with the system on which it is installed. An installed rootkit can hide services, processes, ports, files, directories, and registry keys from the rest of the operating system and from the user.

Notes from the Underground…

Types of Rootkits

Several types of rootkits are currently available:

- **Firmware:** A firmware rootkit is just as it sounds, a rootkit installed with your firmware. This type of rootkit is difficult to detect because you will typically have to inspect the compiled installation package prior to installing it on your firewall, router, switch, or appliance.
- **Virtualized:** A virtualized rootkit installs between the system hardware and the operating system to intercept system calls. This type of rootkit is typically loaded at boot time and treats your operating system as a virtual machine. Any interaction you have with your computer is inspected and silently altered at the leisure of the installed rootkit.
- **Kernel level:** A kernel level rootkit replaces code associated with the system's kernel, typically through device drivers or loadable kernel modules, to hide the rootkit processes from the rest of the system. These rootkits can be very difficult to detect once installed because the kernel level rootkit tricks your system into reporting that nothing is out of the ordinary.
- **Library level:** A library level rootkit will patch or hook into system calls to hide information about the attacker from the system.
- **Application level:** An application level rootkit, one of the most common types of rootkits, replaces a known application binary with the attacker's own copy of the binary. This is commonly referred to as a "trojanized" version of the original binary; drawing reference from the story of the Trojan Horse used to conceal Greek soldiers during the Trojan War.

Active Response

Active response allows you to automatically execute *commands* or responses when a specific event or set of events is triggered. For example, look at Figure 1.8. An attacker launches an attack against your organization's mail server (1). The attack then passes through your firewall (2), and finally, transparently, passes by your deployed network tap that inspects all traffic destined for your mail server (3). Your NIDS happens to have a signature for this particular attack. The NIDS active response service sends a command to your firewall (4) to reset the attacker's session and place a rule blocking that host. When the attacker, whose connection has been reset, tries to initiate the attack again (5), the attacker is blocked.

Figure 1.8 Active Response Example

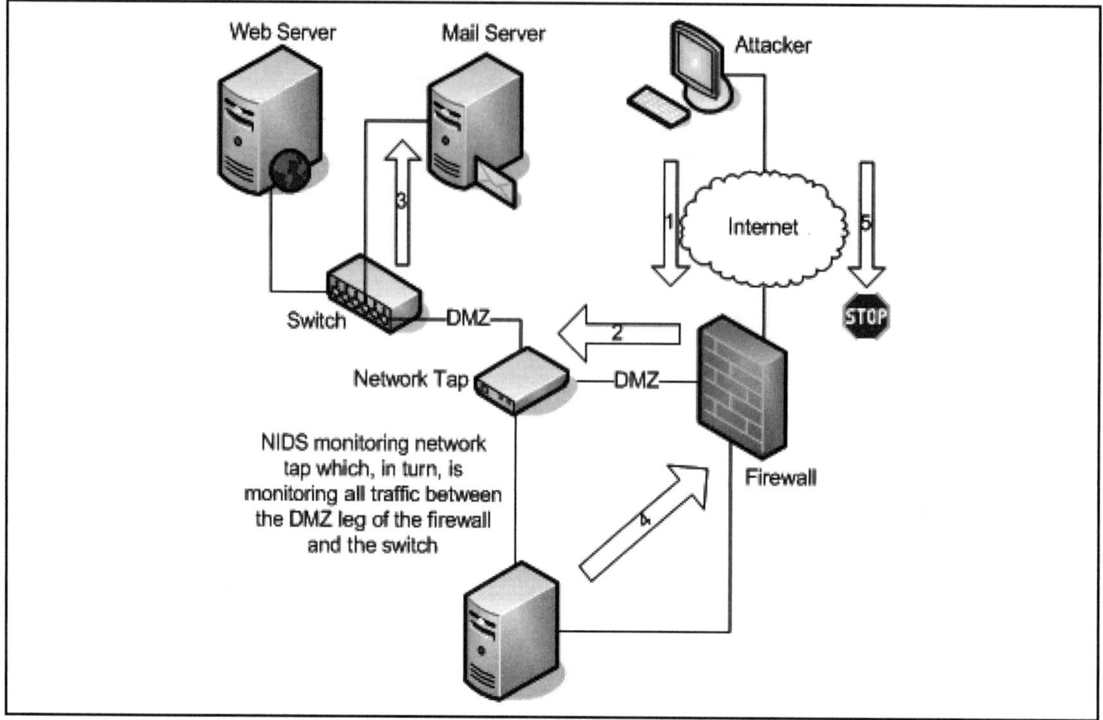

The benefits of active response are enormous, but also risky. For example, legitimate traffic might generate a false positive and block a legitimate user/host if the rules are poorly designed. If an attacker knows that your HIDS blocks a certain traffic signature, the attacker could spoof IP addresses of critical servers in your infrastructure to deny you access. This is essentially a DoS attack that prevents your host from interacting with that IP address.

Introducing OSSEC

OSSEC is a scalable, multiplatform, open source HIDS with more than 5,000 downloads each month. It has a powerful correlation and analysis engine, log analysis integration, file integrity checking, Windows registry monitoring, centralized policy enforcement, rootkit detection, real-time alerting, and active response. In addition to being deployed as an HIDS, it is commonly used strictly as a log analysis tool, monitoring and analyzing firewalls, IDSs, Web servers, and authentication logs. OSSEC runs on most operating systems, including Linux, OpenBSD, FreeBSD, Mac OS X, Sun Solaris, and Microsoft Windows.

OSSEC is free software and will remain so in the future. You can redistribute it and/or modify it under the terms of the GNU General Public License (version 3) as published by the Free Software Foundation (FSF). ISPs, universities, governments, and large corporate data centers are using OSSEC as their main HIDS solution.

The project has contributors from all over the globe and a quarterly release schedule for major fixes, enhancements, and new features. Bugs and feature requests can be sent through the OSSEC bug submission page (www.ossec.net/bugs/) or OSSEC mailing lists (www.ossec.net/main/support/). We will do our best to solve the submitted requests.

If you are interested in being a part of this project, the OSSEC team is always open to new contributors. The easiest way to get involved with OSSEC is by helping to test the product. The OSSEC team is always releasing beta versions and requires good quality control on every supported version before public release. To get involved in the development side you must know C and be willing to take some time (actually quite some time) to understand how the internals work.

Planning Your Deployment

Before starting your OSSEC HIDS installation you must know the differences between the installation types and know how plan your deployment. The OSSEC HIDS can be installed on one system, on multiple systems to provide protection for a large network, or on a few systems with the plan to scale the deployment later to secure your entire organization.

We will discuss three OSSEC installation types to help you understand how to deploy the OSSEC HIDS in your environment:

- **Local installation:** Used to secure and protect a single host
- **Agent installation:** Used to secure and protect hosts while reporting back to a central OSSEC server
- **Server installation:** Used to aggregate information from deployed OSSEC agents and collect syslog events from third-party devices

Are You Owned?

Is It Too Late to Install an HIDS?

When is the best time to install an HIDS? That is a very important question with no easy answer. Ideally, when building a new host, you will follow a checklist to ensure that a common security baseline is enforced across all systems. You will apply the latest patches and hot-fixes for the operating system and applications to ensure that everything is protected against known bugs, exploits, and vulnerabilities.

Continued

During the hardening phase, you prepare the system for deployment by:

- Removing any unwanted applications
- Disabling any unnecessary services
- Adjusting firewall rules to protect the host
- Installing anti-spyware software
- Installing your HIDS solution

You can install an HIDS on an existing host, but there is always the chance that a rootkit has already been installed, compromising the integrity baseline of your HIDS installation. There are several tools available to help you detect rootkits if a fresh installation is not an option:

- **Rootkit Revealer** is an advanced rootkit detection utility. Rootkit Revealer runs on Windows NT 4 and higher and the output lists registry and file system API discrepancies that might indicate the presence of a user-mode or kernel-mode rootkit. More information can be found at www.microsoft.com/technet/sysinternals/Utilities/RootkitRevealer.mspx.
- **GMER** is an application that detects and removes rootkits. It scans for hidden processes, threads, modules, services, files, alternate data streams, and registry keys. GMER also scans for drivers hooking SSDT, hooking IDT, hooking IRP calls, and inline hooks. More information can be found at www.gmer.net.
- **Helios** is designed to detect, remove, and inoculate against modern rootkits. What makes it different from conventional antivirus or anti-spyware products is that it does not rely on a database of known signatures. More information can be found at http://helios.miel-labs.com/.
- **Strider GhostBuster** detects API-hiding rootkits by doing a "cross-view diff" between "the truth" and "the lie." Strider GhostBuster is not based on a known-bad signature and does not rely on a known-good state. It targets the fundamental weakness of hiding rootkits, and turns the hiding behavior into its own detection mechanism. More information can be found at http://research.microsoft.com/rootkit/.
- **ProDiscover Incident Response** can search the suspect system for over 400 known Trojans or rootkits. More information can be found at www.techpathways.com/ProDiscoverIR.htm.
- **Sophos Anti-Rootkit** provides an extra layer of detection, by safely and reliably detecting and removing any rootkit that might already have installed on your system. More information can be found at www.sophos.com/products/free-tools/sophos-anti-rootkit.html.

- **Chrootkit** is a set of utilities to locally check if someone has installed a rootkit on your system. It detects over 50 rootkits, kernel modules, and worms. It also has the capability to check system binaries for rootkit modification, to check if the interface is in promiscuous mode, and check for log deletions. More information can be found at www.chkrootkit.org/.

This is just a small subsection of the anti-rootkit tools available. For more information, please visit Antirootkit.com and browse the full list of Antirootkit Software.

Local Installation

The Local installation type is recommended if you plan to install the OSSEC HIDS on only one system, such as a personal laptop, workstation, or single server. However, if you are administering a network where you have more than one system to secure and monitor, you should consider using the Agent/Server Installation types.

A Local installation is easier to manage and can be customized for the system on which it is installed. This installation also combines all the functionality of the OSSEC HIDS software, including agent and server functionality, on one system (Figure 1.9). The only downside to a Local installation is if you decide later that you want to send your alerts to a central OSSEC server. To do so, you will have to uninstall the Local installation and run an Agent installation.

Figure 1.9 Local Installation Configuration

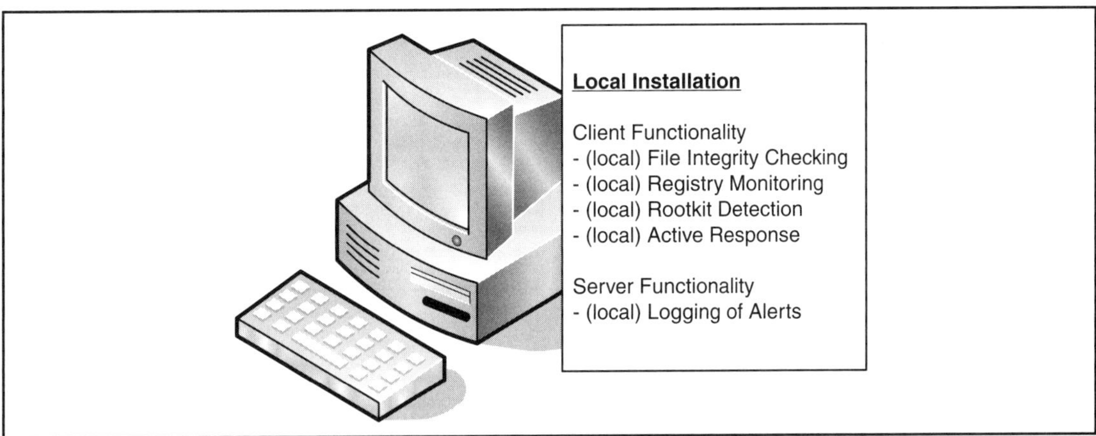

TIP

If you choose the Local installation method and realize that you should have performed an Agent installation, do not panic. It is easy to remove your Local installation and replace it with an Agent installation as you will see in Chapter 2.

Agent Installation

The Agent installation type is recommended if you plan to deploy the OSSEC HIDS on several systems in your organization. This installation type allows you to deploy the security and protection offered by OSSEC on the host of your choosing and centralizes your information by sending alerts back to a single OSSEC server. The Agent installation eliminates the overhead of logging on your deployed agent and ensures that generated alerts are not kept on the system. Figure 1.10 shows the Agent role in a typical Agent/Server type deployment.

Server Installation

The Server installation type is recommended if you already have multiple Agent installations deployed throughout your organization and must collect the host-generated alerts. The role of an OSSEC server is to collect all alerts from deployed Agent installations and provide an overall view of what is being reported by all deployed Agent installations (Figure 1.10).

Figure 1.10 Agent/Server Configuration

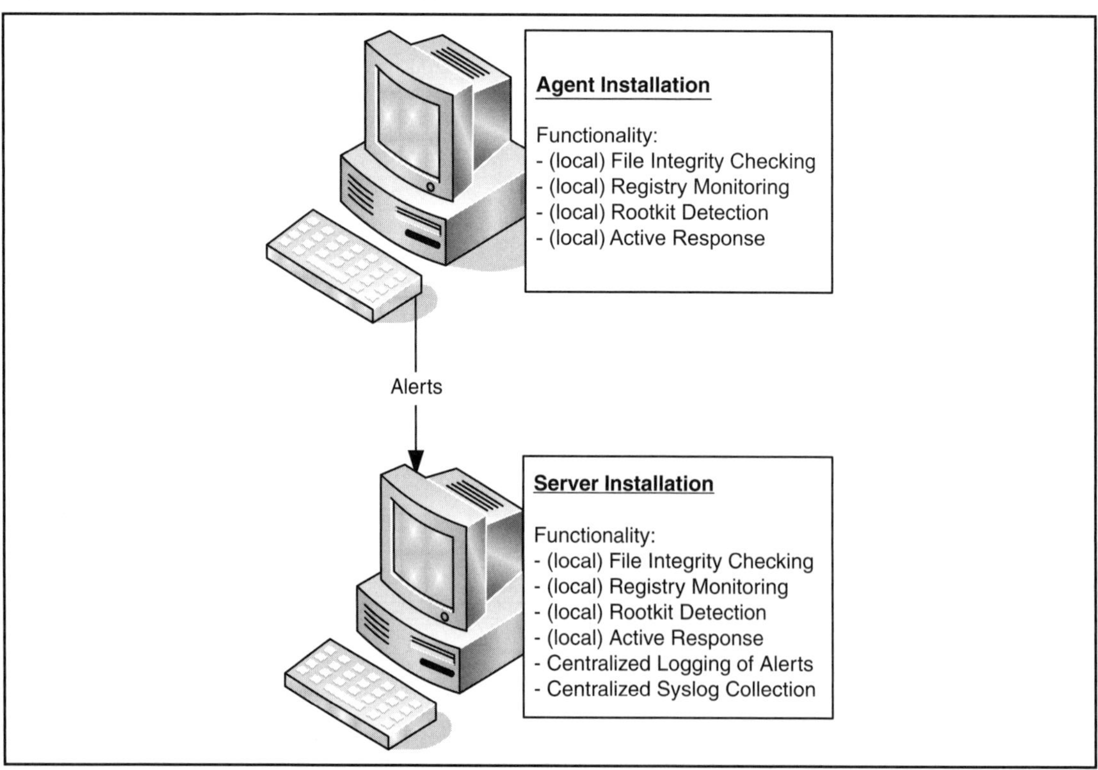

Consider the following situation. You check your assigned issues in the ticketing system and notice that three users have logged issues that morning indicating that their workstations are running slower than usual. The users also indicate that they can hear the computer hard disks working very hard, when they are not doing anything on the system. You decide to walk down and look at the first computer of the first user who reported the issue. After reviewing the OSSEC logs on the system, you notice that a rootkit was detected at 3 A.M. that morning:

```
Received From: rootcheck
Rule: 14 fired (level 8) -> "Rootkit detection engine message' "
Portion of the log(s):
Rootkit 't0rn' detected by the presence of file '/lib/libproc.a'.
```

After reading this information, alarms go off and questions start to go through your mind:

- "Is this rootkit installed on the other two workstations that reported problems this morning?"
- "How many other systems has this rootkit been installed on?"
- "Were the rootkits all installed last night, or have these rootkits been installed over time on various systems?"
- "Is this rootkit only installed on workstations, or has it also been installed on any critical systems?"
- "Should I begin handling this incident on this workstation, or should I check the other workstations first?"

If OSSEC agents were installed on all these systems, instead of Local OSSEC installations, you would have been able to first check the OSSEC server before leaving your desk. This initial check would have allowed you to see if any alerts, such as those generated by the installation of a rootkit, were common across all systems with deployed agents.

This situational awareness provides a method to assist you in determining if an attack is targeting multiple machines or only one host.

Which Type Is Right For Me?

Although we would like to answer that question for you, there are too many factors to consider. However, we have included a helpful table (Table 1.1) to assist you in the decision-making process.

Table 1.1 Installation Suggestions

Scenario	Local Installation	Agent/Server Installation
I only have one system I need to protect.	X	
I have multiple systems that should report back to one location.		X
I have remote users who require protection, but my network isn't the only one they connect to.	X	
My organization is subject to compliance regulations that require centralized log management.		X
I have one server in a different location that cannot communicate with my network where my OSSEC server would be.	X	
I am a "one-person-IT-shop" and need to check for issues on as few systems as possible.		X
I am home based and my laptop can only connect via a slow dial-up connection.	X	
I need to collect syslog events from my firewall.		X

Identifying OSSEC Pre-installation Considerations

Now that you know about the different installation types, it is time to perform the installation, right? Before you rush into installing OSSEC, take a moment to make sure you have all the information you need, especially if you are going to deploy OSSEC agents and OSSEC servers. Depending on the operating system you are looking to install OSSEC on, there might be some dependencies you must satisfy prior to installation.

Supported Operating Systems

The OSSEC HIDS has been tested on the following operating systems:

- OpenBSD 3.5, 3.6, 3.7, 3.8, 3.9, 4.0, 4.1, and 4.2
- GNU/Linux
- Slackware 10.1 and 10.2
- Ubuntu 5.04, 5.10, and 6.06 (32 and 64 bits)
- Red Hat 8.0 and 9.0
- Red Hat Enterprise Linux (RHEL) 4 and 5
- SUSE ES 9 and 10
- Fedora Core 2, 3, 4, and 5
- Debian 3.1 Sarge
- FreeBSD 5.2.1, 5.4-RELEASE, 6.0-STABLE, and 6.1-RELEASE
- NetBSD 3.0
- Solaris 2.8, 2.9 (Sparc) and 10 (x86)
- AIX 5.2 ML-07
- HP-UX 11i v2
- Mac OS X 10.x
- Windows 2000, XP, and 2003 (agent only)

NOTE

The most current list of supported operating systems can be found on the OSSEC Wiki site at www.ossec.net/wiki/index.php/Supported_System.

Special Considerations

Every operating system has specific requirements that must be addressed before new software is installed. We have identified known prerequisites for some of the more popular operating systems here.

Microsoft Windows

Before installation of the OSSEC HIDS software, no additional packages must be installed on a Microsoft Windows platform. Please note that continued development and support are only available for:

- Microsoft Windows 2000 Workstation
- Microsoft Windows 2000 Server
- Microsoft Windows XP Home
- Microsoft Windows XP Professional
- Microsoft Windows 2003 Server

The OSSEC HIDS can only be installed as an Agent at this time because of the reliance on Unix sockets for the server portion. Local and Server type installations are currently being investigated.

NOTE

At the time of writing, OSSEC HIDS support for Microsoft Windows Vista and Microsoft Windows Server 2008 is still being investigated.

Sun Solaris

Before beginning your OSSEC installation on a Sun Solaris platform, ensure that you have installed the SUNWxcu4 package. To check if the SUNWxcu4 package has previously been installed, execute the following from your Solaris command line:

```
$ pkginfo | grep SUNWxcu4
```

If you do not have the SUNWxcu4 package installed, execute the following command to install it:

```
$ pkgadd SUNWxcu4
```

Ubuntu Linux

If using an Ubuntu Linux version before release 7.04 you must ensure that the *build-essential* package is installed before you install the OSSEC HIDS software. To check if the *build-essential* package has already been installed, execute the following from your Ubuntu command line:

```
$ aptitude search build-essential
```

If the *build-essential* package is installed, you will see an *i* beside the package:

```
i build-essential - informational list of build-essential pack
```

If you do not have the *build-essential* package installed, execute the following command to install it:

```
$ sudo apt-get install build-essential
```

If using Ubuntu Linux version 7.04 or later you must ensure that the *gcc* and *glibc-dev* packages are installed before you install the OSSEC HIDS software. These packages are required to properly build the OSSEC HIDS software for your system. If you do not have the *gcc* and *glibc-dev* packages installed, execute the following command to install the packages:

```
$ sudo apt-get install gcc glibc-dev
```

Mac OS X

Before you install the OSSEC HIDS software on a system running Mac OS X, you must ensure that the *Xcode development* package is installed to compile the OSSEC HIDS software. This package can be found on your Mac OS X installation media or at the Apple Developer Connection site.

To install Xcode, you must:

- Download Xcode from the Apple Developer Connection tool site located at http://developer.apple.com/tools/.
- Run the installer to install the packages you need. For the OSSEC HIDS software, at a minimum, you need the Developer Tools Software package, but feel free to install any of the other useful packages contained within the Xcode installer.

NOTE

At the time of writing, the Xcode installation package was a 924MB download from the Apple Developer Connection site. If you are on a slow connection you might want to have someone else download the package for you.

Summary

IDSs act as security guards deployed throughout your network. An IDS watches for intruders on your network in the form of malicious users, bots, and worms, and alerts you as soon as the intrusions are detected.

An NIDS is a powerful monitoring system for your network traffic. When properly deployed, it has the capability to alert you of attacks destined for your critical systems. If an NIDS is incorrectly deployed, you might find yourself chasing down false positives instead of handling valid incidents. Tuning your NIDS solution for your environment is key to reducing false positives. Proper signature creation allows you to mitigate common NIDS evasion techniques such as string matching, session splicing, fragmentation attacks, and DoS attacks. Most network intrusion detection systems currently have a method to mitigate these techniques by reassembling the full traffic session in memory. As you would expect, this can prove dangerous on a busy network or on an NIDS that has not been properly tuned, because it has the potential to exhaust all system resources.

An HIDS is designed to protect the server on which it is installed. It is able to inspect the full communications stream between the local and remote system interacting with the HIDS. NIDS evasion techniques do not cause the same headaches with an HIDS solution because the HIDS is able to inspect the fully recombined session as presented to the operating system. An HIDS is also capable of performing additional system level checks that only IDS software installed on a host machine can do, such as file integrity checking, registry monitoring, rootkit detection, and active response.

OSSEC is a scalable, multiplatform, open source HIDS with more than 5,000 downloads each month. It has a powerful correlation and analysis engine that integrates log analysis, file integrity checking, Windows registry monitoring, centralized policy enforcement, rootkit detection, and real-time alerting and active response. OSSEC runs on most operating systems, including Linux, OpenBSD, FreeBSD, Mac OS X, Solaris, and Windows. In addition to being deployed as an HIDS, it is commonly used strictly as a log analysis tool, to monitor and analyze firewalls, IDSs, Web servers, and authentication logs.

There are three installation types to consider when installing the OSSEC HIDS. The Local installation type is designed to be an all-in-one solution that includes all the protection and logging capabilities the OSSEC HIDS software provides. The Agent installation type protects the host it is installed on, reports all alerts, and logs back to a server installation. The Server installation type protects the system it is installed on and allows you to centralize the alerting and logging of remote agents and third-party devices such as routers, switches, firewalls, and so on.

The OSSEC HIDS software can be installed on every popular operating system currently available. Certain operating systems have dependencies that must be satisfied prior to beginning installation. The most current list of supported operating systems can be found on the OSSEC Wiki site located at www.ossec.net/wiki/index.php/Supported_System.

Solutions Fast Track

Introducing Intrusion Detection

- ☑ Intrusion detection is the act of detecting events deemed inappropriate or unwelcome by the business, organizational unit, department, or group. This can be anything from emailing company secrets to a competitor, malicious attacks from a host on the internet, to viewing inappropriate Web content during your lunch break.
- ☑ An NIDS is typically deployed to passively monitor a sensitive segment of your network.
- ☑ An HIDS detects events on a server or workstation and can generate alerts similar to an NIDS.

Introducing OSSEC

- ☑ OSSEC is a scalable, multiplatform, open source HIDS with a powerful correlation and analysis engine, integrating log analysis, file integrity checking, Windows registry monitoring, centralized policy enforcement, rootkit detection, real-time alerting and active response.
- ☑ You can redistribute and/or modify OSSEC under the terms of the GNU General Public License (version 3) as published by the Free Software Foundation (FSF).
- ☑ The project has contributors from all over the globe and a quarterly release schedule for major fixes, enhancements, and new features.

Planning Your Deployment

- ☑ Local installations of OSSEC are used to secure and protect a single host.
- ☑ Agent installations of OSSEC are used to secure and protect hosts that must report to a central OSSEC server.
- ☑ Server installations of OSSEC are used to aggregate information from deployed OSSEC agents and collect syslog events from third-party devices.
- ☑ You can install an HIDS on an existing host, but there is always the chance that a rootkit has already been installed, compromising the integrity baseline of your HIDS installation.

Identifying OSSEC Pre-installation Considerations

- ☑ Depending on the operating system on which you want to install OSSEC, there might be some dependencies you will need to satisfy prior to installation.
- ☑ No additional packages must be installed before the installation of the OSSEC HIDS software on a Microsoft Windows platform, but development and support are only available for certain Microsoft Windows revisions.
- ☑ The most current list of supported operating systems can be found on the OSSEC Wiki site located at www.ossec.net/wiki/index.php/Supported_System.

Frequently Asked Questions

Q: What is the difference between HIDS and NIDS?

A: An NIDS is deployed to protect your hosts at the network level. An HIDS is deployed to protect the end hosts on your network from malicious traffic that may bypass your NIDS deployments.

Q: What is the best way to catch attackers leveraging common NIDS evasion techniques?

A: The best way, if your NIDS solution supports it, is to keep the state of the connection and reassemble in memory. This allows your NIDS to compare the fully recombined traffic stream, not just the fragments of the connection, against your configured signature set.

Q: Isn't the easiest way to catch all types of malicious traffic to enable every signature in my IDS signature set?

A: Most NIDS and HIDS solutions use a top-down approach when comparing traffic against your deployed signature set. The more signatures you try to compare the monitored traffic against, the more system resources are used. A good system for determining which rules should be enabled is to first take stock of what systems are being monitored by your IDS solution. For example, if your NIDS is deployed to monitor connections to Linux-based Apache Web servers, rules to detect attack attempts against Microsoft IIS Web servers would not provide insight into a Linux or Apache oriented attack.

Q: I really like the functionality of OSSEC and would like to include it in my product. Can I just include the code in my product?

A: Certainly, provided you abide by the terms of the GNU General Public License version 3 (GPLv3). More information on the GPLv3 is provided by the Free Software Foundation (FSF) at http://gplv3.fsf.org/.

Q: I know some free software starts strong and then falls off over time. How do I know that the people behind the OSSEC HIDS will continue to release updates?

A: The OSSEC HIDS project has been around since 2003, has contributors from all over the globe, and is downloaded approximately 5,000 times each month. There is quarterly release schedule for major fixes, enhancements, and new features, and a very active user community.

Q: Can I send firewall/vpn/authentication logs to OSSEC, or does it strictly perform HIDS functions?

A: One of the greatest benefits of the OSSEC HIDS is the capability to receive and process logs from any device that sends logs using the syslog protocol. Detailed rules can be created to extract useful information for analysis and long-term storage. This is discussed in depth in later chapters.

Q: This all sounds great! How do I get involved?

A: The OSSEC team is always looking for contributors. If you are not a developer, we are always looking for people to test new releases, test installations on different operating systems, write documentation, and help on the mailing lists. If you want to contribute to the development of OSSEC, all you have to do is invest some time in learning how the core product functions and sign up on the development mailing list (www.ossec.net/main/support/).

Q: What do I do if I've installed the OSSEC HIDS using the Local type, but need to change it to an Agent installation?

A: To switch your installation type, you must uninstall your Local installation type and reinstall OSSEC as an Agent.

Q: Can I receive syslog data from remote devices if I use the Local or Agent installation types?

A: The Local and Agent installation types are designed to provide HIDS protection to the host on which OSSEC is installed. Even though the Local installation type acts as both an Agent and a Server for the local machine, the capability to receive and process syslog information is reserved solely for the Server installation type. This prevents any scalability issues you may encounter as your deployment grows.

Q: I want to install the OSSEC HIDS, but I cannot reinstall all my systems. How can I ensure that rootkits have not already been installed on my server?

A: There are several tools, far too many to cover within the scope of this book, to help you track down and eliminate rootkits previously installed on your system. We strongly suggest you look at the AntiRootkit.com Web site (www.antirootkit.com) and browse the extensive library of Antirootkit Software and articles relating to rootkit detection and elimination.

Q: What operating system can I install the OSSEC HIDS on?

A: The OSSEC HIDS can be installed on most Unix/Linux distributions and on Microsoft Windows 2000, Windows 2003, or Windows XP. A full list of supported operating systems can be found on the OSSEC Wiki site at www.ossec.net/wiki/index.php/Supported_System.

Q: Can I install the OSSEC HIDS on Microsoft Windows Vista?

A: At the time of writing, the OSSEC team had not yet certified the OSSEC HIDS on Microsoft Windows Vista. Please keep checking the OSSEC Web site (www.ossec.net) for future versions that may support Microsoft Windows Vista.

Q: I don't see my operating system listed. Will OSSEC work on it and, if I run into problems, will you help me?

A: The OSSEC HIDS might work with your operating system but we might not have tested it yet. Unfortunately, we do not have an extensive lab containing every possible operating system available. We rely on our user base to test and provide feedback on experiences. That being said, we will certainly try to assist you with any problems or questions you may run into to the best of our ability.

Chapter 2

Installation

Solutions in this chapter:

- Downloading the OSSEC HIDS
- Building and Installing the OSSEC HIDS
- Performing a Local Installation
- Performing Server-Agent Installations
- Streamlining the Installations

☑ Summary

☑ Solutions Fast Track

☑ Frequently Asked Questions

Introduction

Simran Singh looks at her watch in disgust as she leaves the meeting room. "I told Bob this would happen," she says calmly to Marty Feldman, her second in command and confidant. "But did they listen? Now I have to somehow try to install safeguards on all our systems with what's left of our department's budget."

Simran rose through the ranks of North America's premier defense company due to her mix of business savvy, security knowledge, and track record for fixing impossible solutions. She is known throughout the company for never having to ask for more money than her department is allocated. Simran is also the most respected security mind in the company. During her first week, she was immediately dedicated as part of the incident handling team responsible for handling a companywide worm outbreak. Her superiors were so impressed by the way she operated, before long she was leading the teams of handlers for all the critical incidents in the organization. Within two years, she was head of the department and continued to prove herself by reducing enterprise-wide incidents by 66%. It was no surprise to her employees, peers, and senior managers when she was unanimously nominated for the recently vacated Chief Information Security Officer (CISO) position. Although Simran would prefer to receive the promotion under less hostile circumstances, she completely understands why out-going CISO Bob Rogers is no longer a viable option to continue in the role. Bob spends most of his time on the golf course instead of listening to the department warnings about difficult to protect network entry points. His failure to listen to his team is his downfall. The completely preventable breach, which resulted in the theft of top-secret ballistic missile guidance software, had cost the company its largest contract in 10 years and damaged its reputation with all existing customers.

"What's the plan, boss?" Marty asked Simran, already knowing that her mind was spinning and formulating a plan of attack. "Well, we used our entire budget on those redundant perimeter firewalls and intrusion prevention systems to help mitigate denial of service attacks," mused Simran. "So we have a hard candy shell and a soft, chewy center?" laughed Marty. "And we're all out of money for nougat!" exclaimed Simran. "What about that open source HIDS tool we saw on the SANS Institute webinar a few weeks back?" asked Marty. "Do you think that would do the trick?" Simran remembered that OSSEC sounded like a very capable and feature-rich HIDS, and had jotted some notes in her notebook to follow up on at a later time. "Good idea, Marty," said Simran, thinking that this was the exact reason why you should always surround yourself with smart people. Smart people come up with creative ideas, and creative ideas must be considered. "Can you do some further investigation into this OSSEC application and get back to me by the end of the week?" Marty looked at his Smartphone and noted that it was already

Thursday. Marty didn't miss a beat and simply answered, "Can do, boss!" Marty knows that the end of this week is a hard deadline. He has worked for Simran long enough to know when something was important enough to be asked to pull an all-nighter. As Marty exited the elevator he thought, "If I can't get this done by Friday, there might be another witch hunt upstairs next week." Marty chuckled under his breath, "If I don't play my cards right, then I might be promoted next." Never had the thought of a promotion had such ominous overtones.

"Boss! Boss!!" Marty yelled as he ran across the lobby toward Simran. "Have you been here all night?" asked Simran, already knowing the answer. Marty was unshaved, wearing yesterday's clothes, and had enough caffeine in him that he could probably fly around the world a few times on his own power. "Of course I've been here all night!" raced Marty. His eyes were blinking faster than his lips were moving. Simran laughed and wondered if he was trying to use his eyes to explain his findings using Morse code at the same time he was talking to her. "I listened to the webcast again, went to the OSSEC Web site, downloaded the software, read the documentation, joined the mailing list, and then searched the mailing list archives, and you know what?" Marty said, his mouth starting to get dry, and seemingly waiting for a response. "What, Marty?" asked Simran. "Hey! It's raining out?" asked Marty, staring past Simran. Simran snapped her fingers. "Stay on target, stay on target," said Simran, knowing Marty would appreciate the Star Wars reference. "Ha! Sorry, running on fumes here!" exclaimed Marty. "There are quite a few OSSEC deployments out there and lots of people are using the deployments in an enterprise environment. Even some Telco-sized organizations have deployed OSSEC on thousands of machines and couldn't be happier with it and they say that scalability isn't a problem, which we are always worried about because we're a huge company and we're starting to grow and our number of systems is growing exponentially, am I right or what? Boy I could use a coffee." Simran handed her latte to Marty. "Cheers!" exclaimed Marty, taking a huge gulp. "Will it work in a mixed environment?" asked Simran. "Totally! It works on Windows, Linux, Unix, Solaris, OS X, and a bunch of others!" yelled Marty, oblivious to the stares he was drawing from others in the lobby. "Indoor voice, Marty," said Simran. "So you've already installed it on some test servers, I assume?" Marty took another chug of his newly acquired latte, "Fifty or so…wait…maybe sixty-five…no fifty-five…sixty, definitely sixty!" Simran couldn't believe it. "That's quite the deployment for a test bed." Marty shrugged. "I had the time." He laughed. "It only took about five minutes per machine, which gave me plenty of time to tunnel into my boxes at home and install it on them as well. I guess that makes the total count sixty-five, if we include my systems." Simran smiled. "Marty, I think we've done it again. Let's have these systems run over the weekend and I'll draft a proposal to present on Monday. If all goes well," winked Simran, "we'll be deploying on our production servers in no time at all."

Notes from the Underground ...

Linux, Unix, and BSD ... Oh My!

Throughout this book, we mention the various popular operating systems on which the OSSEC HIDS can be installed. Please keep in mind that when we mention a particular operating system, it typically includes all the associated derivatives, or flavors, of that branch of operating systems, unless expressly stated otherwise.

Unix

When we refer to Unix, we are referring to any Unix-like operating system that does not fall into the BSD or Linux categories described. The Unix operating system was developed by a group of AT&T employees while working at Bell Labs. Examples of popular Unix flavors are:

- Sun Solaris
- OpenSolaris
- HP-UX
- IBM AIX
- IRIX
- Etc.

BSD

When we refer to BSD, we are referring to all Berkeley Software Distributions. BSD is a Unix derivative distributed and maintained by the University of California, Berkeley. Examples of popular BSD flavors are:

- FreeBSD
- NetBSD
- OpenBSD
- DragonFlyBSD
- OpenDarwin
- Mac OS X
- And so on

Linux

When we refer to Linux, we are referring to all Unix-like operating systems that use the GNU/Linux kernel architecture. The Linux kernel, released in 1991, is one of the best examples of a free and open source development initiative. Examples of popular Linux distributions are:

- Slackware
- Debian
- Ubuntu
- Red Hat Enterprise Linux
- CentOS
- Fedore Core
- Mandriva
- openSUSE
- Gentoo
- Linspire
- And so on

If for some reason your operating system does not fall into one of the Unix-like operating system categories, please consult your operating systems documentation and the OSSEC mailing list to find out if an OSSEC installation is possible.

Downloading OSSEC HIDS

The OSSEC HIDS is most commonly downloaded, compiled, and installed from its source code form. Precompiled packages are not currently available from www.ossec.net, with the exception of the Windows agent. However, the compiling, configuring, and installation of the OSSEC HIDS software is all handled with a single and simple to use script.

On Linux- or BSD-based systems, the installation begins the same way regardless of which install type you select. For Windows, an executable installer is provided and performs the agent install type.

NOTE

On most operating systems, the OSSEC HIDS can be installed with any of the three installation types. On Windows, however, only the agent install type is available. This means that protecting Windows hosts with the OSSEC HIDS always requires a server installation on one of the other operating systems.

Getting the Files

All the OSSEC HIDS files needed for installation to any operating system are available at the www.ossec.net/files/ Web site. There are three files of interest to us: the main source tar file, the Windows agent installer, and the checksum file.

The main source tar file contains the complete source code for the OSSEC HIDS, including the Windows agent code. Because Unix- and Linux-based operating systems provide complete development tools, the main source tar file contains everything needed to install the OSSEC HIDS. For Microsoft Windows, the installation is more complex and development tools are not readily available to build the OSSEC HIDS software. Because no development tools are available, an executable, GUI-based installer is provided that installs a precompiled OSSEC HIDS service. The third file is a checksum file used to validate the integrity of the downloaded files.

From the following URLs, download the main source tar file, the Windows agent installer, and the checksum files, using a browser or command-line utility such as wget:

- www.ossec.net/files/ossec-hids-1.4.tar.gz
- www.ossec.net/files/ossec-agent-win32-1.4.exe
- www.ossec.net/files/ossec-hids-1.4_checksum.txt

The checksums are provided to ensure the integrity of the downloaded files and allow you to check for file corruption or unintentional modification. If these checks fail, you will have to try the download again. From the command line, change to the directory where you saved the downloaded files and verify the checksums.

```
# md5sum -c ossec-hids-1.4_checksum.txt
ossec-hids-1.4.tar.gz: OK
ossec-agent-win32-1.4.exe: OK
```

NOTE

On some systems, the command *md5sum* might only be available as *md5*.

Preparing the System

Because the OSSEC HIDS installer must compile the application from source code the first time it runs, a working build environment is required on your system. For most operating systems of the Linux or BSD persuasion, a C compiler and supporting files is already be installed. If not, you must install *gcc* and *development headers* before proceeding.

NOTE

Make sure you review the system requirements in Chapter 1—Getting Started; otherwise, the OSSEC HIDS software might fail to build, causing the installation to abort.

Building and Installing

Whether you are doing a *local* or *server* installation, the first stage is the same. Extract the .tar.gz file, change into the created directory, and then run the install script.

```
# gunzip -c ossec-hids-1.3.tar.gz | tar -xf -
# cd ossec-hids-1.3
# ./install.sh
```

The installation script is divided into several steps to guide you through the installation. The steps are slightly different for each install type. However, the initial screen is the same for all installations and allows you to choose your preferred language. Here we choose the default *en* for English by pressing **Enter**.

NOTE

Values shown within braces, such as [en] on the installation language selection screen, are the default values for the associated installation option. Press **Enter** to confirm using the default option. Typically, the system defaults are sufficient, but please adjust the values as required by your installation requirements.

```
** Para instalação em português, escolha [br].
** 要使用中文进行安装, 请选择 [cn].
** Fur eine deutsche Installation wohlen Sie [de].
** For installation in English, choose [en].
** Para instalar en Español , eliga [es].
** Pour une installation en français, choisissez [fr].
** Per l'installazione in Italiano, scegli [it].
** 日本語でインストールします．選択して下さい [jp].
** Aby instalowa w jzyku Polskim, wybierz [pl].
** Для инструкций по устаноВке на русскоМ ,ВВеДите [ru].
```

```
  ** Za instalaciju na srpskom, izaberi [sr].
  ** Türkçe kurulum için seçin [tr].
(en/br/cn/de/es/fr/it/jp/pl/ru/sr/tr) [en]:
OSSEC HIDS v1.4 Installation Script - http://www.ossec.net
You are about to start the installation process of the OSSEC HIDS.
You must have a C compiler pre-installed in your system.
If you have any questions or comments, please send an e-mail
to dcid@ossec.net (or daniel.cid@gmail.com).
- System: Linux earth 2.6.20-16-generic
- User: root
- Host: earth
-- Press ENTER to continue or Ctrl-C to abort. --
```

Next, we press **Enter** to move to the selection of install type. At this point, you must decide which install type you require. You might now decide to jump ahead in the chapter to a specific install, but be sure to review all installation types because each type provides useful information about OSSEC HIDS components and features.

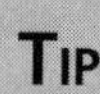

TIP

If you still have not decided which installation types you need, refer back to the section in Chapter 1 titled *Which Type Is Right for Me?*

Performing Local Installation

Local installations can only be done on Linux- and BSD-based operating systems, including Mac OS X. Start by choosing **local** installation in step 1 and then a directory location in step 2. The defaults are shown in square braces and can be accepted by pressing **Enter** or customized as in the case where we have chosen /opt/ossec instead of /var/ossec.

NOTE

The default location for the OSSEC HIDS is the /var/ossec directory. The location is not important as long as it is made to a directory where only the root user has write permissions. Wherever there is a reference to /var/ossec, you can substitute your preference.

```
1- What kind of installation do you want (server, agent, local or help)? local

   - Local installation chosen.

2- Setting up the installation environment.

  - Choose where to install the OSSEC HIDS [/var/ossec]: /var/ossec

    Installation will be made at /var/ossec .
```

Step 3, and the corresponding substeps, deal with notifications and alerts. At this point, you must decide which features you want to enable. You can alter any of the choices later in the ossec.conf file or by reinstalling the OSSEC HIDS.

The OSSEC HIDS communicates alert conditions that require your attention through email. You should specify an email address you check frequently. The sooner you are aware of a new threat, the sooner you can respond before it becomes a major problem.

WARNING

Use caution when choosing an SMTP server for *local* and *server* installations. You must be sure that SMTP relaying is permitted from the host running the OSSEC HIDS. Repeated denials on the SMTP server are likely to annoy your mail administrator. When in doubt, choose 127.0.0.1 and then alter the configuration after the installation, after you are certain of the correct address to use.

```
3- Configuring the OSSEC HIDS.

  3.1- Do you want e-mail notification? (y/n) [y]: y

   - What's your e-mail address? earth@localhost

   - We found your SMTP server as: 127.0.0.1

   - Do you want to use it? (y/n) [y]: y

   --- Using SMTP server: 127.0.0.1
```

The integrity check daemon is responsible for monitoring and reporting changes in system files. The rootkit detection engine regularly performs tests looking for evidence of an installed rootkit. Careful configuration of both services provides granular protection or notification of illicit file modifications, hidden network port activity, and other evidence of intrusion. The details of configuration and rule-tuning are addressed in later chapters. These features are very important for most HIDS solutions and should be enabled.

```
3.2- Do you want to run the integrity check daemon? (y/n) [y]: y

  - Running syscheck (integrity check daemon).

3.3- Do you want to run the rootkit detection engine? (y/n) [y]: y

  - Running rootcheck (rootkit detection).
```

Active response is a very powerful tool for taking automated actions to prevent intrusion or to reduce the extent of an intrusion. Often, an active response will block invasive activity much more quickly than you or your attacker can respond. If misconfigured, however, the active response can also lock you out of your system or interrupt vital services. By default, the OSSEC HIDS active response is quite safe and we recommend enabling it. Be sure, however, to have at least one or two well-trusted IP addresses in the white list so you can always access the system.

```
  3.4- Active response allows you to execute a specific
          command based on the events received. For example,
          you can block an IP address or disable access for
          a specific user.
          More information at:
          http://www.ossec.net/en/manual.html#active-response
   - Do you want to enable active response? (y/n) [y]: y
     - Active response enabled.
   - By default, we can enable the host-deny and the
     firewall-drop responses. The first one will add
     a host to the /etc/hosts.deny and the second one
     will block the host on iptables (if linux) or on
     ipfilter (if Solaris, FreeBSD or NetBSD).
   - They can be used to stop SSHD brute force scans,
     portscans and some other forms of attacks. You can
     also add them to block on snort events, for example.
   - Do you want to enable the firewall-drop response? (y/n) [y]: y
     - firewall-drop enabled (local) for levels >= 6
   - Default white list for the active response:
       - 192.168.65.2
   - Do you want to add more IPs to the white list? (y/n)? [n]: n
  3.6- Setting the configuration to analyze the following logs:
     -- /var/log/messages
     -- /var/log/auth.log
     -- /var/log/syslog
     -- /var/log/mail.info
- If you want to monitor any other file, just change
   the ossec.conf and add a new localfile entry.
   Any questions about the configuration can be answered
   by visiting us online at http://www.ossec.net .
   --- Press ENTER to continue ---
```

After you press **Enter**, the OSSEC HIDS is compiled, installed, and configured with the options you specified. When the installation is complete, the installer script provides you with some final information. You should make note of the information and take any recommended actions. Typically, any platform-specific steps needed to make the OSSEC HIDS operate fully are provided. For example, for the OSSEC HIDS to use the OpenBSD pf firewall, some lines must be added to the /etc/pf.conf script. The lines and instructions are provided in the final information.

TIP

If the compilation of the OSSEC HIDS application fails, you do not get the informational screen indicating how to stop and start the OSSEC HIDS. Instead, you will see the line "Building error. Unable to finish the installation." at the end of the compiler output.

This is typically related to a missing prerequisite. If this occurs, revisit Chapter 1 for tips on installing the correct build environment.

Now that the install is complete, we can start the OSSEC HIDS service by running the following command:

```
# /opt/ossec/bin/ossec-control start
```

Of course, with the initial configuration created by the installation script, the OSSEC HIDS might not do much for you just yet. In the next chapter, we cover altering the configuration to better suit your environment. With just a little more work, the OSSEC HIDS will become a powerful defensive tool against the invading hordes.

Tools & Traps...

Init Scripts—A Question of Timing

Depending on your platform, the OSSEC HIDS installer adds initialization scripts to start the OSSEC HIDS on your system. For systems that use SysV style initialization, primarily Linux, the script is added so that it starts for all common run levels. For BSD-style initializations, the script is added to the end of your /etc/rc.local script. In any case, but especially for BSD, you should review your system initialization to understand when the OSSEC HIDS starts compared with other services.

It is important with any security measure to make sure it is applied at the right point to avoid any unnecessary exposure or lapse in coverage. By ensuring that the OSSEC HIDS starts before network services, such as remote access or Web servers, you can be sure there are few momentary exposures.

With Linux, and other SysV style systems, the OSSEC HIDS has a start order that places it before most common network services for a *local* installation. For a *server* or *agent* installation, the OSSEC HIDS starts after all other network services, which is typically fine. In BSD, because the start is appended to the end of the /etc/rc.local script, the OSSEC HIDS starts after most network services, regardless of the install type. Depending on your system configuration, you might consider starting the OSSEC HIDS earlier, particularly if any other services take a long time to start.

Performing Server-Agent Installations

Server-agent installations are meant for a central controller with multiple agents, which is ideal for providing protection among networked hosts. It provides some advantages over simply having *local* installations on each host. This is because the server performs all log analysis for agents connected to it. Active responses are initiated from the server, but can be executed on an agent or all agents simultaneously.

Because Windows hosts can only be agents, a server is always required prior to installing the OSSEC HIDS on Microsoft Windows. Windows installations are covered separately in this chapter, after a Unix *server-agent* setup.

The *server* and *agent* installations proceed similar to the *local* installation, except that the server is configured to listen for communication from the agents.

Installing the Server

As with the *local* install type, *server* installations can only be done on Linux- and BSD-based operating systems, including Mac OS X. After the initial screen and language selection, we start by choosing ***server*** installation in step 1 and then a directory location in step 2. Defaults are shown in square braces and can be accepted by pressing **Enter**, or customized similar to the following:

```
1- What kind of installation do you want (server, agent, local or help)? server
  - Server installation chosen.
2- Setting up the installation environment.
  - Choose where to install the OSSEC HIDS [/var/ossec]: /var/ossec
    - Installation will be made at /var/ossec .
```

Step 3, and the corresponding sub steps, deal with notifications and alerts. At this point, you must decide which features you want to enable. You can alter any of the choices later in the ossec.conf file or by reinstalling the OSSEC HIDS.

WARNING

Use caution when choosing an SMTP server. You must be sure the SMTP server permits email to be relayed from the host running the OSSEC HIDS. Repeated denials on the SMTP server might annoy your mail administrator. When in doubt, choose 127.0.0.1 and then alter the configuration after you are certain of the correct address to use.

```
3- Configuring the OSSEC HIDS.
  3.1- Do you want e-mail notification? (y/n) [y]: y
    - What's your e-mail address? root@localhost
    - We found your SMTP server as: 127.0.0.1
```

```
   - Do you want to use it? (y/n) [y]: y
--- Using SMTP server: 127.0.0.1
```

The integrity check daemon is responsible for monitoring and reporting changes in system files. The rootkit detection engine regularly performs tests looking for evidence of an installed rootkit. These features are very important on most HIDS solutions and should be enabled. As with the local installation, these services, after being tuned, provide fine-grained protections.

```
3.2- Do you want to run the integrity check daemon? (y/n) [y]: y
  - Running syscheck (integrity check daemon).
3.3- Do you want to run the rootkit detection engine? (y/n) [y]: y
  - Running rootcheck (rootkit detection).
```

Active response is a very powerful tool for taking automated actions to prevent intrusion or reduce the extent of an intrusion. Often, an active response can block invasive activity much more quickly than you or your attacker can respond. If misconfigured, however, active response can also lock you out of your system or interrupt vital services. By default, the OSSEC HIDS active response is quite safe and we recommend enabling it. Be sure, however, to have at least one or two well-trusted IP addresses in the white list so that you can always access the system.

```
3.4- Active response allows you to execute a specific
       command based on the events received. For example,
       you can block an IP address or disable access for
       a specific user.
       More information at:
       http://www.ossec.net/en/manual.html#active-response
  - Do you want to enable active response? (y/n) [y]: y
    - Active response enabled.
  - By default, we can enable the host-deny and the
   firewall-drop responses. The first one will add
   a host to the /etc/hosts.deny and the second one
   will block the host on iptables (if linux) or on
   ipfilter (if Solaris, FreeBSD or NetBSD).
  - They can be used to stop SSHD brute force scans,
   portscans and some other forms of attacks. You can
   also add them to block on snort events, for example.
  - Do you want to enable the firewall-drop response? (y/n) [y]: y
    - firewall-drop enabled (local) for levels >= 6
  - Default white list for the active response:
      - 192.168.65.2
  - Do you want to add more IPs to the white list? (y/n)? [n]: n
```

With a server installation, the OSSEC HIDS can receive alerts through an encrypted channel (port 1514) or through syslog (port 514). Enabling remote syslog allows the OSSEC

HIDS to receive alerts using syslog. Typically, it is better to use encryption for the transport of any security related information; you can choose to disable remote syslog for this reason. Remote syslog can be enabled or disabled at any time in the main configuration file. For the moment, leave it enabled. The significance of providing remote syslog becomes clear after the rule-tuning and log analysis sections of this book.

```
3.5- Do you want to enable remote syslog (port 514 udp)? (y/n) [y]: y
  - Remote syslog enabled.
3.6- Setting the configuration to analyze the following logs:
    -- /var/log/messages
    -- /var/log/auth.log
    -- /var/log/syslog
    -- /var/log/mail.info
  - If you want to monitor any other file, just change
    the ossec.conf and add a new localfile entry.
    Any questions about the configuration can be answered
    by visiting us online at http://www.ossec.net .
--- Press ENTER to continue ---
```

After you press **Enter**, the OSSEC HIDS is compiled, installed, and configured with the options you specified. When the installation is complete, the installer script provides you with some final information. You should make note of the information and take any recommended actions. For example, for the OSSEC HIDS to use the OpenBSD pf firewall, a few lines must be added to the /etc/pf.conf.

TIP

If the compile of the OSSEC HIDS application fails, you do not get the informational screen indicating how to stop and start OSSEC HIDS. Instead, you will see the line "Building error. Unable to finish the installation." at the end of the compiler output.

This is typically always related to a missing prerequisite. If this occurs, revisit Chapter 1 for tips on installing the correct build environment.

You now have a working *server* installation of the OSSEC HIDS. All binaries, scripts, and configurations for the OSSEC HIDS are in the installation directory you specified. To verify that everything is ok, start the OSSEC HIDS and complete the installation.

```
# /opt/ossec/bin/ossec-control start
```

Before moving on to setting up agents, remember that the OSSEC HIDS server needs to receive communication from agents on port 1514 and possibly 514. You must ensure that the firewall or packet filter on the server host machine allows this traffic. Each operating system and software distribution provides a way to do this. You must enable inbound UDP traffic on ports 1514 and 514 from any subnets where agents are installed. The firewall rule must maintain connection state because the agent expects responses from the server.

Managing Agents

Before moving on to another install type, let's review the key management in the OSSEC HIDS. Agents must be able to identify themselves to the server, and the server must be able to validate the identity of the agent. This ensures that illicit messages aren't processed by the server when sent from non-agent hosts.

The server-agent traffic is encrypted and validated using pre-shared keys. These keys must be generated on the server and then *imported* on the agent side. The procedure is the same regardless of the agent platform. All agent key management is done using the *manage_agents* utility in the OSSEC HIDS bin directory.

You must create a key for each agent by adding the agent using the *manage_agents* utility. Run the utility and then choose *Add an agent* by entering **A**.

```
# /opt/ossec/bin/manage_agents
****************************************
* OSSEC HIDS v1.4 Agent manager.       *
* The following options are available: *
****************************************
   (A)dd an agent (A).
   (E)xtract key for an agent (E).
   (L)ist already added agents (L).
   (R)emove an agent (R).
   (Q)uit.
Choose your action: A,E,L,R or Q: A
```

You are prompted for host details and an identifier for the agent. The IP address, not the hostname, of the agent host must be provided. The ID can be any number you choose, but it must be numeric. The name can be any identifying text that is meaningful to you, without spaces, but typically it makes most sense to use the hostname.

```
- Adding a new agent (use '\q' to return to the main menu).
  Please provide the following:
   * A name for the new agent: mars
   * The IP Address of the new agent: 192.168.65.40
   * An ID for the new agent[001]: 001
Agent information:
```

```
    ID:001
    Name:mars
    IP Address:192.168.65.40
Confirm adding it?(y/n): y
Agent added.
```

Repeat this procedure for each agent you must install. After you are done creating keys, restart the OSSEC HIDS service, using /var/ossec/bin/ossec-control, so that the OSSEC HIDS can read the updated keys and permitted agent IP addresses. Failure to restart the OSSEC HIDS server might result in connection failures for the agents. After the OSSEC HIDS software is installed on the agents, you will return to the server to retrieve the keys for each agent using the same *manage_agents* utility.

Installing Agents

Agent installation on Unix/Linux/BSD platforms is performed similar to the other install types. The only notable difference is that you must provide the server IP address. After installation, the agent does not start properly until the key, which is generated on the server, is imported.

For Microsoft Windows, the installation is also simple, but it is performed using a graphical installer. Importing the key from the server to the agent typically requires Secure Shell (SSH) access to the server, so make sure the Windows host has an SSH client.

TIP

After the install.sh script is successfully run once, the files are compiled. The install.sh script has a *binary-install* option that allows you to reinstall without recompiling every time. Also, by copying the install files to another host, you can perform the installation on multiple hosts without recompiling every time. This assumes, of course, that all hosts are of the same operating system.

The hosts still require some build tools, such as *make*, to be installed, but do not require a full build environment.

Installing the Unix Agent

The same installation procedure used for *local* and *server* installations is used for an *agent* installation on Unix- and Linux-based hosts. Start by choosing ***agent*** installation in step 1 and then a directory location in step 2. The defaults are shown in square brackets and can be accepted by pressing **Enter**, or customized as in this case. You will notice that the agent install has fewer options to configure. This is because the server does much of the work.

```
1- What kind of installation do you want (server, agent, local or help)? agent

    - Agent(client) installation chosen.

2- Setting up the installation environment.

  - Choose where to install the OSSEC HIDS [/var/ossec]: /opt/ossec

    - Installation will be made at /opt/ossec .

3- Configuring the OSSEC HIDS.

   3.1- What's the IP Address of the OSSEC HIDS server?: 192.168.65.20

    - Adding Server IP 192.168.65.20

   3.2- Do you want to run the integrity check daemon? (y/n) [y]: y

    - Running syscheck (integrity check daemon).

   3.3- Do you want to run the rootkit detection engine? (y/n) [y]: y

    - Running rootcheck (rootkit detection).
```

On the agent installation, notice that the only options for active response are enable or disable. Enabling active response on an agent allows the server to initiate responses that are executed on this agent. We recommend enabling for all agents.

```
  3.4 - Do you want to enable active response? (y/n) [y]: y

  3.5- Setting the configuration to analyze the following logs:
    -- /var/log/messages
    -- /var/log/authlog
    -- /var/log/secure
    -- /var/log/xferlog
    -- /var/log/maillog

- If you want to monitor any other file, just change
   the ossec.conf and add a new localfile entry.
   Any questions about the configuration can be answered
   by visiting us online at http://www.ossec.net .

--- Press ENTER to continue ---
```

After you press **Enter**, the OSSEC HIDS is compiled, installed, and configured with the options you specified. When the installation is complete, the installer script provides you with some final information. You should make note of the information and take any recommended actions. For example, for the OSSEC HIDS to use the OpenBSD pf firewall, a few lines must be added to the /etc/pf.conf script.

TIP

If the compilation of the OSSEC HIDS application fails, you do not get the informational screen indicating how to stop and start the OSSEC HIDS. Instead, you will see the line "Building error. Unable to finish the installation." at the end of the compiler output.

This is typically always related to a missing prerequisite. If this occurs, revisit Chapter 1 for tips on installing the correct build environment.

Before starting the OSSEC HIDS agent, the key generated on the server must be imported. The *manage_agents* utility is used to import the keys. Because the keys are on the server, the normal method for retrieving the keys is to connect to the server using SSH and run the *manage_agents* utility.

From the manage agents menu, enter **e** to extract a key. You are provided with a list of already configured agents. Choose your agent by entering the correct ID. The key is displayed so you can copy it to your clipboard.

```
# /opt/ossec/bin/manage_agents
****************************************
* OSSEC HIDS v1.3 Agent manager.       *
* The following options are available: *
****************************************
   (A)dd an agent (A).
   (E)xtract key for an agent (E).
   (L)ist already added agents (L).
   (R)emove an agent (R).
   (Q)uit.
Choose your action: A,E,L,R or Q: e
Available agents:
   ID: 001, Name: mars, IP: 192.168.65.40
Provide the ID of the agent to extract the key (or '\q' to quit): 001
Agent key information for '001' is:
MDAxIG1hcnMgMTkyLjE2OC42NS40MCBmY2UzMjM4OTc1ODgzYTU4ZWM3YTRkYWJiZTJmMjQ2Y2ViODhmMzl
mYjE3MmI4OGUzMTE0MDczMzVhYjk2OTRh
** Press ENTER to return to the main menu.
```

Exit from the *manage_agents* utility on the server by entering **q** from the menu, exit the SSH session, and return to the agent host. To import the key, run the *manage_agents* utility on the agent host. The menu for agents is much simpler, because importing keys is the only option. Enter **i** to import and then paste the key value previously saved to your clipboard.

```
# /opt/ossec/bin/manage_agents
****************************************
* OSSEC HIDS v1.3 Agent manager.       *
* The following options are available: *
****************************************
   (I)mport key from the server (I).
   (Q)uit.
```

```
Choose your action: I or Q: i

* Provide the Key generated by the server.
* The best approach is to cut and paste it.
*** OBS: Do not include spaces or new lines.

Paste it here (or '\q' to quit):
MDAxIG1hcnMgMTkyLjE2OC42NS40MCBmY2UzMjM4OTc1ODgzYTU4ZWM3YTRkYWJiZTJmMjQ2Y2ViODhmMzl
mYjE3MmI4OGUzMTE0MDczMzVhYjk2OTRh

Agent information:
  ID:001
  Name:mars
  IP Address:192.168.65.40
Confirm adding it?(y/n): y
Added.
** Press ENTER to return to the main menu.

****************************************
* OSSEC HIDS v1.3 Agent manager.       *
* The following options are available: *
****************************************
  (I)mport key from the server (I).
  (Q)uit.
Choose your action: I or Q: q

** You must restart the server for your changes to have effect.

manage_agents: Exiting ..
```

Now that the agent installation is complete, we can start the OSSEC HIDS service by running the following command:

```
# /opt/ossec/bin/ossec-control start
```

The agent starts and connects to the server. You can verify this by checking the agent logs (/var/ossec/logs/ossec.log) and finding messages similar to the following near the end of the file:

```
2007/10/10 23:25:48 ossec-agentd: Connecting to server (192.168.65.20:1514).
2007/10/10 23:25:48 ossec-agentd(4102): Connected to the server.
```

Installing the Windows Agent

As you have already seen, performing the local, server, and agent installations on Unix-based operating systems is similar and relatively easy. The Windows installation, however, is different. This is because Windows environments do not typically have development tools included. Even when these tools are available, they often require more preparation before use compared with Unix and Linux systems.

Because of these issues, the Windows agent comes precompiled and packaged in a graphical installation wizard. The text menu procedure seen with the other installations is replaced with

GUI screens. Similarly, after the software is installed, there is a GUI version of the manage agents utility.

TIP

Windows operating systems do not come with SSH utilities for remote access to Unix hosts. SSH access to the server host is required to complete the agent install. Fortunately, there is a freely available SSH utility for Windows called PuTTY, which has become exceedingly popular.

PuTTY is an SSH and telnet terminal emulator that can be downloaded from www.chiark.greenend.org.uk/~sgtatham/putty/. You should install an SSH client before installing the OSSEC HIDS just to make the process easier.

Begin by running the installation executable ossec-agent-win32-1.4.exe as seen in Figure 2.1, to open the wizard.

Figure 2.1 Launching the Installer

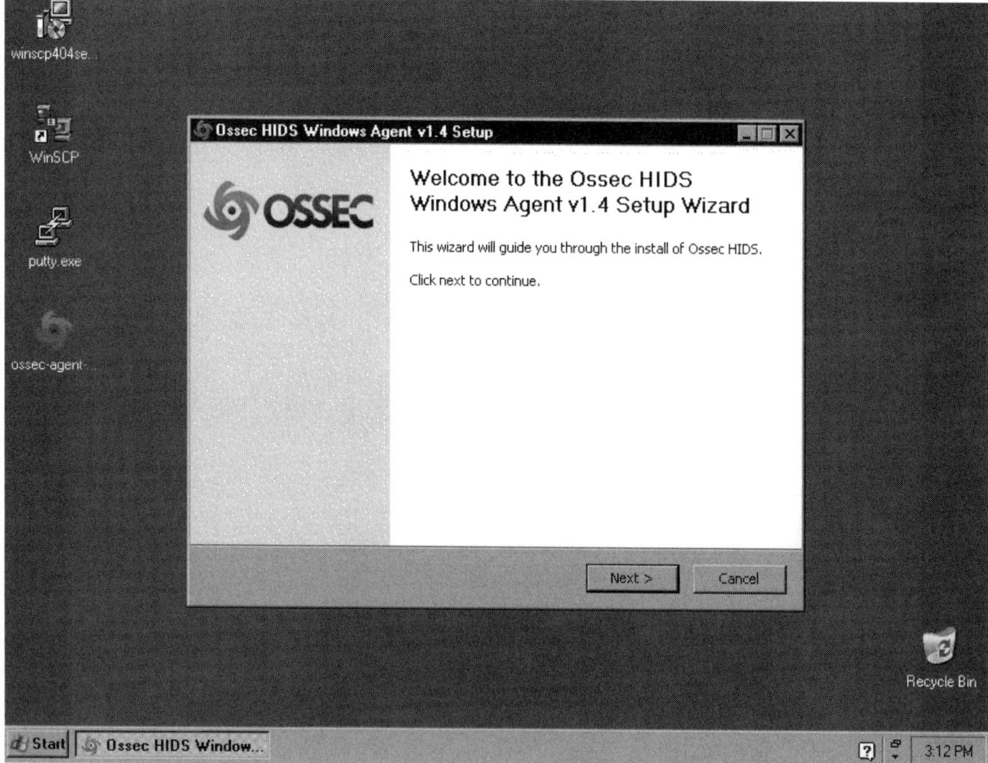

Click **Next** to start the installation.

Review the license agreement and then click **I Agree** to continue (Figure 2.2).

Figure 2.2 Accepting the License Text

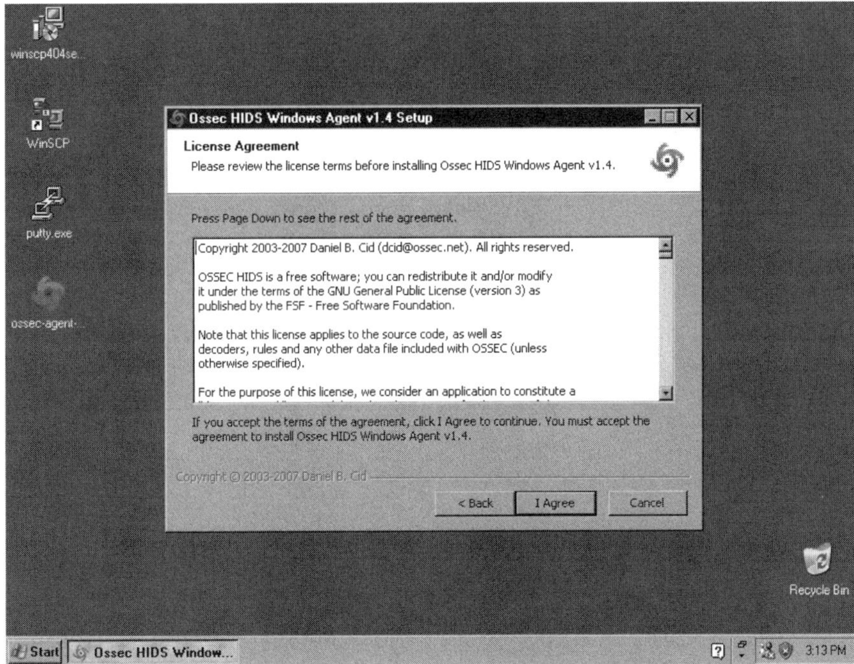

Choose the components you want to install, and click **Next** (Figure 2.3).

Figure 2.3 Selecting Components

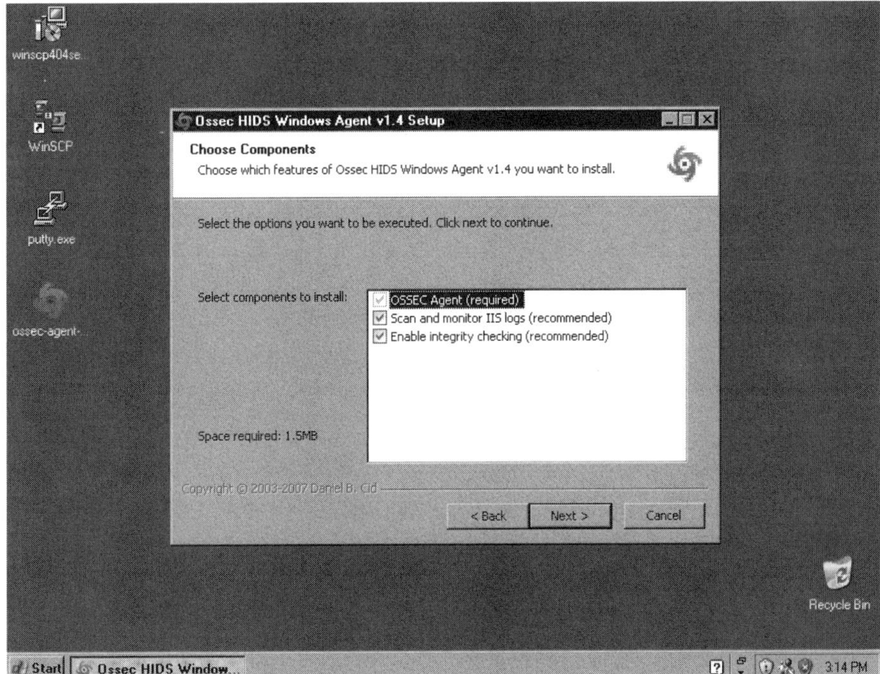

NOTE

The default installation options work in most cases.

Accept the default installation folder, or click **Browse** to specify a new location. Click **Install** to continue (Figure 2.4).

Figure 2.4 Specifying the Location

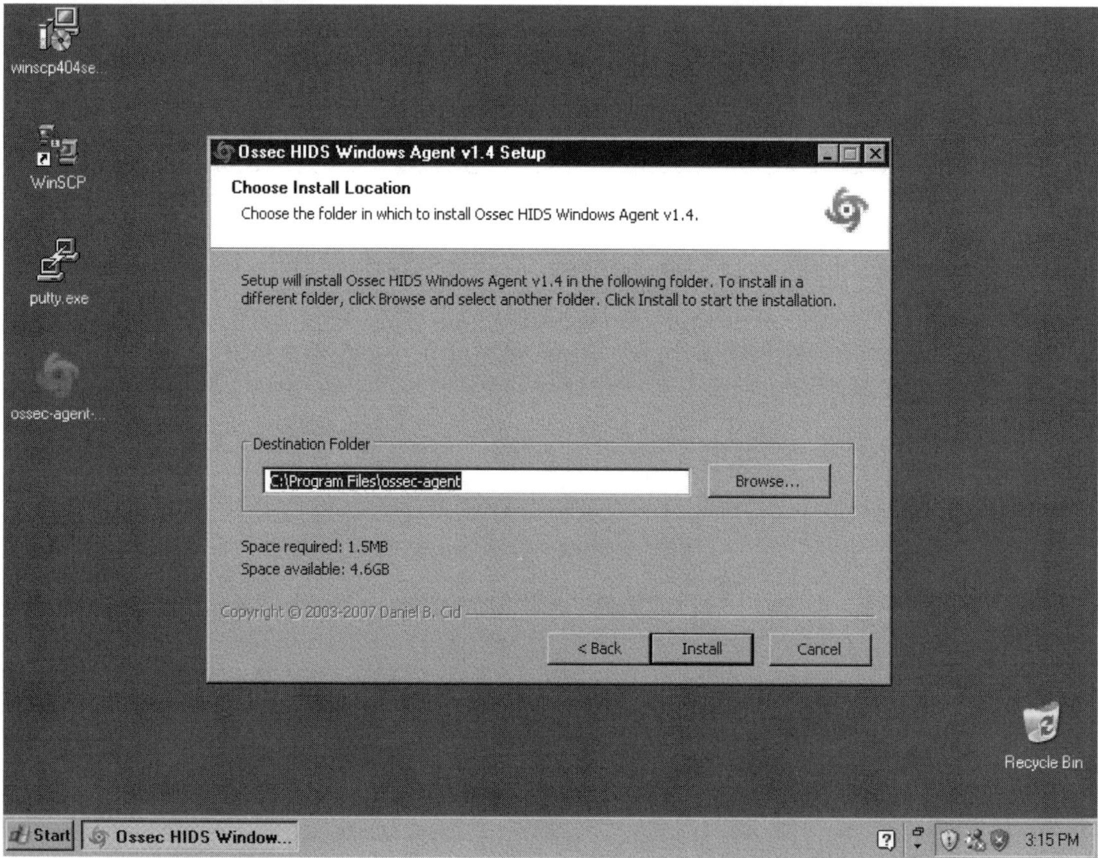

Because this is an agent installation, there are very few questions to answer as part of the installation. Apart from picking the location in Figure 2.3 and importing the agent key in Figures 2.5 through 2.9, the installation on Windows is very simple.

Launch the SSH client on your Windows host and connect to the OSSEC HIDS server. We must use SSH to connect to the OSSEC HIDS server, *Extract* the key for this agent, and then paste the key in the Authentication key field (Figure 2.5).

Figure 2.5 Managing the Agent

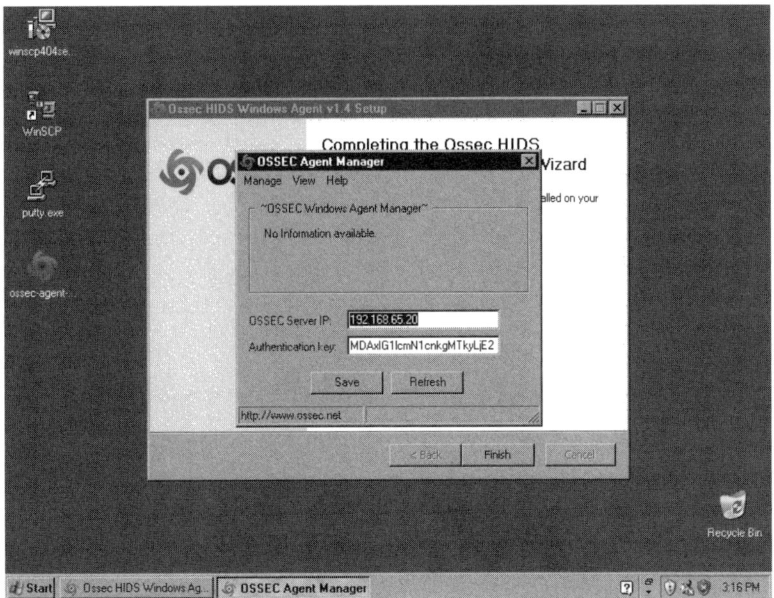

PuTTY is an ideal SSH client and is shown in Figure 2.6. In the Host Name field, type the IP address or hostname of your OSSEC HIDS server and then click **Open**. If this is your first time connecting to the server from this Windows host, you are asked to accept the server SSH identity. Accept the server identity, log in to the server, and then execute the *manage_agents* utility.

Figure 2.6 Connecting to the Server

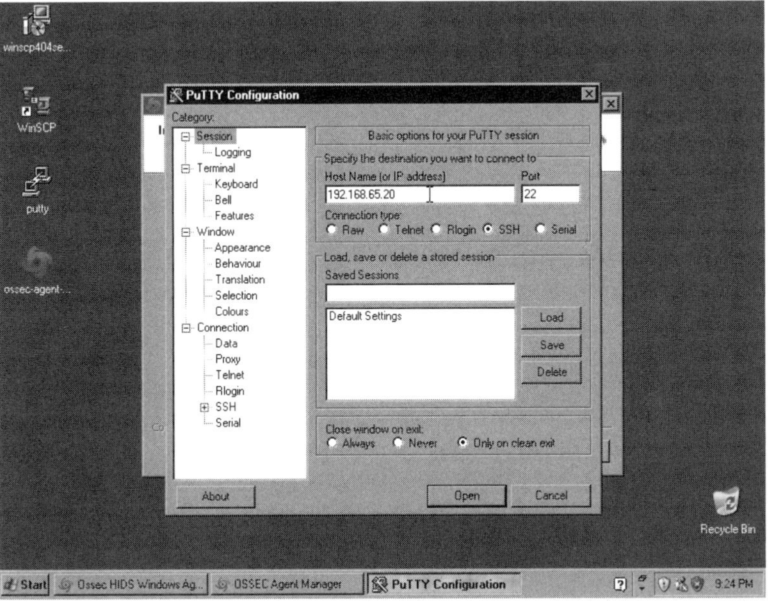

Enter **E** to extract the agent key for the current Windows host (Figure 2.7).

Figure 2.7 Running manage_agents

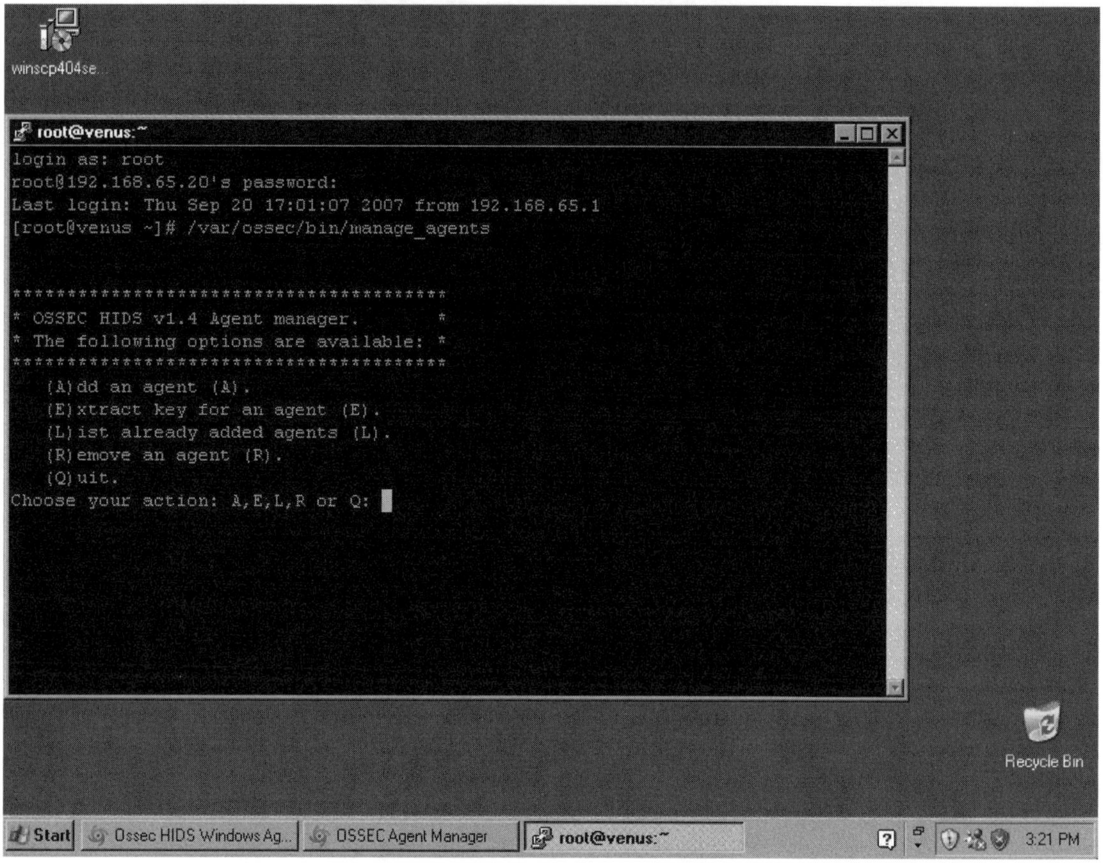

In this case, the host is *mercury*, which has ID 002. Enter **002**, select the key information, and copy it to the clipboard (Figure 2.8).

Now return to the OSSEC HIDS installer.

Type the OSSEC HIDS server IP address and paste the agent key information into the appropriate fields. Click **Save** (Figure 2.9).

You are asked to confirm the values by clicking **OK**. After the values have been confirmed, exit the Agent Manager by clicking the **X** at the top-right corner of the window (Figure 2.10).

Figure 2.8 Copying the Key to the Clipboard

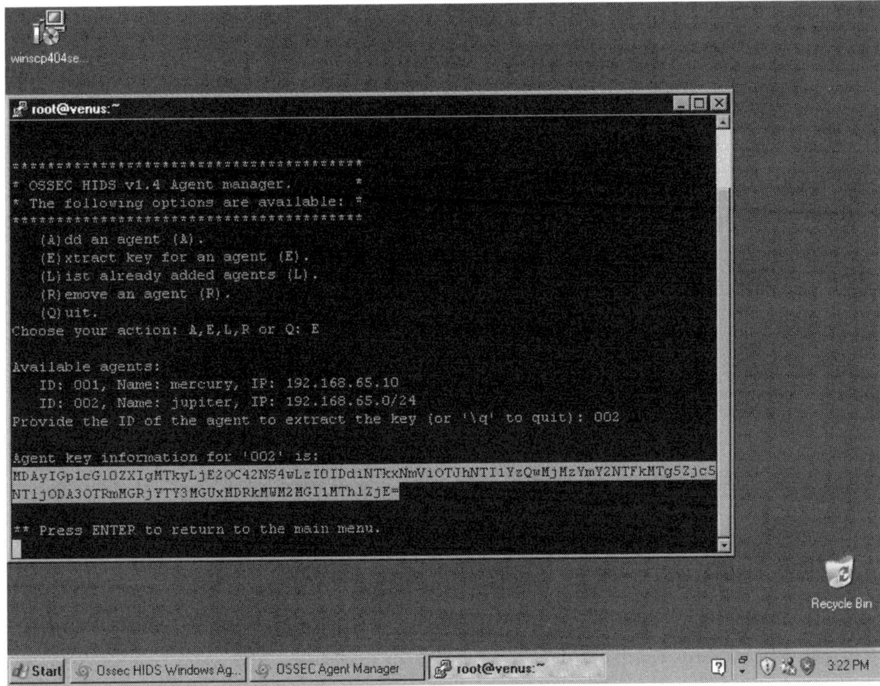

Figure 2.9 Pasting the Key

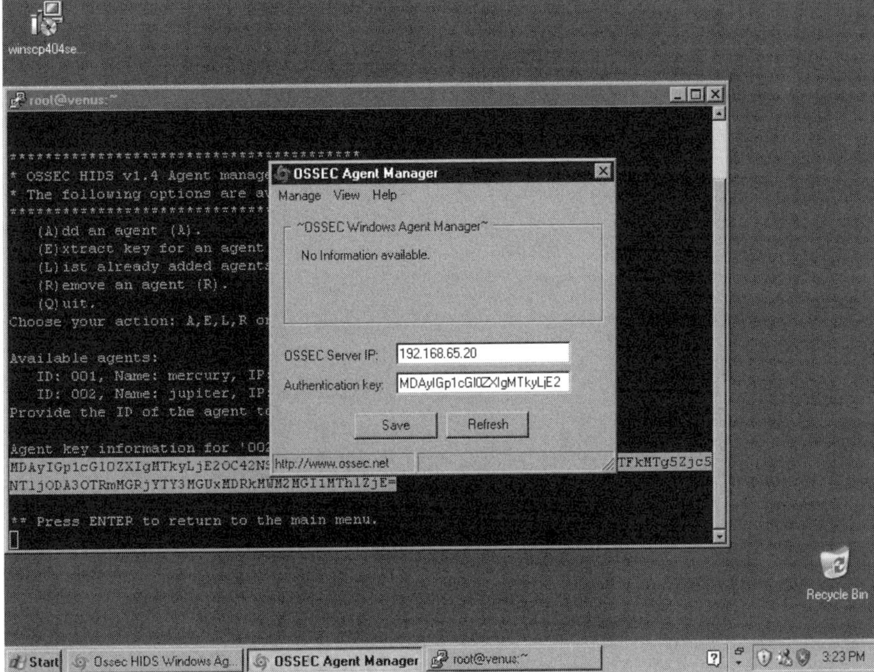

Figure 2.10 Confirming the Import

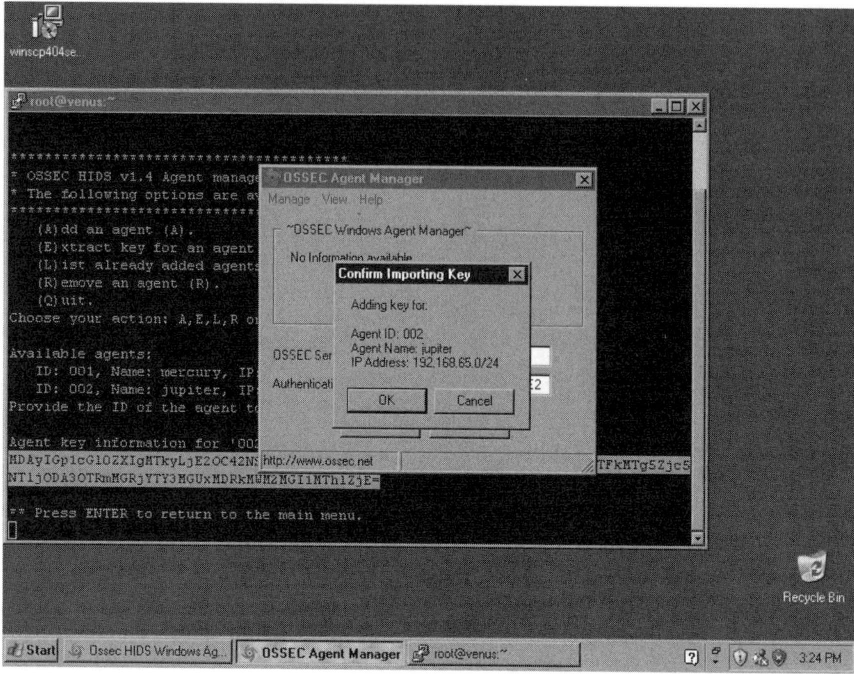

The installer asks if you want to start OSSEC HIDS; click **OK** (Figure 2.11).

Figure 2.11 Starting the OSSEC HIDS

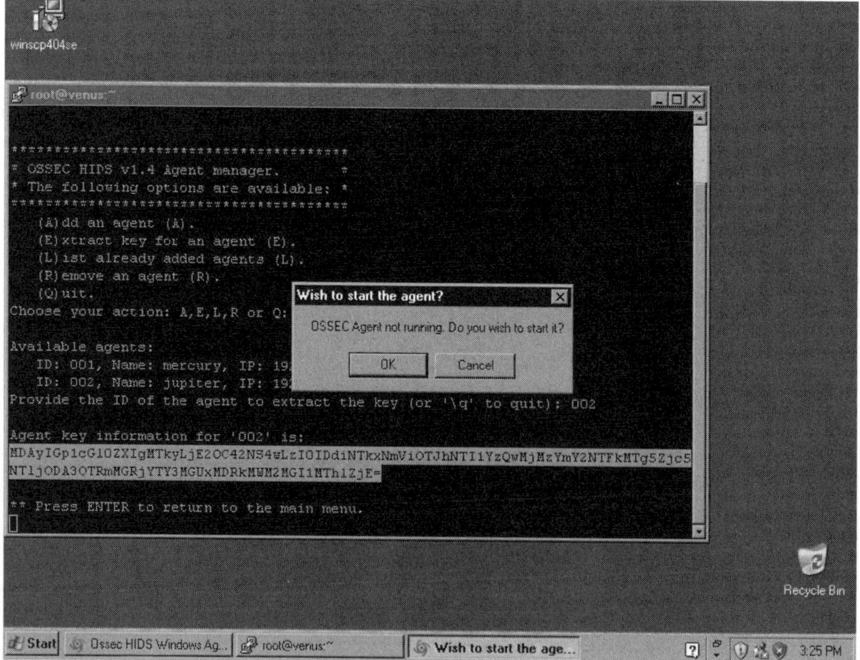

The Windows agent is now installed and running. To confirm that the agent is connected to the server, let's look at the logs for the Windows agent. In Figure 2.12, the two messages *Connecting to server* and *Connected to server* confirm that the agent key is properly imported and the agent is able to connect to UDP port 1514. The Windows agent is successfully installed and communicating with the server.

Figure 2.12 Confirming the Server Connection

```
2007/10/20 21:39:16 ossec-agent: No previous counter available for 'mercury'.
2007/10/20 21:39:16 ossec-agent: Assigning counter for agent mercury: '0:0'.
2007/10/20 21:39:16 ossec-agent: Assigning sender counter: 0:10
2007/10/20 21:39:16 ossec-agent: Connecting to server (192.168.65.20:1514).
2007/10/20 21:39:16 ossec-agent: Starting syscheckd thread.
2007/10/20 21:39:16 ossec-rootcheck: Started (pid: 1980).
2007/10/20 21:39:16 ossec-agent: Monitoring registry entry: 'HKEY_LOCAL_MACHINE\Software\Classes'.
2007/10/20 21:39:16 ossec-agent: Monitoring registry entry: 'HKEY_LOCAL_MACHINE\Software\Microsoft
2007/10/20 21:39:16 ossec-agent: Monitoring registry entry: 'HKEY_LOCAL_MACHINE\Software\Policies'
2007/10/20 21:39:16 ossec-agent: Monitoring registry entry: 'HKEY_LOCAL_MACHINE\System\CurrentCont
2007/10/20 21:39:16 ossec-agent: Monitoring registry entry: 'HKEY_LOCAL_MACHINE\System\CurrentCont
2007/10/20 21:39:16 ossec-agent: Monitoring registry entry: 'HKEY_LOCAL_MACHINE\Security'.
2007/10/20 21:39:16 ossec-agent: Monitoring directory: 'C:\WINDOWS'.
2007/10/20 21:39:16 ossec-agent: Started (pid: 1980).
2007/10/20 21:39:17 ossec-agent(4102): Connected to the server.
2007/10/20 21:39:17 ossec-agent(1951): Analyzing event log: 'Application'.
2007/10/20 21:39:17 ossec-agent(1951): Analyzing event log: 'Security'.
2007/10/20 21:39:17 ossec-agent(1951): Analyzing event log: 'System'.
2007/10/20 21:39:18 ossec-agent: Started (pid: 1980).
```

Streamlining the Installations

Because the installation script is menu-driven, it does not lend itself well to an automated installation. On the server side, this is not a significant issue because there are fewer servers. On the agent side, however, this can be cumbersome. Fortunately, the OSSEC HIDS file structure and configuration is reasonably simple, and therefore there are a few tricks we can play.

Install Once, Copy Everywhere

With the agents in particular, almost all the files are identical for every agent. The one significant exception is the *client.keys* file, which must be unique for each host. Assuming a mass installation is required and that the host operating system is virtually identical for all agents, we can install to one agent and then replicate the files to all agents.

Similarly, if you or your organization has a standard system image, the files can be added to the image and therefore automatically installed on each host. This is a common strategy for many organizations or enterprises, and works well for the OSSEC HIDS. The only customization required is to properly import the agent key on each host. This, too, can be done more directly than with the cut-and-paste method, which is difficult to automate.

In the case of Unix-based hosts, SSH is used for file transfers and remote access. Virtually every Unix administrator is familiar with its use and utility.

Unix, Linux, and BSD

Because all of the OSSEC HIDS files (excluding the initialization scripts) are contained the directory where it is installed, we can copy this entire directory structure (excluding etc/client.keys) to each host using whichever file transfer method is most convenient. It is important, however, to preserve file permissions and ownership during the transfer. Typically, this means using tar to package the files, transferring the tar file to the destination host, and then extracting on the host. Assuming the OSSEC HIDS is installed at /var/ossec and the agent hosts are all Linux, the tar file can be created using:

```
# cd /; tar -exclude client.keys -cf /tmp/ossec.tar var/ossec \
etc/init.d/ossec 'find etc -name "S[0-9][0-9]ossec"' \
'find etc -name "K[0-9][0-9]ossec"'
```

Now, assuming that the target host is 192.168.65.30, we can transfer the full OSSEC HIDS install in one long line. The *ossec* user must be created on the target to preserve permission so this is included:

```
# cat /tmp/ossec.tar | ssh root@192.168.65.30 \
"groupadd ossec; useradd -g ossec -d /var/ossec ossec; cd / ; tar -xf - "
```

The full OSSEC HIDS installation, configuration, and rules have been transferred to the remote agent, including initialization scripts and proper permissions. These commands also work similarly with any Unix-based operating system that has SSH installed. All that remains now is to import the keys to each agent.

Push the Keys

With all the files in place on the agents, each agent needs a key. The only difference between the client.keys file on the server and the file on an agent host is the number of lines. The server copy of the client.keys file has all agent keys, with one per line. The agent client.keys file has only the one line belonging to that agent.

Configuring the keys on the agent simply requires you to extract the single line for that agent to a file and then copy that file to the agent host. On the server side, because it is always Unix or Linux based, extracting the key for a single agent is the first step. Assuming the agent name provided when creating the key is *mars* and that the OSSEC HIDS is installed at /var/ossec:

```
# grep 192.168.65.30 /var/ossec/etc/client.keys > /tmp/agent.key
```

Unix, Linux, and BSD

Pushing the key to a Unix- or Linux-based host is also a one-line command. Assuming the OSSEC HIDS is installed to /var/ossec on the agent:

```
# scp /tmp/agent.key root@192.168.65.30:/var/ossec/etc/client.keys
```

Alternatively, if the agent is accessible using a networked file system, a file copy can be performed. While this approach does not provide a complete solution, you can see that the steps required to perform a remote installation and configuration of the OSSEC HIDS are easy.

Summary

The OSSEC HIDS is an easily accessible HIDS solution, offering a simple, menu-driven installation. It can be downloaded from the OSSEC Web site as uncompiled source code, allowing you to build and compile the application for any operating system, or as a binary executable file specifically for Windows agent deployments.

To build and compile the OSSEC source code you must first ensure that the necessary development tools are installed. The two modes of installation, *local* and *server-agent*, provide the flexibility to plan complex deployments. While the *server-agent* installation requires minor extra effort, getting the agents connected to the servers is a simple task.

The OSSEC HIDS server must receive communication from agents on port 1514 and possibly 514. You must ensure that the firewall or packet filter on the OSSEC server allows this traffic. Each operating system and software distribution provides a way to do this, so please consult your operating system documentation.

Installing the OSSEC HIDS on multiple hosts can be automated using a combination of the SSH protocol and some Unix commands. This allows you to deploy OSSEC HIDS agents to multiple hosts without having to physically sit at every computer you must configure.

At this point, you have seen that performing an OSSEC HIDS installation takes minimal time and effort. Local installations are effortless and a great way to get functioning with the OSSEC HIDS quickly. With this introduction to the accessibility of the OSSEC HIDS, you are now ready to examine more information about this remarkable security solution.

Solutions Fast Track

Downloading the OSSEC HIDS

☑ The OSSEC HIDS is most commonly downloaded, compiled, and installed from the source code available on the OSSEC Web site (www.ossec.net).

☑ Because Unix- and Linux-based operating systems provide complete development tools, the main OSSEC source tar file contains everything needed to install the OSSEC HIDS.

☑ Because the OSSEC HIDS installer must compile the application from source code the first time it runs, a working build environment is required on your system. For most Linux and BSD operating systems, a C compiler and supporting files are already installed. If the files are not installed, you must install gcc and development headers before proceeding.

☑ Because development tools are not typically installed on most Microsoft Windows systems, an executable, GUI-based installer is provided that installs a precompiled OSSEC HIDS service.

Building and Installing the OSSEC HIDS

- ☑ The installation script is divided into several easy steps to guide you through the installation.
- ☑ The steps are slightly different for each of the install types, however; the initial screen is the same for all installations.
- ☑ The OSSEC HIDS installer allows you to choose your installation language of choice from one of 12 supported languages, including English, Brazilian Portuguese, Chinese, German, Spanish, French, Italian, Japanese, Polish, Russian, Serbian, and Turkish.

Performing a Local Installation

- ☑ Local installations can only be done on Linux-, Unix-, and BSD-based operating systems.
- ☑ The integrity check daemon is responsible for monitoring and reporting changes in system files.
- ☑ The rootkit detection engine regularly performs tests looking for evidence of an installed rootkit.
- ☑ Careful configuration of both services provides fine-grained protection or notification of illicit file modifications, hidden network port activity, and other evidence of intrusion.
- ☑ Depending on your platform, the OSSEC HIDS installer adds initialization scripts to start the OSSEC HIDS on your system.

Performing Server-Agent Installations

- ☑ Server-agent installations are meant for a central controller with multiple agents.
- ☑ Because Microsoft Windows hosts can only be agents, a server is always required prior to installing the OSSEC HIDS on Windows.
- ☑ The OSSEC HIDS server must receive communication from agents on port 1514 and possibly 514, so firewall rules might need to be adjusted in your environment to allow this communication.
- ☑ Agents must be able to identify themselves to the server, and the server must be able to validate the identity of the agent. This ensures that illicit messages are not processed by the server when sent from non-agent hosts.
- ☑ Importing the key from the server to the agent typically requires SSH access to the server.

- ☑ The OSSEC HIDS Windows agent comes precompiled and packaged in a graphical installation wizard. The text menu procedure seen with the other installations is replaced with GUI screens. Similarly, after the software is installed, there is a GUI version of the *manage_agents* utility.

Streamlining Installation

- ☑ Using SSH and some simple Unix commands, you can install and configure multiple OSSEC HIDS agents from one central location.
- ☑ The *ossec* user must be created on every remote host to ensure file permissions are synchronized across your deployment.
- ☑ If the agent is accessible using a networked file system, the *client.keys* file can be copied from one file system to the networked file system.

Frequently Asked Questions

Q: Where can I download the OSSEC HIDS files I need?

A: All files needed for your OSSEC HIDS installation can be found at the OSSEC Web site at www.ossec.net.

Q: What files do I need to install the OSSEC HIDS?

A: If you plan to install the OSSEC HIDS on a Unix, Linux, or BSD operating system, you need the source code tar.gz archive. If you plan to install the OSSEC HIDS on a Microsoft Windows system, you can download the precompiled Windows agent installation executable. Regardless of the file you download, it is strongly reccomended that you also download the checksum text file to validate the integrity of your downloads prior to installation.

Q: I don't have development tools installed on my Unix, Linux, or BSD machine. Is there a precompiled OSSEC HIDS executable for Unix, Linux, or BSD operating systems?

A: At the time of this writing, there were no officially supported OSSEC HIDS packages available for download. The OSSEC HIDS team, however, is investigating packages for Debian/Ubuntu, Mac OS X, and Red Hat based operating systems as a future roadmap item.

Q: What languages does the OSSEC HIDS installer support?

A: The OSSEC HIDS installer allows you to choose your installation language of choice from one of 12 supported languages, including English, Brazilian Portuguese, Chinese, German, Spanish, French, Italian, Japanese, Polish, Russian, Serbian, and Turkish.

Q: I don't see my native language listed. How can I get support for my language into the OSSEC HIDS?

A: The OSSEC HIDS team is always looking for translators for documentation and the user interface. If you, or someone you know, is capable of translating from one of the currently supported languages, please contact the OSSEC HIDS development team.

Q: The installer wants me to install the OSSEC HIDS in the /var/ossec directory, but I want to put it somewhere else. Does it matter what directory I install to?

A: You can install the OSSEC HIDS to any directory on your system as long as the root user has write access to that directory.

Q: If I did not enable one of the features during installation, can I enable that feature later?

A: Yes, you can run the installer script as many times as you like to make changes to the current configuration or edit the existing configuration. The configuration of the OSSEC HIDS is covered in greater depth later in this book.

Q: Active response sounds potentially dangerous. Should I still enable it?

A: Even though active response could be potentially dangerous, we still recommend that you enable it. It is a very powerful feature of the OSSEC HIDS and its configuration is discussed in greater detail later in this book.

Q: When the installation completed there was a message indicating that a startup script could not be created. What do I do now?

A: The OSSEC HIDS installer is able to create a startup script on most operating systems, but if one is not created, you can create your own initialization script to launch the OSSEC HIDS on system boot.

Q: How do I manually start the OSSEC HIDS processes?

A: If you want to start the OSSEC HIDS manually, you can run *ossec-control start* from the bin directory where your OSSEC HIDS installation is located. Please note that the OSSEC HIDS might need to be started as the root user, so you might have to log in as a user with root permissions or leverage *sudo* to run the command.

Q: When should I install my OSSEC HIDS server—before or after my agents?

A: When installing your OSSEC HIDS agents, you are asked to supply the IP address for your OSSEC HIDS server. It is always recommended that your OSSEC HIDS server be installed prior to deploying your agents.

Q: How do I manage my agents?

A: On Unix, Linux, and BSD operating systems you can run the *manage_agents* utility to add new agents, extract keys for agents, list agents, and remove existing agents. On a Windows agent, you can click on the Manage Agents icon where your *ossec* start menu group is located.

Q: The agent is not able to connect to the server, what's wrong?

A: There are two common issues. If there are no messages in the server log regarding the agent, chances are there is a firewall blocking port 1514 between the server and agent. If you see a message similar to:

```
2007/05/23 09:27:35 ossec-remoted(1403): Incorrectly formated message from
'xxx.xxx.xxx.xxx'.
```

there is an issue with the key on the agent. Either the key is used by another agent or the IP address configured in the key is incorrect.

Q: When copying the OSSEC HIDS files from one system to another, are there any files I shouldn't copy?

A: Because each OSSEC HIDS agent requires its own generated *client.keys* file, and the OSSEC HIDS server copy of *client.keys* contains all agent keys, it is recommended that you exclude this file from your copy.

Q: How can I get the OSSEC HIDS files to the remote systems?

A: Depending on your environment, you might be able to use SSH to securely transfer the files from one system to the other. If you have a networked file system, you can copy the files from one file system to the other. Alternately, if no connection is available, you can simply copy the files to a floppy, CD-ROM, or DVD, and then copy the files to the system.

Q: Which command can I use to securely copy the key from the OSSEC HIDS server to the remote agent?

A: You can use the *grep* command to extract the OSSEC HIDS agent key from the OSSEC HIDS server *client.keys* file, and use SCP to copy it to the other system.

Chapter 3

OSSEC HIDS Configuration

Solutions in this chapter:

- Understanding the OSSEC HIDS Configuration File
- Configuring Logging/Alerting Options
- Declaring Rule Files
- Reading Log Files
- Configuring Integrity Checking
- Configuring an Agent
- Configuring Advanced Options

☑ Summary

☑ Solutions Fast Track

☑ Frequently Asked Questions

Introduction

After a long and restful weekend, Marty rushed into work to check on the newly deployed OSSEC HIDS agents and servers. To his pleasant surprise, all the test servers were still running and there were no indications of any errors. Looking at the logs collected by the OSSEC HIDS servers, Marty also noted that his scripted attacks were detected by the OSSEC HIDS agents and reported to the OSSEC HIDS server. His scripted modifications to critical system files and brute force authentication attacks were also reported. "I can't wait to tell Simran!" Marty thought. Marty scheduled a meeting to talk to Simran about the results of his testing, and she suggested involving the heads of some of the other departments, namely David Schuster and Antoine Joseph. David Schuster, the department head of operations, was responsible for the installation and maintenance of all servers, desktops, and networking equipment within the organization. Antoine Joseph, the department head for incident handling and response, was responsible for the monitoring of all systems within the organization and the teams deployed to "fight fires" in the event of an incident.

With Simran, Antoine, and David in the room, Marty began his presentation by familiarizing everyone with the current challenges and introducing the OSSEC HIDS as a solution. He explained how easy it is to deploy the OSSEC HIDS on multiple servers with different operating systems, how all events can be centralized to a single server, how additional servers can be added as the event load increased, and how alerts can be generated from the received events. "I've heard of applications like this in the past," said Antoine. "What benefit does my team get from this product besides something else to support? I need something that's going to alert me to potential incidents and not force me to sit someone in front of a dashboard 24/7." Marty smiled, as he knew Antoine was going to raise this question early in the meeting. "Actually Antoine, the OSSEC HIDS allows you to configure alerts to be sent to individual email addresses, email groups, and even SMS-enabled devices like a cell phone or pager." Marty paused to take a sip of water. "You can also configure the OSSEC HIDS to generate emails based on the severity of the alerts, the alert groupings, the subnet, or the agent. You can even limit the number of emails sent per hour so your analyst isn't inundated with emails about the same issue." Antoine nodded a couple of times to let everything sink in.

"OK," said David, "how does this OSSEC HIDS thing communicate between the agents and the server? I don't want to have to open up all kinds of special ports just so these things can communicate." Marty did his best not to roll his eyes, sigh, or react negatively in any way. In dealing with David before, Marty knew that David's primary concern was always opening new ports between network segments to allow communication between client and server application deployments. Marty understood that it was David's job to have such concerns, but that sometimes got in Marty's way when deploying new technologies around the network. "Well, I have good news for you, David!" exclaimed Marty with a smile. "This time, we can change the communication port on the agent and the server to whatever you need so we don't need to open any additional firewall rules if we don't want to." David smiled and started to formulate his next question. "And if we pick a port that the firewall or NIDS tries to inspect" Marty jumped in to cut David's next question off before he asked it, "We can just create exclusion rules for those agents and the server." David let his smile slip away and tried to ask his final question, but Marty jumped in again. "And to answer your last question, David, the communication channels are encrypted so you don't have to worry about someone seeing the generated alerts from, say, the Web servers out on the DMZ." Simran looked at David and noticed he wasn't smiling, but, at the same time, wasn't upset. "Sounds good, Marty," said David. "It's also good to see you did your homework this time. An outsider might think that we may have had conversations like this before."

"What's the next step, Marty?" asked Simran. "Well, I think we should expand our test bed and get Antoine's team involved in some of the rule writing," responded Marty. "David, can you work with Marty on expanding this test environment?" Simran said, looking at David, "Involve whomever you need on your team to get this rolling." " Antoine," Simran shifted her focus, "once David and Marty have the agents and servers installed, can you bring your team together for a session so Marty can show them how to write the rules for alert generation?" Both David and Antoine looked at each other, nodded, and exclaimed "Can do, boss."

As with any intrusion detection system, or security software for that matter, there are important post-installation configurations you must perform. After you install the OSSEC HIDS, you might need to tweak and tune it according to your needs. The OSSEC HIDS has multiple configuration options that are covered this chapter. Additional configuration steps relating to specific parts of the OSSEC HIDS are covered in later chapters in this book.

Tools & Traps...

OSSEC HIDS File Locations

On a Unix, Linux, or BSD installation of the OSSEC HIDS, your default installation path is /var/ossec. Whichever directory was specified during installation, the OSSEC HIDS will chroot to that directory during startup and read the configuration files and rules from it.

Here is a list of all the OSSEC HIDS directories and files on a typical Unix, Linux, or BSD installation:

- */var/ossec/bin*—Directory containing all binaries used by the OSSEC HIDS.
- */var/ossec/etc*—Directory containing all configuration files needed by the OSSEC HIDS.

Continued

- *ossec.conf*—The main OSSEC HIDS configuration file.
- *internal_options.conf*—A file with additional configuration options.
- *decoders.xml*—A file containing decoders used to normalized the logs.
- *client.keys*—A file containing authentication keys used in agent/server communication.

- */var/ossec/logs*—Directory containing all OSSEC HIDS related log files.
  - *ossec.log*—OSSEC HIDS main logs (error, warn, info, and so on).
  - *alerts/alerts.log*—OSSEC HIDS alert log.
  - *active-responses.log*—OSSEC HIDS active response logs.
- */var/ossec/queue*—Directory containing OSSEC HIDS queue files.
  - *agent-info*—Directory containing agent specific information (operating system, OSSEC HIDS version, and so on).
  - *syscheck*—Directory containing integrity checking data with a separate log file for each agent.
  - *rootcheck*—Directory containing rootkit information and policy monitoring data for each agent.
  - *rids*—Directory containing agent message IDs.
  - *fts*—File containing first time seen (FTS) entries. For more information on FTS, see Chapter 4.
- */var/ossec/rules*—Directory containing all OSSEC HIDS rules.
- */var/ossec/stats*—Directory containing OSSEC HIDS statistical information such as number of logs per second, and so on.

On the Windows installation, everything is located under *C:\Program Files\ossec-agent*, unless a different path is specified during installation:

- *C:\Program Files\ossec-agent\ossec.conf*—Main OSSEC HIDS configuration file.
- *C:\Program Files\ossec-agent\internal_options.conf*—Additional configuration options.
- *C:\Program Files\ossec-agent\ossec.log*—OSSEC HIDS main logs (*error*, *warn*, *info*, and so on).

Understanding the OSSEC HIDS Configuration File

To fully understand the OSSEC HIDS configuration file, we will start with the configuration options for the local/server installations on Unix, Linux, and BSD. After we thoroughly understand how local/server configurations are performed, we will discuss OSSEC HIDS agent configuration on Unix and Windows.

The main OSSEC HIDS configuration file, named *ossec.conf*, is an Extensible Markup Language (XML) based file. XML was chosen instead of a flat text configuration file for a couple of reasons. The primary reason is that XML files are easy to read and those with a working knowledge of the OSSEC HIDS should be able to find the section they're looking for. Another reason is that the XML format allows for easy-to-follow hierarchical nesting of tags, which makes it easier to figure out where the configuration starts, where it ends, and what section it's associated with. In addition, XML files are designed to be written programmatically and are able to be edited in anything from a text editor to an XML editing application.

TIP

If you are not familiar with XML, try some of the resources available at xml.org: www.xml.org/xml/resources_focus_beginnerguide.shtml.

The OSSEC HIDS configuration options are located in the *<ossec_config></ossec_config>* root tag. The configuration options are further divided into a series of subelements. Table 3.1 shows the subelement tags and what is contained in each section.

Table 3.1 ossec.conf Subelements

Subelement	Description
<global>	Global (general) configuration options used in server/ local installations
<alerts>	Email and log alerting options
<email_alerts>	Granular email alerting options
<remote>	Configuration options related to remote connections and agents (server only)
<database_output>	Database output options
<rules>	List of included rules

Continued

Table 3.1 Continued. ossec.conf Subelements

Subelement	Description
<client>	Agent related configuration options
<localfile>	Configuration options for monitored log files
<syscheck>	Configuration options for integrity checking
<rootcheck>	Configuration options for rootkit detection and policy monitoring
<command>	Configuration options for active-response
<active-response>	Additional configuration options for active-response

Configuring Logging/Alerting Options

The first step in configuring your OSSEC HIDS deployment is tuning the alert and log capabilities of the system. The OSSEC HIDS provides powerful email alerting capabilities with very granular control of the alert types generated.

Also included with the OSSEC HIDS is the ability to centralize events and logs from deployed OSSEC HIDS agents. Each agent can be configured to send events to an OSSEC HIDS server for further analysis and alert generation. If your deployment becomes quite large, or the events require long-term storage, the OSSEC HIDS can be configured to log to a database. Storing this information becomes important for your incident handling team to analyze large amounts of data. In addition, if your organization must achieve certain regulatory compliance goals, this long-term event storage becomes a requirement.

Alerting with Email

Every alert has a severity level from 0 to 15, with 15 being the highest and 0 the lowest. By default, the OSSEC HIDS logs every alert with a severity level of 1 to 15. In addition, the OSSEC HIDS generates email messages for every alert above a 7 severity level.

If you want to change how severity levels are handled, you must change the *<log_alert_level></log_alert_level>* and *<email_alert_level></email_alert_level>* tags in the *<alerts></alerts>* section. In the following example, we have switched the configuration to only log for severities above 2 and only send emails for severities above 8.

```
<ossec_config>
  <alerts>
    <log_alert_level>2</log_alert_level>
    <email_alert_level>8</email_alert_level>
  </alerts>
</ossec_config>
```

In addition to logging for every alert, or logging for every event that matches specific rules, you can configure the OSSEC HIDS to log everything received. Certain compliance regulations and industry standards, such as the Payment Card Industry (PCI) data security standard, Sarbanes-Oxley Act (SOX), and Health Insurance Portability and Accountability Act (HIPAA), among others, have specific requirements surrounding log collection and retention. Each regulation and act has detailed requirements, but if you decide to log everything, you can specify *yes* between the *<logall></logall>* tag in the *<global></global>* section.

```
<ossec_config>
  <global>
    <logall>yes</logall>
  </global>
</ossec_config>
```

WARNING

Just because you can log everything, does not mean you should. Storing information uses disk space, and the more information you log, the more space your saved logs use.

Configuring Email

Email alerts are an integral part of the OSSEC HIDS because email allows for rapid response in the event of an incident. Why would you want to wait until your administrator discovers an error, when you can send him an email immediately letting him know what happened?

Basic Email Configuration

In the *<global></global>* configuration section, you can specify which email addresses receive the generated email alerts.

NOTE

Whenever an alert has a severity higher than the *<log_alert_level>* option, an email is sent.

In the following example, we will configure the OSSEC HIDS to send emails to John and Mike, who are the security administrators of our fake company *fakeinc.com*. First, we must enable email notification using the *<email_notification></email_notification>* tag. Changing the tag from *no* to *yes* enables the email notification functionality. After the tag is set to yes, we must then indicate the email addresses to receive our email alerts. We use the *<email_to> </email_to>* tag to specify each alert recipient email address. The Simple Mail Transfer Protocol (SMTP) server must also be specified. Using the *<smtp_server></smtp_server>* tag, you can indicate which outbound SMTP server to use. The SMTP server can be specified using a fully qualified hostname or valid IPv4 IP address. Specify who is sending the email alert by using the *<email_from></email_from>* tag. Within the tag, specify an email address to associate with generated email alerts. This email address is the *From:* or *Sender:* address, depending on your email client, in the received email alert.

Finally, to safeguard our email server and avoid a flood of emails, we have configured a maximum threshold of 20 emails per hour using the *<email_maxperhour></email_maxperhour>* tag. If, within an hour, more than 20 emails are generated, the emails are grouped and sent together at the end of the hour.

```
<ossec_config>
  <global>
    <email_notification>yes</email_notification>
    <email_to>john@fakeinc.com</email_to>
    <email_to>mike@fakeinc.com</email_to>
    <smtp_server>smtpserver.fakeinc.com.</smtp_server>
    <email_from>ossecm@fakeinc.com</email_from>
    <email_maxperhour>20</email_maxperhour>
  </global>
</ossec_config>
```

To disable email notifications, simply change the *<email_notification></email_notification>* tag to *no*:

```
<ossec_config>
  <global>
    <email_notification>no</email_notification>
  </global>
</ossec_config>
```

Granular Email Configuration

If the basic email options are not enough, other options provide more granular email alerting capabilities. If you need your alert emails in a format suitable for Short Message Service (SMS), or text messaging for a cell phone or pager, or if you must alert only one administrator, there are granular email options to suit your needs.

In our company, *fakeinc.com*, we have an administrator, Peter, whose only responsibility is the security of Web servers on a network segment. Because his only responsibility is for those servers, we only want to alert him of Apache HTTP server alerts. The following granular email configuration allows us to only send Peter email alerts for alerts that fall into the *apache* group of rules. Using the *<group></group>* tag, we can easily indicate what grouping of alerts should be sent to the specified email address:

```
<ossec_config>
  <email_alerts>
    <email_to>peter@fakeinc.com</email_to>
    <group>apache</group>
  </email_alerts>
</ossec_config>
```

We might also want to send an SMS for the on-call administrator, if the alert severity is above *10*. Using the *<level></level>* tag, we can indicate which severity level of email alerts should be emailed to the on-call administrator. The *sms* value, specified within the *<format></format>* tag, ensures that the sent emails are formatted for an SMS-capable device.

```
<ossec_config>
  <email_alerts>
    <email_to>oncall@fakeinc.com</email_to>
    <level>10</level>
    <format>sms</format>
  </email_alerts>
</ossec_config>
```

Finally, we have a Windows administrator who is responsible for the entire 10.1.1.0/24 network. His primary concern, however, is two critical Windows servers. The Windows servers, configured within the OSSEC HIDS as *win2k1* and *winxpAD*, both have OSSEC HIDS agents installed, as does every other server in the 10.1.1.0/24 subnet. Using the *<event_location></event_location>* tag ensures that an email alert is generated for any alert that occurs on the 10.1.1.0/24 subnet, the *win2k1* server, or the *winxpAD* server:

```
<ossec_config>
  <email_alerts>
    <email_to>cc@fakeinc.com</email_to>
    <event_location>win2k1|winxpAD|10.1.1</event_location>
  </email_alerts>
</ossec_config>
```

NOTE

Use the pipe "|" character to separate multiple event locations.

Receiving Remote Events with Syslog

An OSSEC HIDS server type installation allows for the collection of events from remote agents, as explained in Chapter 2, and from any system using syslog (TCP and UDP). To receive events from additional remote agents, you must add a new *<remote></remote>* section with *secure* defined within the *<connection></connection>* tag. This tag should already exist if you selected the server type installation.

```
<ossec_config>
  <remote>
    <connection>secure</connection>
  </remote>
</ossec_config>
```

We can also use the *<allowed-ips></allowed-ips>* tag to explicitly state which IP address we allow connections from. In the following example, we used the *<allowed-ips></allowed-ips>* tag in conjunction with the *<connection></connection>* tag to indicate that we expect OSSEC HIDS agent connections from the 192.168.10.0/24 network:

```
<ossec_config>
  <remote>
    <connection>secure</connection>
    <allowed-ips>192.168.10.0/24</allowed-ips>
  </remote>
</ossec_config>
```

For remote syslog, instead of specifying *secure* within the *<connection></connection>* tag, you must change it to *syslog*. Additionally, you must specify which IP addresses (or networks) are allowed to send syslog data to your OSSEC HIDS server. In the following example, we used the *<connection>syslog</connection>* tag to indicate that we allow syslog messages, and the *<allowed-ips></allowed-ips>* tag to define networks 192.168.2.0/24 and 192.168.1.0/24.

```
<ossec_config>
  <remote>
    <connection>syslog</connection>
    <allowed-ips>192.168.2.0/24</allowed-ips>
    <allowed-ips>192.168.1.0/24</allowed-ips>
  </remote>
</ossec_config>
```

Configuring Database Output

The OSSEC HIDS does not require a database to function, but you could find it useful to have all your alerts in a database. If you have multiple servers, it is beneficial to centralize all your collected alert information. Table 3.2 shows the available options for configuring your OSSEC HIDS server to log to a database.

Table 3.2 Database Logging Configuration Options

Variable	Value	Description
<hostname>	Any valid IP address	IP address of the database server
<username>	Any valid username	Username to access the database
<password>	Any password	Password to access the database
<database>	Database name	Database name to store the alerts
<type>	Database type, options are *mysql* or *postgresql*	Type of database to use

Before you configure the database output, you must make sure the OSSEC HIDS is compiled to support database logging. To see how your OSSEC HIDS install was configured, run *ossec-dbd* with the *-V* flag. This indicates which database your currently installed OSSEC HIDS server will support.

```
# /var/ossec/bin/ossec-dbd -V
  OSSEC HIDS v1.4 - Daniel B. Cid
  Compiled with MySQL support.
  Compiled with PostgreSQL support.
```

If, for any reason, it says **Compiled without any Database support.**, you must reinstall the OSSEC HIDS with database support.

NOTE

Before you reinstall, make sure you have the necessary database libraries. See Chapter 1 for more information.

To enable database support during installation, you must run the following commands before the *install.sh* script:

```
$ cd ossec-hids-1.4
$ cd src; make setdb; cd ..
$ ./install.sh
```

To enable the database after the installation is complete, run the following command:

```
# /var/ossec/bin/ossec-control enable database
```

To configure the database support within the OSSEC HIDS, we must define the database settings using the *<database_output></database_output>* tag. In our example, we are using the server 192.168.2.32 as indicated by the *<hostname></hostname>* tag. We have also indicated that we are logging in to a MySQL server, as the *db_test* user, with password *db_pass1*, as noted within the *<type></type>*, *<username></username>*, and *<password></password>* tags. We also specify the database we want to connect to, *ossecdb*, within the *<database></database>* tag.

```
<ossec_config>
  <database_output>
    <hostname>192.168.2.32</hostname>
    <username>db_test</username>
    <password>db_pass1</password>
    <database>ossecdb</database>
    <type>mysql</type>
  </database_output>
</ossec_config>
```

NOTE

At the time of this writing, only the MySQL and PostgreSQL database are supported as valid database *<type>* variables.

After you have configured and restarted the OSSEC HIDS, you should see the following message in the /var/ossec/logs/ossec.log file, indicating that the OSSEC HIDS was successful in connecting to your specified database:

```
# /var/ossec/bin/ossec-control restart
# grep ossec-dbd /var/ossec/logs/ossec.log
2007/11/26 11:31:22 ossec-dbd: Connected to database 'ossecdb' at '192.168.2.32'.
2007/11/26 11:31:38 ossec-dbd: Started (pid: 8242).
```

Declaring Rule Files

The rules section, defined by the *<rules></rules>* tag, is used to declare which rule files are loaded when the OSSEC HIDS starts. Typically, these declarations will not need to be changed. There is only one valid tag, *<include></include>*, which allows you to specify which rule file to load. Please note that every rule file must be located within the rules directory at /var/ossec/ rules/.

An example, from our default configuration, shows how these rule declaration statements are used.

```
<ossec_config> <!- rules global entry ->
  <rules>
    <include>rules_config.xml</include>
    <include>pam_rules.xml</include>
    <include>sshd_rules.xml</include>
  </rules>
<ossec_config>
```

To add more rules, you must add new *<include></include>* tag and specify the rule filename and extension. For example, the OSSEC HIDS policy rules ship disabled by default. To enable these rules, you must add a new *<include></include>* tag and specify the *policy_rules.xml* policy rules file.

```
<ossec_config> <!- rules global entry ->
  <rules>
    <include>policy_rules.xml</include>
  </rules>
<ossec_config>
```

If you want to know which rules are loaded when the OSSEC HIDS starts, you can investigate the *ossec.conf* file or look at your *ossec.log* file. When the OSSEC HIDS starts, a log entry is generated as each rule file is successfully loaded:

```
# grep "Reading rules file" /var/ossec/logs/ossec.log
...
2007/10/30 00:10:24 ossec-analysisd: Reading rules file: 'pix_rules.xml'
2007/10/30 00:10:24 ossec-analysisd: Reading rules file: 'named_rules.xml'
2007/10/30 00:10:24 ossec-analysisd: Reading rules file: 'smbd_rules.xml'
2007/10/30 00:10:24 ossec-analysisd: Reading rules file: 'vsftpd_rules.xml'
2007/10/30 00:10:24 ossec-analysisd: Reading rules file: 'pure-ftpd_rules.xml'
..
```

NOTE

The OSSEC HIDS rules are explained in more detail in Chapter 4.

Reading Log Files

When you install the OSSEC HIDS, a number of files, typically existing on the specified operating system, are automatically monitored. In some circumstances, depending on your operating system and file system structure, some files might not be automatically monitored. You do, however, have the ability to specify additional files for monitoring by the OSSEC HIDS.

NOTE

The ability to specify additional files is true of all OSSEC HIDS installation types.

To configure the OSSEC HIDS to monitor additional files, you must first use the *<localfile></localfile>* tag. After you have indicated that you want to monitor a new system file, you must specify the log format and file location. To specify the log format, you must use the *<log_format></log_format>* tag. Table 3.3 indicates the possible values for the *<localfile></localfile>* section, and Table 3.4 indicates the possible values for the *<log_format></log_format>* tag. The *<location></location>* tag allows you to indicate the location of the new file for monitoring. The following example shows how you would configure the OSSEC HIDS to monitor the /var/log/messages file:

```
<ossec_config>
  <localfile>
    <log_format>syslog</log_format>
    <location>/var/log/messages</location>
  </localfile>
</ossec_config>
```

The following example shows how you can configure the OSSEC HIDS to monitor a custom Apache log file; in this case, the /var/www/logs/server1/error_log file. Because this is an Apache log file, we can specify the corresponding value, *apache*, within the *<log_format></log_format>* tag:

```
<ossec_config>
  <localfile>
    <log_format>apache</log_format>
    <location>/var/www/logs/server1/error_log</location>
  </localfile>
</ossec_config
```

NOTE

If you have an application that logs one log entry per line to a file, you can use the *syslog* log format within the *<log_format></log_format>* tag. This ensures that the file is properly handled by the OSSEC HIDS.

Another powerful feature of the OSSEC HIDS is the ability to specify *strftime* variables within the *<location></location>* tag. If you have a log file with a date as part of the filenaming scheme, and the file follows the format /var/log/custom-*YYYY-Mmm-DD*.log (for example, /var/log/custom-2007-Nov-06.log), you can easily monitor the file using:

```
<ossec_config>
  <localfile>
    <log_format>syslog</log_format>
    <location>/var/log/custom-%Y-%b-%d.log</location>
  </localfile>
</ossec_config
```

Tools & Traps…

Using *strftime* Expressions

The *strftime()* function within the C/C++ programming language allows you to return a string from your input data and format it according to the conversion specifiers you use. The conversion specifiers are typically seen as a percent sign, %, followed by a single uppercase or lowercase character. The OSSEC HIDS *<location></location>* tag allows you use these conversion specifiers to match on filenames. The supported conversion specifiers are:

%a—Abbreviated weekday name (e.g., **Thu**)
%A—Full weekday name (e.g., **Thursday**)
%b—Abbreviated month name (e.g., **Aug**)
%B—Full month name (e.g., **August**)
%c—Date and time representation (e.g., **Thu Sep 22 12:23:45 2007**)
%d—Day of the month (01–31) (e.g., **20**)
%H—Hour in 24h format (00–23) (e.g., **13**)
%I—Hour in 12h format (01–12) (e.g., **02**)
%j—Day of the year (001–366) (e.g., **235**)

Continued

%*m*—Month as a decimal number (01–12) (e.g., **02**)
%*M*—Minute (00–59) (e.g., **12**)
%*p*—AM or PM designation (e.g., **AM**)
%*S*—Second (00–61) (e.g., **55**)
%*U*—Week number with the first Sunday as the first day of week one (00–53) (e.g., **52**)
%*w*—Weekday as a decimal number with Sunday as 0 (0–6) (e.g., **2**)
%*W*—Week number with the first Monday as the first day of week one (00–53) (e.g., **21**)
%*x*—Date representation (e.g., **02/24/79**)
%*X*—Time representation (e.g., **04:12:51**)
%*y*—Year, last two digits (00–99) (e.g., **76**)
%*Y*—Year (e.g., **2008**)
%*Z*—Timezone name or abbreviation (e.g., **EST**)
%%—A % sign (e.g., %)

More information can be found at the following Web sites:

- http://msdn.microsoft.com/library/default.asp?url=/library/en-us/vclib/html/_crt_strftime.2c_.wcsftime.asp
- www.php.net/strftime
- www.cplusplus.com/reference/clibrary/ctime/strftime.html

Table 3.3 <localfile> Options

Options	Values	Description
<location>	Any log file (e.g., */var/log/messages*)	The full path and filename of file to be monitored by the OSSEC HIDS.
<log_format>	*syslog* *snort-full* *snort-fast* *squid* *iis* *eventlog* *nmapg* *mysql_log* *postgresql_log* *apache*	The format of the log file being read. If the log has one entry per line, the syslog type is recommended. Table 3.4 provides more details on each log format type.

Table 3.4 <log_format> Types

<log_format> **Type**	**Description**
syslog	Used to read generic syslog messages and any one-line-per-message log file (includes IIS, squid, apache, snort-fast, etc).
snort-full	Used to read Snort formatted logs that use the FULL output format.
snort-fast	Used to read Snort formatted logs that use the FAST output format.
squid	Used to read squid proxy server formatted logs.
iis	Used to read IIS formatted logs.
eventlog	Used to read Windows Event logs.
nmapg	Used to read nmap "greppable" formatted logs.
mysql_log	Used to read MySQL server formatted logs.
postgresql_log	Used to read PostgreSQL server formatted logs.
apache	Used to read Apache HTTP server formatted logs.

Configuring Integrity Checking

Integrity checking can be enabled on all OSSEC HIDS installation types (server, local, and agent). Integrity checking comes with a feature-rich default configuration that monitors all configuration files and binaries on Unix, Linux, and BSD operating systems (/etc, /bin, and so on), and monitors the system directory on Windows (C:\Windows\System32). The default configuration also monitors some key Windows registry entries for changes.

The integrity checking configuration is separated into three main tags. The *<frequency></frequency>* tag indicates how often syscheck should scan the system, in seconds, looking for changes.

The *<directories></directories>* tag lists the directories to monitor. Additional *checks* can be specified to only check file size changes, group ownership changes, etc. Table 3.5 explains all possible variable options for the <directories></directories> tag.

The *<ignore></ignore>* tag allows to you exclude files or directories from file integrity checks. The *<ignore></ignore>* tag has an additional simple regular expression variable called *sregex*. Table 3.6 explains the possible *sregex* options.

Table 3.5 *<directories></directories>* Options

Option	Description
check_all	Perform all available integrity checks
check_sum	Use MD5/SHA1 to check the integrity of files
check_size	Check files for size changes
check_owner	Check files for ownership changes
check_group	Check files for group ownership changes
check_perm	Check files for permission changes

Table 3.6 sregex Options

Option	Description
^	Specify the beginning of the text; e.g., <ignore type="sregex">^apache</ignore>
$	Specify the end of the text; e.g., <ignore type="sregex">.log$</ignore>
|	Specify an *OR* between multiple patterns; e.g., <ignore type="sregex">.log$\|.htm$</ignore>

The default configuration to monitor a Unix, Linux, or BSD operating system is:

```
<ossec_config>
  <syscheck>
    <frequency>86400</frequency>
    <directories check_all="yes">/etc,/usr/bin,/usr/sbin</directories>
    <directories check_all="yes">/bin,/sbin</directories>
    <ignore>/etc/mtab</ignore>
    <ignore>/etc/mnttab</ignore>
  </syscheck>
</ossec_config>
```

NOTE

Multiple directories can be specified using a comma-separated list.

For example, if you wanted to monitor your Apache HTTP Web server files in the /var/www/htdocs/ directory, you would configure the *<syscheck></syscheck>* section and *<directories></directories>* tag as follows:

```
<ossec_config>
  <syscheck>
    <directories check_all="yes">/var/www/htdocs</directories>
  </syscheck>
</ossec_config>
```

On Windows, there are some more options available to monitor the Windows registry. The *<windows_registry></windows_registry>* tag allows you to specify a list of registry keys to monitor.

The *<registry_ignore></registry_ignore>* tag allows you to specify registry keys to exclude from integrity checking.

A sample configuration to monitor the *HKEY_LOCAL_MACHINE\Security* Registry key is:

```
<ossec_config>
  <syscheck>
    <windows_registry>HKEY_LOCAL_MACHINE\Security</windows_registry>
  </syscheck>
</ossec_config>
```

NOTE

The HKEY_LOCAL_MACHINE subtree contains information about the local computer system, including hardware and operating system data, such as bus type, system memory, device drivers, and startup control parameters. The Security key contains security information used by the system and network.

Tools & Traps...

Files Monitored in Windows by Default

The OSSEC HIDS monitors several key directories, files, and registry keys by default. The first declaration is that anything in the *system32* directory should be monitored.

Continued

The default Windows directory is called by using the %WINDIR% system variable.

```
<!-- Default files to be monitored - system32 only. -->
  <directories check_all="yes">%WINDIR%/system32</directories>
```

Several files within the system32 directory are excluded as they are constantly changing. If these directories were monitored, they might generate an excessive amount of events. Depending on your environment, you may choose to remove some of these exclusions so the files changes are reported to your OSSEC HIDS server.

```
<!-- Default files to be ignored. -->
  <ignore>%WINDIR%/System32/LogFiles</ignore>
  <ignore>%WINDIR%/system32/wbem/Logs</ignore>
  <ignore>%WINDIR%/system32/config</ignore>
  <ignore>%WINDIR%/system32/CatRoot</ignore>
  <ignore>%WINDIR%/system32/wbem/Repository</ignore>
  <ignore>%WINDIR%/system32/dllcache</ignore>
  <ignore>%WINDIR%/system32/inetsrv/History</ignore>
  <ignore type="sregex">.log$|.htm$|.jpg$|.png$|.chm$|.pnf$</ignore>
```

Several important Windows registry keys are monitored for changes. These registry keys are related to policy, version, services, control, and security information. The Internet Explorer Registry information is also monitored.

```
<!-- Windows registry entries to monitor. -->
<windows_registry>HKEY_LOCAL_MACHINE\Software\Policies</windows_registry>
<windows_registry>HKEY_LOCAL_MACHINE\Software\Microsoft\Windows NT\
CurrentVersion</windows_registry>
<windows_registry>HKEY_LOCAL_MACHINE\Software\Microsoft\Windows\
CurrentVersion</windows_registry>
<windows_registry>HKEY_LOCAL_MACHINE\Software\Microsoft\Internet Explorer
</windows_registry>
<windows_registry>HKEY_LOCAL_MACHINE\Software\Classes</windows_registry>
<windows_registry>HKEY_LOCAL_MACHINE\System\CurrentControlSet\Control
</windows_registry>
<windows_registry>HKEY_LOCAL_MACHINE\System\CurrentControlSet\Services
</windows_registry>
<windows_registry>HKEY_LOCAL_MACHINE\Security</windows_registry>
```

Quite a few registry keys are excluded, as they frequently change through regular use of a Windows operating system. Depending on your environment, you may choose to remove some of these exclusions so the registry key changes are reported to your OSSEC HIDS server.

```
<!-- Windows registry entries to ignore. -->
<registry_ignore>HKEY_LOCAL_MACHINE\Software\Microsoft\Windows\
CurrentVersion\Installer\UserData</registry_ignore>
<registry_ignore>HKEY_LOCAL_MACHINE\Software\Microsoft\Windows\
CurrentVersion\Group Policy\State</registry_ignore>
<registry_ignore>HKEY_LOCAL_MACHINE\Software\Microsoft\Windows\
CurrentVersion\WindowsUpdate</registry_ignore>
<registry_ignore>HKEY_LOCAL_MACHINE\Software\Microsoft\Windows\
CurrentVersion\Internet Settings\Cache</registry_ignore>
<registry_ignore>HKEY_LOCAL_MACHINE\Software\Microsoft\Windows NT\
CurrentVersion\ProfileList</registry_ignore>
<registry_ignore>HKEY_LOCAL_MACHINE\Software\Microsoft\Windows NT\
CurrentVersion\Prefetcher</registry_ignore>
<registry_ignore>HKEY_LOCAL_MACHINE\Software\Classes\Interface
</registry_ignore>
<registry_ignore>HKEY_LOCAL_MACHINE\Software\Classes\TypeLib
</registry_ignore>
<registry_ignore>HKEY_LOCAL_MACHINE\Software\Classes\MIME</registry_ignore>
<registry_ignore>HKEY_LOCAL_MACHINE\Software\Classes\Software
</registry_ignore>
<registry_ignore>HKEY_LOCAL_MACHINE\Software\Classes\CLSID</registry_ignore>
<registry_ignore>HKEY_LOCAL_MACHINE\Security\Policy\Secrets</registry_
ignore>
<registry_ignore>HKEY_LOCAL_MACHINE\Security\SAM\Domains\Account\Users
</registry_ignore>
<registry_ignore>HKEY_LOCAL_MACHINE\System\CurrentControlSet\Control\
DeviceClasses</registry_ignore>
<registry_ignore>HKEY_LOCAL_MACHINE\System\CurrentControlSet\Control\
Watchdog</registry_ignore>
<registry_ignore>HKEY_LOCAL_MACHINE\System\CurrentControlSet\Control\
MediaCategories</registry_ignore>
<registry_ignore>HKEY_LOCAL_MACHINE\System\CurrentControlSet\Control\
Windows</registry_ignore>
<registry_ignore>HKEY_LOCAL_MACHINE\System\CurrentControlSet\Control\
hivelist</registry_ignore>
<registry_ignore>HKEY_LOCAL_MACHINE\System\CurrentControlSet\Control\
ServiceCurrent</registry_ignore>
<registry_ignore>HKEY_LOCAL_MACHINE\System\CurrentControlSet\Control\Print
</registry_ignore>
<registry_ignore>HKEY_LOCAL_MACHINE\System\CurrentControlSet\Control\Session
Manager</registry_ignore>
```

Continued

```
<registry_ignore>HKEY_LOCAL_MACHINE\System\CurrentControlSet\Services\
Eventlog</registry_ignore>
<registry_ignore>HKEY_LOCAL_MACHINE\System\CurrentControlSet\Services\
RemoteAccess\Performance</registry_ignore>
<registry_ignore>HKEY_LOCAL_MACHINE\System\CurrentControlSet\Services\
W32Time\TimeProviders\NtpClient</registry_ignore>
<registry_ignore type="sregex">\Enum$</registry_ignore>
```

Configuring an Agent

The OSSEC HIDS agent does not perform any analysis or processing of alerts. All collected information is forwarded to the server for further processing and alert generation. The *<client> </client>* configuration section allows you to specify your OSSEC HIDS server IP or hostname and the port used to send events.

The *<server-ip></server-ip>* tag allows you to specify the IP address of your OSSEC HIDS server using any valid IPv4 address. The *<server-hostname></server-hostname>* tag allows you to use a fully qualified hostname instead of an IP address. The *<port></port>* tag allows you to specify any port number, from 1 to 65535, to send events to your OSSEC HIDS server. This port number, that has a default value of 1514 if not explicitly defined, has to be the same port that is configured on your OSSEC HIDS server.

For example, to tell your agent that the OSSEC HIDS server is located at 192.168.1.1, and is configured to receive events on port 1519 instead of the default 1514 port, you can use the configuration as follows:

```
<client>
  <server-ip>192.168.1.1</server-ip>
  <port>1519</port>
</client>
```

If you know the fully qualified hostname, in this case *os1.fakeinc.com*, of your OSSEC HIDS server, you can use the configuration as follows:

```
<client>
  <server-hostname>os1.fakeinc.com</server-hostname>
  <port>1519</port>
</client>
```

Configuring Advanced Options

The main configuration of the OSSEC HIDS is located within the *ossec.conf* file. However, some advanced configuration features are located within the *internal_options.conf* file. These options, as stated within the configuration file, should be handled with care, as they are responsible for runtime configurations. Any errors within this file may cause your OSSEC HIDS agent or server to not start if not properly configured.

Typically, this file is only used to enable advanced debugging of OSSEC HIDS issues. Table 3.7 describes the options and provides the default values in case you need to revert your changes.

Table 3.7 *internal_options.conf* Options

Option	Default Value	Description
analysisd.default_timeframe=	360	Default frequency used by rules that have "frequency" enabled. Default 360, Min 60, Max 3600.
analysisd.stats_maxdiff=	25000	Maximum difference on the number of alerts per hour in the stats alerting. Default 25000, Min 10, Max 99999.
analysisd.stats_mindiff=	250	Minimum difference on the number of alerts per hour in the stats alerting. Default 250, Min 10, Max 99999.
analysisd.stats_percent_diff=	30	How much to differ from the average number of alerts before alerting. Default 30, Min 5, Max 999.
analysisd.fts_list_size=	32	Size of the FTS list in memory. It is recommended that you do not change this value.
analysisd.fts_min_size_for_str=	14	FTS minimum string size. It is recommended that you do not change this value.
logcollector.loop_timeout=	2	How often *logcollector* checks for new entries in the logs. Default 2, Min 1, Max 999.
logcollector.open_attempts=	8	Number of attempts to open a file. Default 8, Min 0, Max 999.
remoted.recv_counter_flush=	128	How often *remoted* flushes agent message id counter entries to disk. It is recommended that you do not change this value.

Continued

Table 3.7 Continued. *internal_options.conf* Options

Option	Default Value	Description
remoted.comp_average_printout=	19999	How often *remoted* should print the agent message id counter. It is recommended that you do not change this value.
maild.strict_checking=	1	Specifies if the internal OSSEC HIDS mail server should perform strict checking of the SMTP connection. This is enabled by default.
maild.groupping=	1	Specifies if the internal OSSEC HIDS mail server should group and send multiple alerts into one email message. This is enabled by default.
maild.full_subject=	0	Specifies if the internal OSSEC HIDS mail server should send the alert email with a verbose subject. This is disabled by default.
monitord.day_wait=	10	Amount of seconds to wait before compressing and signing the files. Default 10 seconds, Min 1, Max 999.
monitord.compress=	1	If the OSSEC HIDS should compress the logs after each day. This is enabled by default.
monitord.sign=	1	If the OSSEC HIDS should sign the logs at the end of each day. This is enabled by default.
monitord.monitor_agents=	1	If the OSSEC HIDS should monitor the agents and alert if any go offline. This is enabled by default.
syscheck.sleep=	2	Syscheck checking/usage speed. To avoid large CPU/memory usage, you can specify how long to sleep after generating the checksum of the specified number of files. The default sleep time is 2 seconds.

Continued

Table 3.7 Continued. *internal_options.conf* Options

Option	Default Value	Description
syscheck.sleep_after=	15	The number of files to generate checksums for before sleeping. The default number of files is 15.
dbd.reconnect_attempts=	10	Maximum number of reconnect attempts to the database. Default 10, Min 0, Max 999.
windows.debug=	0	Used to enable the debugging of Windows agents. This is disabled by default.
syscheck.debug=	0	Used to enable the debugging of the *syscheck* daemon. This is disabled by default.
remoted.debug=	0	Used to enable the debugging of the *remoted* daemon. This is disabled by default.
analysisd.debug=	0	Used to enable the debugging of the *analysisd* daemon. This is disabled by default.
logcollector.debug=	0	Used to enable the debugging of the *logcollector* daemon. This is disabled by default.
agent.debug=	0	Used to enable the debugging of the *agent* daemon. This is disabled by default.

NOTE

It is always good practice to back up your configuration file prior to making changes to it.

Summary

The OSSEC HIDS main configuration file, named *ossec.conf*, is an XML-based file that contains several sections and tags for configuring logging and alerting options, rule and log files, integrity checking and agents. To be able to fully use the OSSEC HIDS, you must have a thorough understanding of how the *ossec.conf* file is used.

With the *ossec.conf* file, you can set specific alerts to email specific people and log the alerts to a database for further analysis. For best support and response, the *ossec.conf* file can be set up for email notifications to a cell phone or pager using SMS.

The *<include>* tag within the *<rules>* section allows you to specify which rule files to load when the OSSEC HIDS starts. By declaring each file in the rule section, and placing each file in the */var/ossec/rules* directory, you ensure that alerts will be generated as defined by the selected rules.

The OSSEC HIDS can also be configured to read other, typically operating system specific, local log files. You simply specify the log format and file location in the *<localfile>* tag of the *ossec.conf* file to include a file for monitoring.

Integrity checking for all operating systems is handled by the *<syscheck>* section of the *ossec.conf* file. There are three main tags: *<frequency>*, *<directories>*, and *<ignore>* for all operating systems. On a Windows system, there are two additional tags, *<windows_registry>* and *<registry_ignore>*, which can be used to include or exclude specific registry keys for monitoring.

Because the OSSEC HIDS agent does not perform any analysis or processing of alerts, you must use the *<server-ip>* or *<server-hostname>* and *<port>* tags to indicate where the agent events are sent. These values represent the IP address and port of your OSSEC HIDS server.

Solutions Fast Track

Understanding the OSSEC HIDS Configuration File

☑ The main OSSEC HIDS configuration file is called *ossec.conf* and is typically located in the *etc/* directory where your OSSEC HIDS software is installed.

☑ The configuration file is an Extensible Markup Language (XML) based file to make it easy for users to tailor their OSSEC HIDS deployment for their environment.

☑ The OSSEC HIDS configuration options are located within the *<ossec_config>* tag. Additional configuration tags are divided into subelements within this root tag.

Configuring Logging/Alerting Options

- ☑ The OSSEC HIDS provides powerful email alerting capabilities with very granular control of the alert types generated.
- ☑ Events are sent to an OSSEC HIDS server, and alerts can be sent to recipients via email or SMS notifications. These alerts can also be written to a database.
- ☑ Remote events from deployed OSSEC HIDS agents or syslog events from third-party devices can be received by your OSSEC HIDS server.

Declaring Rule Files

- ☑ The rules section, defined by the *<rules></rules>* tag, is used to declare which rule files are loaded when the OSSEC HIDS starts.
- ☑ To add more rules, you must add a new *<include></include>* tag and specify the rule file name and extension.
- ☑ If you want to know which rules are loaded when the OSSEC HIDS starts, you can investigate the *ossec.conf* file or look at your *ossec.log* file.

Reading Log Files

- ☑ When you install the OSSEC HIDS, a number of files, typically existing on the specified operating system, are automatically monitored.
- ☑ To configure the OSSEC HIDS to monitor additional files, you must first use the *<localfile></localfile>* tag.
- ☑ If you have an application that logs one log entry per line to a file, you can use the syslog log format within the *<log_format></log_format>* tag. This ensures that the file is properly handled by the OSSEC HIDS.

Configuring Integrity Checking

- ☑ Integrity checking can be enabled on all OSSEC HIDS installation types (server, local, and agent).
- ☑ The integrity checking configuration is separated into three main tags: *<frequency>*, *<directories>*, and *<ignore>* for all operating systems.
- ☑ The *<windows_registry></windows_registry>* tag allows you to specify a list of registry keys to monitor, while the *<registry_ignore></registry_ignore>* tag allows you to specify a list of keys to ignore.

Configuring an Agent

- ☑ The OSSEC HIDS agent does not perform any analysis or processing of alerts.
- ☑ The *<server-ip></server-ip>* tag allows you to specify the IP address of your OSSEC HIDS server using any valid IPv4 address, while the *<server-hostname> </server-hostname>* tag allows you to use a fully qualified hostname instead of an IP address.
- ☑ The *<port></port>* tag allows you to specify any port number, from 1 to 65535, to send events to your OSSEC HIDS server.

Configuring Advanced Options

- ☑ Some advanced configuration features are located within the *internal_options.conf* file.
- ☑ Any errors within this file may cause your OSSEC HIDS agent or server to not start if not properly configured.
- ☑ It is always good practice to back up your configuration file prior to making changes to it.

Frequently Asked Questions

Q: Will I ever have to modify the *internal_options.conf* file?

A: It is very rare that you will ever have to modify the *internal_options.conf* file. It is recommended that you don't modify the file, as it contains internal options that, if edited incorrectly, might cause your OSSEC HIDS to not function properly. Generally, the *internal_options.conf* file is reserved for troubleshooting and debugging issues you might be having.

Q: Could the *ossec.conf* file ever get corrupted?

A: Like any text file, the *ossec.conf* could become corrupt if improperly modified. It is generally a good idea to back up your configurations to avoid any long-term downtime resulting from a corrupted configuration file.

Q: What will happen if the *ossec.conf* file is corrupted?

A: If your *ossec.conf* file becomes corrupted, the OSSEC HIDS will fail to start. The configuration file is needed for the OSSEC HIDS to function properly.

Q: If I have a remote agent, what information do I place within the *<remote>* tags? Is it an IP address?

A: The *<remote>* tag is used to declare what type of events the OSSEC HIDS server is receiving from that particular source. Using the *<connection>* tag, you can specify if the events are coming from an OSSEC HIDS agent using the **secure** option. To indicate that the source of the events is a syslog-based device, you must use the **syslog** option. To identify the source of the events, you must use the *<allowed-ips>* tag. This tag allows you to specify the IP address or network range, using CIDR notation, the events will be coming from.

Q: What type of information is emailed to a person when an alert is triggered?

A: The agent location, filename, description, rule level, rule description, rule id, event time, and the log (or message) that caused the alert.

Q: Can I customize the information that is emailed?

A: At the time of this writing, the OSSEC HIDS does not provide a mechanism to change the information that is sent in the alert email. This is, however, on the roadmap for a future release.

Q: If I decide to log all information to a database, is the information encrypted?

A: The information logged by the OSSEC HIDS is not encrypted in the database. This is being investigated further as a future possibility.

Q: When declaring rules files, what specific file types are supported?

A: The OSSEC HIDS rules files can have any file extension provided they are written using the OSSEC HIDS XML syntax.

Q: Is there a limit to the number of rules files I can include?

A: The OSSEC HIDS does not limit the number of rules you can use.

Q: How will I know if a rules file does not load successfully?

A: If a rules file fails to load, a corresponding message will be seen in the *ossec.log*.

Q: Can I monitor any type of local file?

A: Any type of local file can be monitored by the OSSEC HIDS.

Q: On a Windows system, do I have to give a specific location of the local file for monitoring?

A: When defining a local file for monitoring, you must ensure that you use the full path and filename.

Q: Can I monitor specific local files?

A: Yes, you can configure the OSSEC HIDS to monitor any file on the local file system where the agent is installed.

Q: Are spaces, periods, or any special characters acceptable when defining your directories in the integrity checking section?

A: When defining your *<directories></directories>* entries, you must ensure that you define valid directories. You can, however, use PATH variables (e.g., SYSTEM_ROOT) on Windows systems to specify directory locations.

Q: How will I know if I have incorrectly typed a registry key for integrity checking?

A: A corresponding log will be shown in the *ossec.log* indicating that the OSSEC HIDS was unable to read the registry key in question.

Q: When specifying information in the syscheck section, are the variables case sensitive?

A: If you are configuring your syscheck section for a Linux system, the variables are case sensitive. On Windows, they are not.

Q: Can I configure an agent for alert processing?

A: Only the OSSEC HIDS server can be configured for alert processing.

Q: If I have a remote agent, is there any special configuration I must perform other than specifying the server IP and port?

A: Only the OSSEC HIDS server IP address and port need be defined. You must, however, ensure that the authentication keys are properly created for the agent on the OSSEC HIDS server.

Q: For a remote agent, can I use the fully qualified hostname of the OSSEC HIDS server?

A: Yes, you can use the *<server-hostname></server-hostname>* tag in place of the *<server-ip></server-ip>* tag.

Chapter 4

Working with Rules

Solutions in this chapter:

- Introducing Rules
- Understanding the OSSEC HIDS Analysis Process
- Predecoding Events
- Decoding Events
- Understanding Rules
- Working with Real World Examples
- Writing Decoders/Rules for Custom Applications

☑ Summary

☑ Solutions Fast Track

☑ Frequently Asked Questions

Introduction

David and his team, under the guidance of Marty, installed the OSSEC HIDS agents on roughly 100 servers and about 50 workstations in the lab environment. Because this was a test environment, Marty deployed only three OSSEC HIDS servers to centralize the events from the deployed agents. He knew that in the corporate environment he would require many more OSSEC HIDS servers. The lab environment was a scaled down clone of the corporate production environment but the same event rate was impossible to simulate given his smaller lab budget. David's team consisted of his three most senior engineers: Ming Tsai, Mark Olyphant, and Sergei Zbruyev. David and Sergei configured five Cisco PIX firewalls, two Juniper Netscreen firewalls, and seven Cisco IOS based routers to send their logs to the first OSSEC HIDS server, named Saturn. Mark handled the OSSEC HIDS agent installations on Windows systems. Ming and Sergei handled the OSSEC HIDS agent installations on all the Linux, UNIX, and BSD systems in the lab environment. Under the guidance of Marty, Mark configured the agents to monitor the mail logs on the Microsoft Exchange server and the FTP logs on the Microsoft FTP servers. All the Windows agents were configured to send their logs to Mars, the second OSSEC HIDS server. Ming and Sergei ensured that the OSSEC HIDS agents were monitoring all the MySQL and PostgreSQL database server logs, Apache HTTPD server logs, Snort IDS logs, Sendmail logs, and Squid proxy server logs on the deployed hosts. All the Linux, UNIX, and BSD agents were configured to send their logs to Venus, the third OSSEC HIDS server.

The configuration in the lab took about two days and, to the surprise of David, there were no issues. He and his team monitored the systems closely for any errors, crashes, or reboots and, in a quick meeting with Marty, he gave his blessing to continue to the next phase.

"They're all yours Marty," said David. "You should have more than enough logs for your proof of concept and rule writing session with Antoine and his team." Marty shook David's hand.

"Thanks for all your help on this one Dave." David shook his head.

"You don't need to thank me!" exclaimed David. "Anything I can do to help prevent another embarrassment like that last breach and ensure my continued employment is no waste of time in my books." Marty thanked David and went to Simran's office to provide an update.

"I'm going to schedule the meeting with Antoine and his team tomorrow to review the rule configuration options with the OSSEC HIDS," said Marty. "I figure I should plan on taking the whole day so we can create a thorough library of alert rules from our lab environment traffic." Marty put his hands in his pockets and looked around the room, hesitant to ask his next question. "So....I can expense lunch for the team right?" asked Marty. Simran looked up from her paperwork at Marty. "Oh come on! I can't be responsible for Antoine's team being malnourished." Marty smiled. "How could I live with myself?" Simran rolled her eyes.

"Fine, have lunch brought in. But," Simran paused, "make sure you save me a salad."

Marty wasn't sure if it was the promise of a free lunch or the topic of discussion that brought so many of Antoine's team to the meeting. "I guess if it was the lunch then they would have just showed up at noon," Marty thought to himself. Antoine had brought seven of his senior incident handlers and three of his senior forensic analysts who were the most familiar with the types of systems used in the lab environment. They were also well versed in the types of information required to perform a proper incident handling exercise. They knew what to look for, where to look for it, and how to preserve it in case it had to be used as evidence.

"Well, Marty," said Antoine "You've got our full attention. I want to make sure that everyone in this room is up to speed by the end of the day." Marty nodded in agreement. He provided an overview of the OSSEC HIDS, its capabilities, how to write predecoders, decoders, and rules. He also discussed where the OSSEC HIDS fits into the current incident handling model. As Marty spoke he noticed that everyone in the room looked interested but he could tell that people were still exhausted from the last breach. Marty made sure to highlight how the OSSSEC HIDS could have helped shave valuable hours off their investigation and perhaps even prevent the breach altogether.

When the overview was complete Marty divided everyone up into three teams.

"Alpha team," Marty pointed to a network diagram showing the installed OSSEC HIDS agents. "You're responsible for configuring rules for the firewall and router logs being sent to Saturn. Bravo team," Marty pointed to another area of the diagram. "You need to handle the Windows system and application events coming into Mars." Marty pointed to the final area of the diagram. "Charlie team, you need to handle the Linux, Unix, BSD system, and application events." Marty took a sip of his coffee. "I want to see e-mails and SMS pages for high-priority alerts. Think real-world incidents everyone," Marty said. "You need to create rules that will make all of our jobs easier in the long run." Marty sat down and noticed an instant message on his laptop from Simran:

```
Simran> How's it going?
Marty>  Good, after lunch we'll get into the syscheck and rootkit discovery.
Simran> Excellent, is everyone participating?
Marty>  Yes, everyone is in their teams and plugging away at the rules.
Simran> Good…and my salad?
Marty>  Operation "Salad Grab" is still a go!
```

Introducing Rules

Now that you are familiar with the installation and configuration of the OSSEC HIDS it's time to move onto the most powerful features of the product. The decoders and rules give the OSSEC HIDS its power. When combined they allow you to configure and tune every alert from the OSSEC HIDS, including those generated for integrity checking alerts, syslog and agent log events, and rootkit detection alerts.

Every OSSEC rule is stored inside the *rules/* directory of your OSSEC HIDS installation. This is typically in */var/ossec/rules/*. Each rule is defined in a separate XML file and is named accordingly. For example, all rules for the Apache HTTP server are located within the *apache_rules.xml* file just as all rules for the Cisco PIX firewall are located within the *pix_rules.xml* file. The default installation of the OSSEC HIDS contains 43 rules files, described in Table 4.1.

Table 4.1 Default OSSEC HIDS Rules

Rule Name	Description
apache_rules.xml	Apache HTTP server rules
arpwatch_rules.xml	Arpwatch rules
attack_rules.xml	Common attack rules
cisco-ios_rules.xml	Cisco IOS firmware rules
courier_rules.xml	Courier mail server rules
firewall_rules.xml	Common firewall rules
ftpd_rules.xml	Rules for the ftpd daemon
hordeimp_rules.xml	Horde Internet Messaging Program rules
ids_rules.xml	Common IDS rules
imapd_rules.xml	Rules for the *imapd* daemon
local_rules.xml	OSSEC HIDS local, user-defined rules
mailscanner_rules.xml	Common mail scanner rules
msauth_rules.xml	Microsoft Authentication rules
ms-exchange_rules.xml	Microsoft Exchange server rules
netscreenfw_rules.xml	Juniper Netscreen firewall rules
ms_ftpd_rules.xml	Microsoft FTP server rules
mysql_rules.xml	MySQL database rules
named_rules.xml	Rules for the *named* daemon
ossec_rules.xml	Common OSSEC HIDS rules
pam_rules.xml	Pluggable Authentication Module (PAM) rules
pix_rules.xml	Cisco PIX firewall rules
policy_rules.xml	Policy specific event rules
postfix_rules.xml	Postfix mail transfer agent rules
postgresql_rules.xml	PostgerSQL database rules

Continued

Table 4.1 Continued. Default OSSEC HIDS Rules

Rule Name	Description
proftpd_rules.xml	ProFTPd FTP server rules
pure-ftpd_rules.xml	Pure-FTPd FTP server rules
racoon_rules.xml	Racoon VPN device rules
rules_config.xml	OSSEC HIDS Rules configuration rules
sendmail_rules.xml	Sendmail mail transfer agent rules
squid_rules.xml	Squid proxy server rules
smbd_rules.xml	Rules for the *smbd* daemon
sonicwall_rules.xml	SonicWall firewall rules
spamd_rules.xml	Rules for the *spamd* spam-deferral daemon
sshd_rules.xml	Secure Shell (SSH) network protocol rules
symantec-av_rules.xml	Symantec Antivirus rules
symantec-ws_rules.xml	Symantec Web Security rules
syslog_rules.xml	Common syslog rules
telnetd_rules.xml	Rules for the telnetd daemon
vpn_concentrator_rules.xml	Cisco VPN Concentrator rules
vpopmail_rules.xml	Rules for the *vpopmail* virtual mail domain application
vsftpd_rules.xml	Rules for the vsftpd FTP server
web_rules.xml	Common web server rules
zeus_rules.xml	Zeus web server rules

Each rule file contains multiple rule definitions for the application or device. This provides you with over 600 rules for anything from ProFTPD logs, to Snort NIDS alerts, to Cisco VPN Concentrator messages, to OSSEC HIDS Integrity Checking and rootkit detection logs.

Coupled with the rules, we have the *decoders*, which are defined within the *decoders.xml* file in the */etc* directory of your OSSEC HIDS installation. This typically is found in */var/ossec/etc/decoders.xml*. Decoders are designed to extract data from the raw events, which enables the OSSEC HIDS to correlate disparate events received from multiple sources.

Every rule has a unique ID that is assigned when it is first created. For each log type, a range of IDs have been assigned to ensure that OSSEC HIDS released decoders are not overwritten by mistake. The OSSEC HIDS team does, however, provide you with a dedicated range of IDs to be used for user created rules. This range is 100,000 to 119,999, inclusive. Table 4.2 shows the current reserved ID assignments.

TIP

Within the OSSEC HIDS world, user-created rules are referred to as *local rules*. Local rules should range from 100,000 to 119,999. If you choose any other ID you might cause a conflict with the official rules from the OSSEC HIDS project. A complete list with all current ranges is available at the OSSEC HIDS Web site: *www.ossec.net/wiki/index.php/Know_How:RuleIDGrouping*.

Table 4.2 Reserved ID Assignments

Rule ID Range	General Category
00000–00999	Reserved for internal OSSEC HIDS rules
01000–01999	General syslog rules
02100–02299	Network File System (NFS) rules
02300–02499	xinetd rules
02500–02699	Access control rules
02700–02729	mail/procmail rules
02800–02829	*smartd* rules
02830–02859	*crond* rules
02860–02899	Mount/Automount rules
03100–03299	Sendmail mail server rules
03300–03499	Postfix mail server rules
03500–03599	*spamd* filter rules
03600–03699	*imapd* mail server rules
03700–03799	Mail scanner rules
03800–03899	Microsoft Exchange mail server rules
03900–03999	Courier mail rules (*imapd/pop3d/pop3-ssl*)
04100–04299	Generic firewall rules
04300–04499	Cisco PIX/FWSM/ASA firewall rules

Continued

Table 4.2 Continued. Reserved ID Assignments

Rule ID Range	General Category
04500–04699	Juniper Netscreen firewall rules
04700–04799	Cisco IOS rules
04800–04899	SonicWall firewall rules
05100–05299	Linux, UNIX, BSD kernel rules
05300–05399	Switch user (*su*) rules
05400–05499	Super user do (*sudo*) rules
05500–05599	Unix pluggable authentication module (*PAM*) rules
05600–05699	*telnetd* rules
05700–05899	*sshd* rules
05900–05999	Add user or user deletion rules
07100–07199	Tripwire rules
07200–07299	*arpwatch* rules
07300–07399	Symantec Antivirus rules
07400–07499	Symantec Web Security rules
09100–09199	Point-to-point tunneling protocol (*PPTP*) rules
09200–09299	Squid syslog rules
09300–09399	Horde IMP rules
09900–09999	*vpopmail* rules
10100–10199	FTS rules
11100–11199	*ftpd* rules
11200–11299	ProFTPD rules
11300–11399	Pure-FTPD rules
11400–11499	vs-FTPD rules
11500–11599	MS-FTP rules
12100–12299	*named* (BIND DNS) rules
13100–13299	Samba (*smbd*) rules
14100–14199	Racoon SSL rules
14200–14299	Cisco VPN Concentrator rules
17100–17399	Policy rules
18100–18499	Windows system rules
20100–20299	IDS rules

Continued

Table 4.2 Continued. Reserved ID Assignments

Rule ID Range	General Category
20300–20499	IDS (Snort specific) rules
30100–30999	Apache HTTP server error log rules
31100–31199	Web access log rules
31200–31299	Zeus web server rules
35000–35999	Squid rules
40100–40499	Attack pattern rules
40500–40599	Privilege escalation rules
40600–40999	Scan pattern rules
50100–50299	MySQL database rules
50500–50799	PostgreSQL database rules
100000–109999	User-defined rules

Every local rule should go in the *local_rules.xml* file located within the *rules/* directory of your OSSEC HIDS installation. This typically is found in */var/ossec/rules/local_rules.xml.*

TIP

The other rules files should not be modified because they could impact how the core OSSEC HIDS rules function.

During the upgrade process, the scripts overwrite all rules files, except the *local_rules.xml* file. If you need to tweak or tune a specific rule that is shipped with the OSSEC HIDS, the *local_rules.xml* can be used to override how the standard rule functions. This is discussed later in this chapter.

Understanding the OSSEC HIDS Analysis Process

The first thing to understand is how the OSSEC HIDS handles every event received. Figure 4.1 shows this event flow.

Figure 4.1 Event Flow Diagram

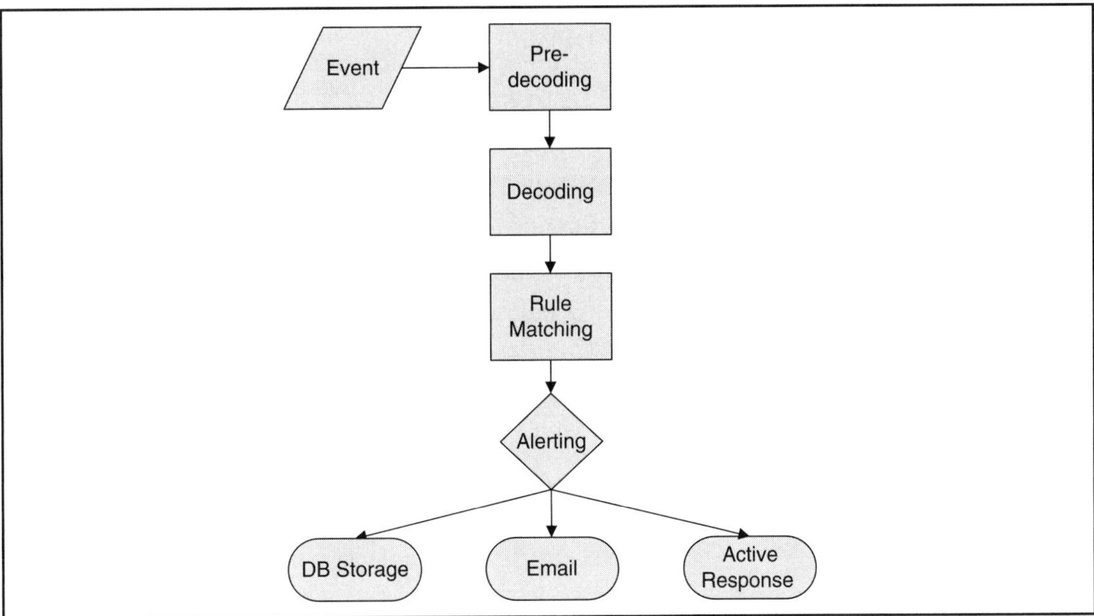

As soon as an event is received, the OSSEC HIDS tries to decode and extract any relevant information from it. Decoding or normalization of the event is done in two parts, called predecoding and decoding. The fields used to decode these events are shown in Table 4.3.

Table 4.3 Decoded Fields

Field	Description
log	The message section of the event.
full_log	The entire event.
location	Where the log came from.
hostname	Hostname of the event source.
program_name	Program name. This is taken from the syslog header of the event.
srcip	The source IP address within the event.
dstip	The destination IP address within the event.
srcport	The source port within the event.

Continued

Table 4.3 Continued. Decoded Fields

Field	Description
dstport	The destination port within the event.
protocol	The protocol within the event.
action	The action taken within the event.
srcuser	The originating user within the event.
dstuser	The destination user within the event.
id	Any ID decoded as the ID from the event.
status	The decoded status within the event.
command	The command being called within the event.
url	The URL within the event.
data	Any additional data that you want to extract from the payload of the event.
systemname	The system name within the event.

After this data is extracted, the rule-matching engine is called to verify if an alert should be created.

Predecoding Events

The process of predecoding is very simple and is meant to extract only static information from well-known fields of an event. It generally is used with log messages that follow widely used protocols, like Syslog or the Apple System Log (ASL) formats. The information extracted during this phase is time, date, hostname, program name, and the log message.

The following log indicates that the syslog daemon has stopped. The predecoder can inspect this log and extract important information from it as seen in Table 4.4.

```
Apr 13 13:00:01 linux_server syslogd: stopped
```

Table 4.4 Predecoded Example (syslogd)

Field	Description
hostname	linux_server
program_name	syslogd
log	stopped
time/date	13:00:01, Apr 13

As you can see, only the static information from the log is extracted. Dealing with additional fields, like usernames or source IP addresses, are performed later in the *decoding* part of the process.

Another example of predecoding can be seen in the following log generated by the *sshd* daemon:

```
Apr 14 17:32:06 linux_server sshd[1025]: Accepted password for dcid from
192.168.2.180 port 1618 ssh2
```

Table 4.5 shows how this log would be predecoded.

Table 4.5 Predecoded Example (sshd)

Field	Description
hostname	linux_server
program_name	sshd
log	Accepted password for dcid from 192.168.2.180 port 1618 ssh2
time/date	Apr 14 17:32:06

The last example, a failed authentication log from an ASL-enabled system, is shown here:

```
[Time 2006.12.28 15:53:55 UTC] [Facility auth] [Sender sshd] [PID 483]
[Message error: PAM: Authentication failure for username from 192.168.0.2]
[Level 3] [UID -2] [GID -2] [Host mymac]
```

Table 4.6 shows how this log would be predecoded.

Table 4.6 Predecoded Example (ASL sshd)

Field	Description
hostname	mymac
program_name	sshd
log	error: PAM: Authentication failure for username from 192.168.0.2
time/date	Dec 28, 2006 15:53:55

When you compare a Syslog message and an ASL message, they look very different. Within the OSSEC HIDS, however, they would be normalized in a way that the same rule can be written to match both message formats. Another benefit is that you are able to write rules looking for each of these fields separately, like looking for any log from *hostname X* or any log with *program_name Y*.

Decoding Events

Decoding is the next step in the process, following predecoding. The goal of decoding is to extract nonstatic information from the events that we can use in our rules later in the process. Generally we want to extract IP address information, usernames, and similar data.

Let's revisit our previously discussed *sshd* message:

```
Apr 14 17:32:06 linux_server sshd[1025]: Accepted password for dcid from
192.168.2.180 port 1618 ssh2
```

The message is predecoded as previously explained in Table 4.5, but we could user our decoder to extract the fields as shown in Table 4.7 if the log message contained the information.

Table 4.7 Decoded Example (sshd)

Field	Description
srcip	192.168.2.180
user	dcid

The decoders, unlike the predecoders, are not static, and can vary from event to event. All decoders are user-configured in the *decoder.xml* file in the etc/ directory of your OSSEC HIDS installation. This typically is located in */var/ossec/etc/decoder.xml*. There are several *decoder* options available and these are explained in Table 4.8.

Table 4.8 Available Decoder Options

Field	Description
program_name	Executes the decoder if the *program_name* matches the syslog program name.
prematch	Executes the decoder if *prematch* matches any portion of the *log* field.

Continued

Table 4.8 Continued. Available Decoder Options

Field	Description
regex	Regular expression to specify where each field is.
offset	Attribute of regex. It can be *after_prematch* or *after_parent*. It essentially tells the regex where to start computing the expression.
order	Order within the regular expression. It can be all the fields in the normalized event (*srcip*, *user*, *dstip*, *dstport*, etc.)
parent	Parent decoder that must be matched for this decoder to be called.

To start, each decoder is delimited by a *<decoder></decoder>* tag, where the name of the decoder is specified. Within the *<decoder></decoder>* tag the fields explained in Table 4.8 can be used.

```
<decoder name="decoder-test"></decoder>
```

We will now walk through several decoder examples to help you fully understand the decoder process.

Decoder Example: sshd Message

In this example, we have a decoder to extract the Source IP address and username from a the following *sshd* log message:

```
Apr 14 17:32:06 linux_server sshd[1025]: Accepted password for dcid from
192.168.2.180 port 1618 ssh2
```

To extract the information we must define our decoder. The first step is to create the decoder, named sshd-test. The *name* attribute is mandatory so that your decoder can be properly identified.

```
<decoder name="sshd-test">
</decoder>
```

Within the decoder we need to define the <program_name></program_name> tag so that this decoder is called only if the program_name matches sshd in the syslog header.

```
<program_name>sshd</program_name>
```

To extract the user and port information from the message we must use the *<regex></regex>* tag. The *\S+* will match any sequence of consecutive nonwhite space characters (i.e., spaces and tabs).

The two capture groups (in parenthesis) will match the username and IP address part of the message, respectively.

```
<regex>^Accepted \S+ for (\S+) from (\S+) port </regex>
```

We must also specify the order to tell the OSSEC HIDS the field that we are parsing out of the message. In this case, the order is a username followed by a source IP address.

```
<order>user, srcip</order>
```

Our completed decoder is:

```
<decoder name="sshd-test">
  <program_name>sshd</program_name>
  <regex>^Accepted \S+ for (\S+) from (\S+) port </regex>
  <order>user, srcip</order>
</decoder>
```

Decoder Example: vsftpd Message

In addition to the program_name, we can use the <prematch> conditional tag to specify when the decoder should be called. It can be used with the program_name to have two conditionals or by itself on non-syslog messages (only syslog can have a program_name). The following is an example to match a vsftpd message.

The following log is a vsftpd login message that we want to decode:

```
Sun Jun 4 22:08:39 2006 [pid 21611] [dcid] OK LOGIN: Client "192.168.1.1"
```

To extract the information we must define our decoder. The first step is to create the decoder, named **vsftpd**. The *name* attribute is mandatory so that your decoder can be properly identified.

```
<decoder name="vsftpd">
</decoder>
```

Within the decoder we need to define the *<prematch></prematch>* tag so when the prematch matches what is in the log, the regex is going to be called to extract the user and source IP address.

In this example, the pattern will match if the line starts with (^) one or more word characters (*w*+), followed by a space then one or more word characters (*w*+), one or more white-space characters (*s*+), one or more digits (*d*+), and a space. Next, is one or more nonwhite-space characters (*S*+), a space then the *pid* section where the *pid* has one or more digits (*d*+).

```
<prematch>^\w+ \w+\s+\d+ \S+ \d+ [pid \d+] </prematch>
```

The *offset* option must be used within the <regex></regex> tag to make sure our regular expression is compared only after what was read from this prematch. This saves a lot of time when computing the regular expressions. In this example, the expression matches a line beginning with a word in braces followed by *OK LOGIN: Client* and then an IP address in dotted quad notation.

```
<regex offset="after_prematch">^[(\w+)] OK LOGIN: Client "(\d+.\d+.\d+.\d+)"$</regex>
```

We need to also specify the order to tell the OSSEC HIDS what each field is that we are parsing out of the message. In this case the order is a username followed by a source IP address.

```
<order>user, srcip</order>
```

Our completed decoder is:

```
<decoder name="vsftpd">
  <prematch>^\w+ \w+\s+\d+ \S+ \d+ [pid \d+] </prematch>
  <regex offset="after_prematch">^[(\w+)] OK LOGIN: Client
"(\d+.\d+.\d+.\d+)"$</regex>
  <order>user, srcip</order>
</decoder>
```

Tools & Traps...

Using Offsets

Offsets should be used whenever you can. They specify where in the string OSSEC should start evaluating the regular expression. For example, imagine you have a log:

```
Sun Jun 4 22:08:39 2007 test: Login USER dcid
```

and you write a simple <prematch> looking for the date and time format:

```
<prematch>\w+ \w+ \d+ \S+ \d\d\d\d </prematch>
```

When the <prematch> finishes evaluating, it will read everything up to "Sun Jun 4 22:08:39 2007 ", so there is no point in reading it all again. Because of that, in our regex, we use:

```
<regex offset="after_prematch">^test: Login USER (\w+)</regex>
```

so that it starts reading at "test: Login USER dcid" instead of the whole log.

If your decoder has a "parent" decoder (explained later), you can use "after_\parent" to make sure your decoder does not read everything that the parent already did.

Using the <*parent*> Option

The next step of *decoding* is to use the <*parent*></*parent*> option to create trees of *decoders*, where each extracts parts of the event. Imagine a case where you need to extract the username and source IP address from both a successful login event and a failed login event. Instead of checking each every time, a *parent decoder* can be written that looks for a specific *program_name* or part of the log. This allows you to create *subdecoders* to extract the data you need. Using the following sshd log messages:

```
Apr 14 17:32:06 linux_server sshd[1025]: Accepted password for dcid from
192.168.2.180 port 1618 ssh2

Apr 14 17:33:09 linux_server sshd[1231]: Failed password for invalid user lcid
from 192.168.2.180 port 1799 ssh2
```

We could write two decoders, but the *prematches* and *program_name* would be checked multiple times, slowing OSSEC down. With a parent decoder we can look for *sshd* within the program name of the log messages:

```
<decoder name="sshd">
  <program_name>^sshd</program_name>
</decoder>
```

Now that we have a parent decoder created we can create a separate decoder for each log message. One decoder can be created for the successful authentication and another for the failed authentication message.

```
<decoder name="sshd-success">
  <parent>sshd</parent>
  <prematch>^Accepted</prematch>
  <regex offset="after_prematch">^ password for (\S+) from (\S+) port </regex>
  <order>user, srcip</order>
</decoder>

<decoder name="ssh-failed">
  <parent>sshd</parent>
  <prematch>^Failed password </prematch>
  <regex offset="after_prematch">^for invalid user \S+ from (\S+) </regex>
  <order>srcip</order>
</decoder>
```

Note how on each one we have a different <*prematch*></*prematch*> value specified. If a message contains the string **Accepted** the regex for success is going to be extracted. Conversely if the message contains the string **Failed**, the regex for the failed decoder is called. Figure 4.2 shows how the event would flow, if subject to the preceding <*prematch*></*prematch*> configuration.

Figure 4.2 <prematch> Event Flow

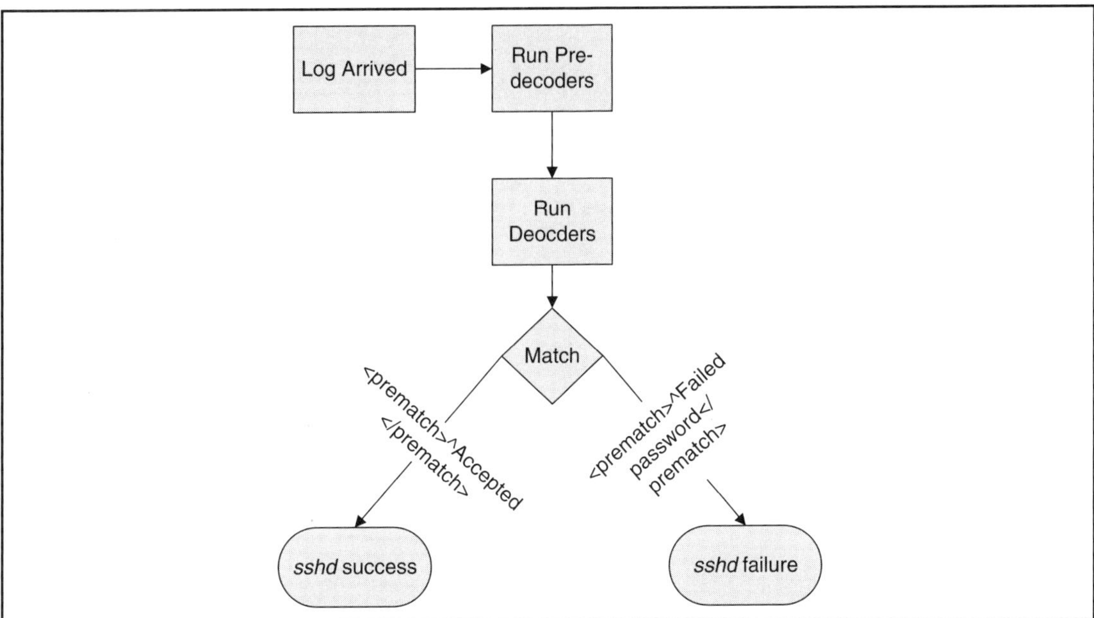

Decoder Example: Cisco PIX Message

In this example we need to create a decoder for the following Cisco PIX message:

```
%PIX-2-106001: Inbound TCP connection denied from 165.139.46.7/3854 to
165.189.27.70/139 flags
```

Because we might have to write *decoders* for different PIX IDs at a later time we should first create a *parent decoder* for all PIX messages:

```
<decoder name="pix">
  <prematch>^%PIX-</prematch>
</decoder>
```

Any additional PIX decoders we create should reference this parent decoder for consistency. We should also use the *after_parent* option to make sure we are not reading the message more times then we should:

```
<decoder name="pix-fw1">
  <parent>pix</parent>
  <prematch offset="after_parent">^2-106001</prematch>
  <regex offset="after_parent">^(\S+): \w+ (\w+) \S+ (\S+) from </regex>
  <regex>(\S+)/(\S+) to (\S+)/(\S+)</regex>
  <order>id, protocol, action, srcip, srcport, dstip, dstport</order>
</decoder>
```

Our regular expression is a bit more complex, but it extracts everything from the event, including protocol, action, source and destination IP addresses, and ports.

Decoder Example: Cisco IOS ACL Message

In this example we need to extract the action, source IP address, source port, destination IP address, and destination port for use in Cisco IOS access control list (ACL) rules.

WARNING

The following example does not need to be created within the *decoder.xml* file since it is already present. The example is presented so that you might understand how to create your own advanced decoders.

The following log is a Cisco IOS ACL message that we want to decode:

```
%SEC-6-IPACCESSLOGP: list 102 denied tcp 10.0.6.56(3067) -> 172.36.4.7(139),
  1 packet
%SEC-6-IPACCESSLOGP: list 199 denied tcp 10.0.61.108(1477) -> 10.0.127.20(44
5), 1 packet
```

To extract the information we must define our decoder. The first step is to create the decoder, named **cisco-ios-acl**. The *name* attribute is mandatory so that your decoder can be properly identified.

```
<decoder name="cisco-ios-acl">
</decoder>
```

The Cisco IOS ACL decoder relies on the already created Cisco IOS decoder named *cisco-ios*. As such we must defined the *<parent></parent>* tag to reference the other decoder.

```
<parent>cisco-ios</parent>
```

Because this is an ACL rule we can identify this *type* of message as a *firewall* message using the *<type></type>* tag. The *<type></type>* tag can be syslog, firewall, ids, web-log, squid, windows, or ossec, and are defined in the *rules_config.xml* file.

```
<type>firewall</type>
```

Within the decoder we need to define the *<prematch></prematch>* tag so when the prematch matches what is in the log, the regex is going to be called to extract the user and source IP address.

```
<prematch>^%SEC-6-IPACCESSLOGP: </prematch>
```

The *offset* option must be used within the <regex></regex> tag to make sure our regular expression is compared only after what was read from the earlier prematch. This saves a lot of time when computing the regular expressions. The regular expression used matches any string beginning with *list*, followed by multiple nonwhite-space and two more space-separated words. The two words are captured in groups *denied* and *tcp*.

```
<regex offset="after_prematch">^list \S+ (\w+) (\w+) </regex>
```

Anther regular expression must be created to locate the source IP address (*srcip*), source port (*srcport*), destination IP address (*dstip*), and destination port (*dstport*) so another *<regex></regex>* tag must be used.

```
<regex>(\S+)\((\d+)\) -> (\S+)\((\d+)\),</regex>
```

We also need to specify the order to tell the OSSEC HIDS what each field is that we are parsing out of the message. In this case the order is an action, protocol, source IP address, source port, destination IP address, and destination port.

```
<order>action, protocol, srcip, srcport, dstip, dstport</order>
```

Our completed decoder appears as follows:

```
<decoder name="cisco-ios-acl">
  <parent>cisco-ios</parent>
  <type>firewall</type>
  <prematch>^%SEC-6-IPACCESSLOGP: </prematch>
  <regex offset="after_prematch">^list \S+ (\w+) (\w+) </regex>
  <regex>(\S+)\((\d+)\) -> (\S+)\((\d+)\),</regex>
  <order>action, protocol, srcip, srcport, dstip, dstport</order>
</decoder>
```

Understanding Rules

The OSSEC HIDS evaluates the rules to see if the received event should be escalated to an alert or if it should be part of a composite alert (with multiple events). As we mentioned earlier, the rules are stored in XML files located within the *rules/* directory of your OSSEC HIDS installation directory. These typically are found in the */var/ossec/rules/* directory.

There are two types of OSSEC HIDS rules: atomic and composite. Atomic rules are based on single events, without any correlation. For example, if you see an authentication failure, you can alert on that unique event. Composite rules are based on multiple events. For example, if you want an alert after 10 authentication failures, from the same source IP address, then a composite rule would be required.

Atomic Rules

We will begin by explaining how atomic rules work and then expand on your knowledge of rules by working with the advanced composite rules.

Writing a Rule

Each rule, or grouping of rules, must be defined within a *<group></group>* element. Your attribute *name* must contain the rules you want to be a part of this group. In the following example we have indicated that our group contains the **syslog** and **sshd** rules.

```
<group name="syslog,sshd,">
</group>
```

NOTE

A trailing comma in the group name definition is required if additional rules will append groups into the rule.

A group can contain as many rules as you require. The rules are defined using the *<rule></rule>* element and must have at least two attributes, the **id** and the **level**. The **id** is a unique identifier for that signature and the **level** is the severity of the alert. In the following example, we have created two rules, each with a different rule id and level.

```
<group name="syslog,sshd,">
<rule id="100120" level="5">
  </rule>
  <rule id="100121" level="6">
  </rule>
</group>
```

NOTE

User-defined rules should range from 100,000 to 119,999. If you choose any other ID, it might collide with the official ones from the OSSEC HIDS project.

Tools & Traps...

OSSEC HIDS Severities

The OSSEC HIDS severities (levels) range from 0 to 15, with 0 being the lowest and 15 the highest. When the rules are written, they are stored using a hierarchical model, where the rules with higher severity are evaluated first. The only exception is the severity 0, which is evaluated before all other severities.

The severities can be changed on a case-by-case basis but the default OSSEC HIDS severities are defined as follows:

Level 0: Ignored, no action taken
Primarily used to avoid false positives. These rules are scanned before all the others and include events with no security relevance.

Level 2: System low priority notification
System notification or status messages that have no security relevance.

Level 3: Successful/authorized events
Successful login attempts, firewall allow events, etc.

Level 4: System low priority errors
Errors related to bad configurations or unused devices/applications. They have no security relevance and are usually caused by default installations or software testing.

Level 5: User-generated errors
Missed passwords, denied actions, etc. These messages typically have no security relevance.

Level 6: Low relevance attacks
Indicate a worm or a virus that provide no threat to the system such as a Windows worm attacking a Linux server. They also include frequently triggered IDS events and common error events.

Level 9: Error from invalid source
Include attempts to login as an unknown user or from an invalid source. The message might have security relevance especially if repeated. They also include errors regarding the *admin* or *root* account.

Level 10: Multiple user generated errors
Include multiple bad passwords, multiple failed logins, etc. They might indicate an attack, or it might be just that a user forgot his or her credentials.

Continued

Level 12: High-importance event
Include *error* or *warning* messages from the system, kernel, etc. They might indicate an attack against a specific application.

Level 13: Unusual error (high importance)
Common attack patterns such as a buffer overflow attempt, a larger than normal syslog message, or a larger than normal URL string.

Level 14: High importance security event.
Typically the result of the correlation of multiple attack rules and indicative of an attack.

Level 15: Attack successful
Very small chance of false positive. Immediate attention is necessary.

You can define additional subgroups within the parent group using the *<group></group>* tag. This subgroup can reference any of the predefined OSSEC HIDS groups listed in Table 4.9. A description is also required in the *<description></description>* tag so that you can differentiate between rules as you create them.

```
<group name="syslog,sshd,">
  <rule id="100120" level="5">
    <group>authentication_success</group>
    <description>SSHD testing authentication success</description>
  </rule>
  <rule id="100121" level="6">
    <description>SSHD rule testing 2</description>
  </rule>
</group>
```

Table 4.9 OSSEC HIDS Groups

Group Type	Group Name	Description
Reconnaissance	connection_attempt	Connection attempt
	web_scan	Web scan
	recon	Generic scan
Authentication Control	authentication_success	Success
	authentication_failed	Failure
	invalid_login	Invalid
	login_denied	Login denied
	authentication_failures	Multiple failures

Continued

Table 4.9 Continued. OSSEC HIDS Groups

Group Type	Group Name	Description
	adduser	User account added
	account_changed	User account changed or removed
Attack/Misuse	automatic_attack	Worm (nontargeted attack)
	exploit_attempt	Exploit pattern
	invalid_access	Invalid access
	spam	Spam
	multiple_spam	Multiple spam messages
	sql_injection	SQL injection
	attack	Generic attack
	rootcheck	Rootkit detection
	virus	Virus detected
Access Control	access_denied	Access denied
	access_allowed	Access allowed
	unknown_resource	Access to nonexistent resource
	firewall_drop	Firewall drop
	multiple_drops	Multiple firewall drops
	client_misconfig	Client misconfiguration
	client_error	Client error
Network Control	new_host	New host detected
	ip_spoof	Possible ARP spoofing
System Monitor	service_start	Service start
	service_availability	Service availability at risk
	system_error	System error
	system_shutdown	Shutdown
	logs_cleared	Logs cleared
	invalid_request	Invalid request
	promisc	Interface switched to promiscuous mode
	policy_changed	Policy changed
	config_changed	Configuration changed

Continued

Table 4.9 Continued. OSSEC HIDS Groups

Group Type	Group Name	Description
	syscheck	Integrity checking
	low_diskspace	Low disk space
	time_changed	Time changed
Policy Violation	login_time	Login time
	login_day	Login day

Another important tag is the *<decoded_as></decoded_as> tag*. This explicitly states that the rule will be evaluated only if the specified decoder decoded it. As an example, using the *<decoded_as></decoded_as>* tag, we can explicitly state that the rule will execute only if the event is decoded by the *sshd* decoder. As you can see, we also have created a *<description></description>* tag detailing that this rule will log every decoded *sshd* message.

```
<rule id="100123" level="5">
  <decoded_as>sshd</decoded_as>
  <description>Logging every decoded sshd message</description>
</rule>
```

The previous rule is not necessarily a very useful rule. We can, however, expand it a bit further by using the *<match></match>* tag to evaluate parts of the log. For example, if we are interested in capturing failed attempts to log into a server due to incorrect SSH passwords, a rule could be created to match for certain strings in the event. For example, take a look at the following Linux *sshd* failed password log:

```
Apr 14 17:33:09 linux_server sshd[1231]: Failed password for invalid user lcid
from 192.168.2.180 port 1799 ssh2
```

Using the *<match></match>* tag we can search through the log and use the *Failed password* part of the message as a key to detect all events of this type. As you can see in the following example we have also updated the *<description></description>* tag to describe our new rule.

```
<rule id="100124" level="5">
  <decoded_as>sshd</decoded_as>
  <match>^Failed password</match>
  <description>Failed SSHD password attempt</description>
</rule>
```

If you want to alert on the successful password attempts and log with a lower severity, we would need three additional rules. Since these rules are looking at the same data, we can create a rule tree for the *sshd* logs. The rule tree organizes our rules and increases the speed at which they are parsed.

For this to work properly, you must use the *<if_sid></if_sid>* tag. This tag adds a rule to the tree under the signature specified. In the following example we use the *<if_sid></if_sid>* tag to indicate that this rule is a child of the parent *100123* rule in the tree. We also use the *<match></match>* tag to search through the log and use the *Accepted password* part of the message as a key to detect all events of this type. The *<group></group>* tag is used to associate this rule with the internal OSSEC HIDS *authentication_success* group. Finally, a meaningful description is added to identify this rule using the *<description></description>* tag.

```
<rule id="100125" level="3">
  <if_sid>100123</if_sid>
  <match>^Accepted password</match>
  <group>authentication_success</group>
  <description>Successful SSHD password attempt</description>
</rule>
```

The following example shows our entire tree for this group. The first *Logging every decoded sshd message* rule (100123), our *Failed SSHD password attempt* rule (100124), and finally our *Successful SSHD password attempt* rule (100125) are shown. Please note that rules *100124* and *100125* have been modified to be children of the 100123 rule using the *<if_sid></if_sid>* tag and have been associated with the *authentication_failure* and *authentication_success* OSSEC HIDS groups, respectively, using the *<group></group>* tag.

```
<group name="syslog,sshd,">
  <rule id="100123" level="2">
    <decoded_as>sshd</decoded_as>
    <description>Logging every decoded sshd message</description>
  </rule>

  <rule id="100124" level="7">
    <if_sid>100123</if_sid>
    <match>^Failed password</match>
    <group>authentication_failure</group>
    <description>Failed SSHD password attempt</description>
  </rule>

  <rule id="100125" level="3">
    <if_sid>100123</if_sid>
    <match>^Accepted password</match>
    <group>authentication_success</group>
    <description>Successful SSHD password attempt</description>
  </rule>
</group>
```

Figure 4.3 shows the rule hierarchy of the preceding group.

Figure 4.3 SSH Rule Hierarchy

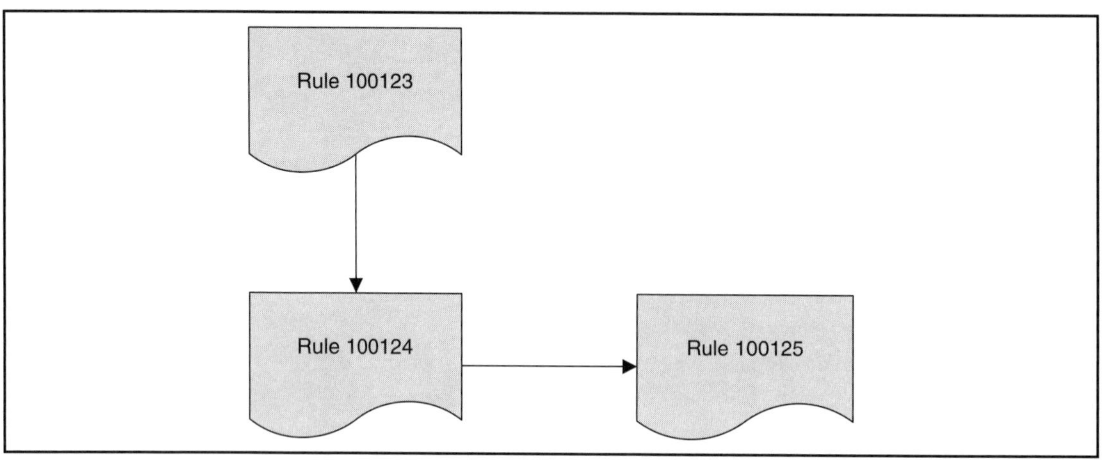

If the following three logs were recorded by the OSSEC HIDS:

```
Apr 14 17:32:06 linux_server sshd[1025]: Accepted password for dcid from
192.168.2.180 port 1618 ssh2

Apr 14 17:33:09 linux_server sshd[1231]: Failed password for invalid user
lcid from 192.168.2.180 port 1799 ssh2

Apr 14 17:33:12 linux_server sshd[1231]: SSHD debug: key shared.
```

then the rules that we had just created would ensure that the events were recorded as alerts and written to the */var/ossec/logs/alerts.log* log as follows:

```
** Alert 1199140087.788: - syslog,sshd,authentication_success,

2007 Apr 14 17:32:06 linux_server->/var/log/auth.log

Rule: 100125 (level 3) -> '>Successful SSHD password attempt'

Src IP: 192.168.2.180

User: dcid

Apr 14 17:32:06 linux_server sshd[1025]: Accepted password for dcid from
192.168.2.180 port 1618 ssh2

** Alert 1199140089.788: - syslog,sshd,authentication_failure,

2007 Apr 14 17:33:09 linux_server->/var/log/auth.log

Rule: 100124 (level 7) -> 'Failed SSHD password attempt'
```

```
Src IP: 192.168.2.180
User: lcid
Apr 14 17:33:09 linux_server sshd[1231]: Failed password for invalid user lcid
from 192.168.2.180 port 1799 ssh2
```

NOTE

Because we did not create a rule to look for the *SSHD debug* log, an alert was not generated.

We can use the *<hostname></hostname>* and *<srcip></srcip>* tags to create more granular rules. Imagine that our company, *fakeinc.com,* has a very important server whose hostname is *main_sys*. Because this server contains highly sensitive customer information we want to record a high severity alert (12) for every authentication failure from outside of the corporate 192.168.2.0/24 network.

Our new rule uses the *<if_sid></if_sid>* tag to define the rule as a child of rule 100124. Because rule 100124 already looks for *Failed password* events, we do not need to parse them again. The new conditions that we want to use to increase the severity of the event are the hostname of the server being accessed and source IP address from which the users are attempting to authenticate. We can define these two conditions using the *<hostname></hostname>* and *<srcip></srcip>* tags, respectively.

```
<rule id="100126" level="12">
  <if_sid>100124</if_sid>
  <group>authentication_failure</group>
  <hostname>main_sys</hostname>
  <srcip>!192.168.2.0/24</srcip>
  <description>Severe SSHD password failure.</description>
</rule>
```

The new rule hierarchy is shown in Figure 4.4.

Figure 4.4 SSH Rule Hierarchy

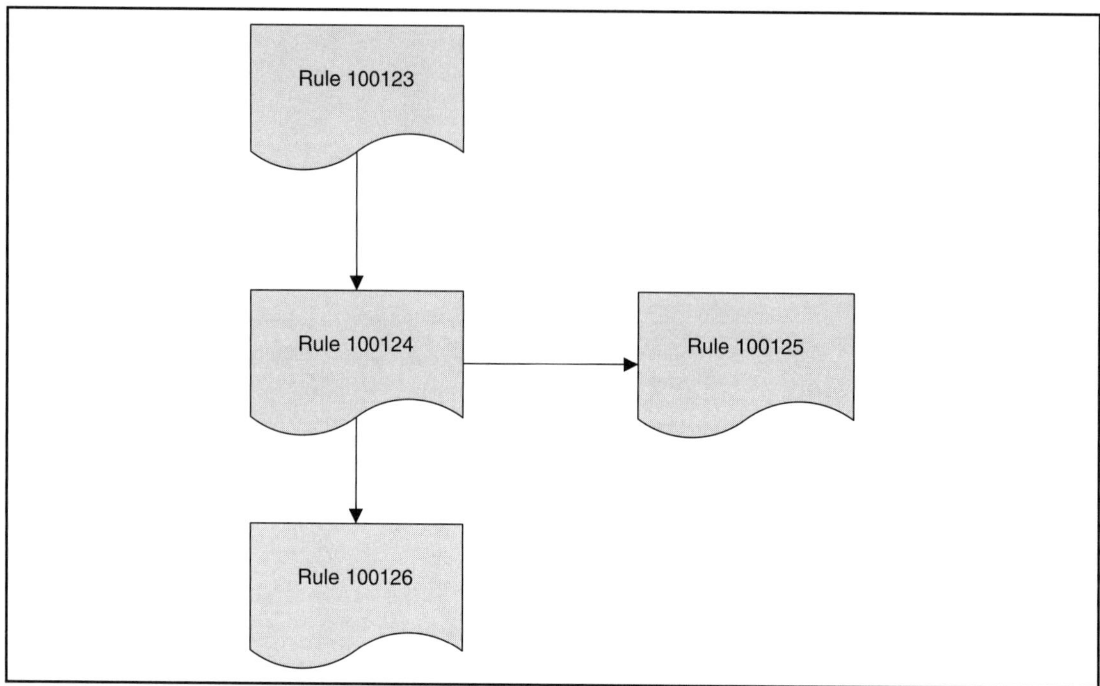

The benefit of this hierarchical tree structure is that our parsing engine operates more efficiently. With more than 600 rules by default, only eight or nine rules are checked for every log instead of all 600. This structure is the main difference between the *linear* and *tree-based* analysis used by the OSSEC HIDS.

Using the *<time></time>* conditional atomic rule tag, we can alert on every successful login outside business hours and increase the severity of the alert. A full list of available atomic rule conditional options are shown in Table 4.10. We use the *<if_sid>100125</if_sid>* tag to make this rule depend on the 100125 rule. This rule will be checked only for *sshd* messages that already matched the successful login rule.

```
<rule id="100127" level="10">
  <if_sid>100125</if_sid>
  <time>6 pm - 8:30 am</time>
  <description>Login outside business hours.</description>
  <group>policy_violation</group>
</rule>
```

Table 4.10 Atomic Rule Conditional Options

Option	Value	Description
match	Any pattern	Any string to match against the event (log).
regex	Any regular expression	Any regular expression to match against the event(log).
decoded_as	Any string	Any prematched string. For more information see the *decoders* section of this chapter.
srcip	Any source IP address	Any IP address that is decoded as the source IP address. Use "!" to negate the IP address.
dstip	Any destination IP address	Any IP address that is decoded as the destination IP address. Use "!" to negate the IP address.
srcport	Any source port	Any source port (match format).
dstport	Any destination port	Any destination port (match format).
user	Any username	Any username that is decoded as a username.
program_name	Any program name	Any program name that is decoded from the syslog process name.
hostname	Any system hostname	Any hostname that is decoded as a syslog hostname.
time	Any time range in the format hh:mm - hh:mm or hh:mm am - hh:mm pm	The time range that the event must fall within for the rule to alert.
weekday	Any week day (sunday, monday, weekends, weekday, etc)	Day of the week that the event must fall on for the rule to alert.
id	Any ID	Any ID that is decoded from the event.
url	Any URL	Any URL that is decoded from the event.

The final rule hierarchy is shown in Figure 4.5.

Figure 4.5 SSH Rule Hierarchy with Policy Violation

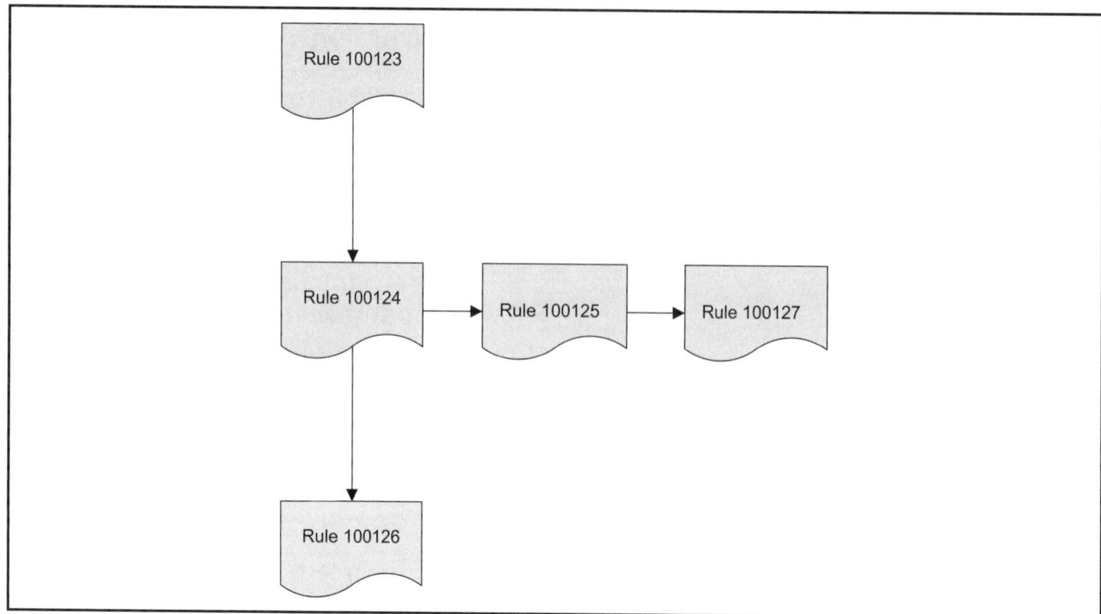

Notes from the Underground...

After-Hours Attacks

When is the best time to attack a network? Is it during the day when the organization has the majority of their staff working and analyzing potential intrusions into their network? Perhaps it's better to wait for everyone to go home and attack outside of regular business hours.

Typically, an attacker would want to breach your network when there is a lesser chance of being detected. This provides them a certain level of anonymity to perform their covert action while your security staff is fast asleep. With no analysts in the office to track and action the associated alerts(provided alerts are generated) until the next morning, the attacker gains some room in which to work.

Using the *<time></time>* tag in your OSSEC HIDS rules allows you to increase the severity of alerts if they happen outside of regular operational hours. Take the following scenario as an example:

Abdalah works a typical Monday to Friday 9 A.M. to 5 P.M. job. Because Abdalah's job as a corporate accountant has him dealing with sensitive accounting records for the company, he is not permitted to bring his work home with him. He does, however, have a corporate laptop so that he can log into the company VPN and check e-mail and perform other duties. All the corporate accounting information is stored on a central server that he, and other accountants, can collaboratively work on.

Taking this into consideration, there should never be a reason for Abdul to log into the accounting server outside of regular business hours. With this information you could create your own rule to create a high severity alert if Abdalah logs into the server between 5:30 P.M. and 8:30 A.M. The following example shows one way of accomplishing this by using our already created *SSH* rules.

```
<group name="syslog,sshd,">
  <rule id="100123" level="2">
    <decoded_as>sshd</decoded_as>
    <description>Logging every decoded sshd message</description>
  </rule>
  <rule id="100124" level="7">
    <if_sid>100123</if_sid>
    <match>^Failed password</match>
    <group>authentication_failure</group>
    <description>Failed SSHD password attempt</description>
  </rule>
  <rule id="100125" level="3">
    <if_sid>100123</if_sid>
    <match>ÐAccepted password</match>
    <group>authentication_success</group>
    <description>Successful SSHD password attempt</description>
  </rule>
  <rule id="100130" level="12">
    <if_sid>100125</if_sid>
    <time>5:30 pm - 8:30 am</time>
    <description>Accounting access outside of regular business
hours.</description>
    <user>abdalahg035</user>
    <group>policy_violation</group>
    <hostname>accounting01</hostname>
  </rule>
</group>
```

As you can see, we have created a rule that relies on the successful SSH authentication rule. It will alert only if the event occurs between the hours of 5:30 P.M. and 8:30 A.M. and is a successful authentication by *abdalahg035* to the *accounting01* server. This rule could be made even more granular with additional atomic rule attributes as defined in Table 4.11.

Another way of writing the 100127 rule would be to include it under every rule in the *successful_login* group replacing the *<if_sid></if_sid>* tag with the *<if_group></if_group>* tag. Extending the rule in this way allows us to create an alert if **any** logins, reported from any device or agent, occur outside of regular business hours. A full listing of the available tree-based options is shown in Table 4.12.

```
<rule id="100127" level="10">
  <if_group>successful_login</if_group>
  <time>6 pm - 8:30 am</time>
  <description>Login outside business hours.</description>
  <group>policy_violation</group>
</rule>
```

NOTE

Only one alert is generated per event. So, for our rule looking for logins outside business hours, only the 100127 rule is going alert if the time is between 6 P.M. and 8:30 A.M. The same applies for rule 100126.

Table 4.11 Atomic Rule Values

Option	Value	Description
level	Any number (0 to 15)	Specifies the severity level of the rule.
id	Any number (100 to 999999)	Specifies the unique ID of the rule.
maxsize	Any number (1 to 99999)	Specifies the maximum size of the log event.

Table 4.12 Tree-Based Options

Option	Value	Description
if_sid	Any rule ID	Adds this rule as a child rule of the rules that match the specified signature ID.
if_group	Any group ID	Adds this rule as a child rule of the rules that match the specified group.

Continued

Table 4.12 Continued. Tree-Based Options

Option	Value	Description
if_level	Any level	Adds this rule as a child rule of the rules that match the specified severity level.
description	Any string	A description of the rule.
info	Any string	Extra information about the rule.
cve	Any CVE number	Any Common Vulnerabilities and Exposures (CVE) number that you would like associated with the rule.
options	alert_by_email no_email_alert no_log	Additional rule options to indicate if the alert should generate an e-mail, *alert_by_email*, should not generate an email, *no_email_alert*, or should not log anything at all, *no_log*.

Composite Rules

So far we have covered the options for single events. If we want to correlate multiple events, there are a few other options that we need to understand with composite rules. Composite rules are supposed to match the current event with those already received by the OSSEC HIDS. To have our rule maintain state, our rule needs two additional options. The *frequency* option specifies how many times an event/pattern must occur before the rule generates an alert. The *timeframe* option tells the OSSEC HIDS how far back, in seconds, it should look for the events. All composite rules have the following structure:

```
<rule id="100130" level="10" frequency="x" timeframe="y">
</rule>
```

For example, you could create a composite rule that creates a higher severity alert after five failed passwords within a period of 10 minutes. Using the *<if_matched_sid></if_matched_sid>* tag you can indicate which rule needs to be seen within the desired frequency and timeframe for your new rule to create an alert. In the following example, we have used the *level* option to set the severity level to **10**. The *frequency* option is configured to alert when five of the events are seen by the OSSEC HIDS and the *timeframe* option is used to specify our time window as **600** seconds (10 minutes).

The *<if_match_sid></if_match_sid>* tag is used to define which rule we want our composite rule to watch. In this case, we want to look for single failed password alerts, which is OSSEC HIDS rule **100124**. A meaningful description is also added using the *<description>* *</description>* tag.

```
<rule id="100130" level="10" frequency="5" timeframe="600">
  <if_matched_sid>100124</if_matched_sid>
  <description>5 Failed passwords within 10 minutes</description>
</rule>
```

If we send the following logs to our OSSEC HIDS server:

```
Apr 14 17:33:09 linux_server sshd[1231]: Failed password for invalid user lcid
from 192.168.2.180 port 1799 ssh2
Apr 14 17:33:09 linux_server sshd[1231]: Failed password for invalid user lcid
from 192.168.2.180 port 1729 ssh2
Apr 14 17:33:09 linux_server sshd[1231]: Failed password for invalid user lcid
from 192.168.2.180 port 1749 ssh2
Apr 14 17:33:09 linux_server sshd[1231]: Failed password for invalid user lcid
from 192.168.2.180 port 1729 ssh2
Apr 14 17:33:09 linux_server sshd[1231]: Failed password for invalid user lcid
from 192.168.2.180 port 1819 ssh2
Apr 14 17:33:09 linux_server sshd[1231]: Failed password for invalid user lcid
from 192.168.2.180 port 1909 ssh2
```

we would see the following alert generated by our composite rule:

```
# tail /var/ossec/logs/alerts/alerts.log
** Alert 1199697806.0: - syslog, sshd,authentication_failures,
2008 Jan 01 05:23:26 linux_server->/var/log/auth.log
Rule: 100130 (level 10) -> '5 Failed passwords within 10 minutes.'
Src IP: 192.168.2.180
User: lcid
Apr 14 17:33:09 linux_server sshd[1231]: Failed password for invalid user lcid
from 192.168.2.180 port 1799 ssh2
Apr 14 17:33:09 linux_server sshd[1231]: Failed password for invalid user
lcid from 192.168.2.180 port 1729 ssh2
Apr 14 17:33:09 linux_server sshd[1231]: Failed password for invalid user
lcid from 192.168.2.180 port 1749 ssh2
Apr 14 17:33:09 linux_server sshd[1231]: Failed password for invalid user
lcid from 192.168.2.180 port 1729 ssh2
Apr 14 17:33:09 linux_server sshd[1231]: Failed password for invalid user
lcid from 192.168.2.180 port 1819 ssh2
```

NOTE

The logs that triggered the alert are shown within the composite alert.

There are several additional tags that we can use to create more granular composite rules. These rules, as shown in Table 4.13, allow you to specify that certain parts of the event must be the same. This allows us to tune our composite rules and reduce false positives.

Table 4.13 Composite Rule Tags

Tag	Description
same_source_ip	Specifies that the *source IP address* must be the same.
same_dest_ip	Specifies that the *destination IP address* must be the same.
same_src_port	Specifies that the *source port* must be the same.
same_dst_port	Specifies that the *destination port* must be the same.
same_location	Specifies that the location (*hostname* or *agent name*) must be the same.
same_user	Specifies that the decoded *username* must be the same.
same_id	Specifies that the decoded *id* must be the same.

Looking back at our composite rule to alert on multiple failed passwords, we can improve it to restrict it to the same source IP address using the *<same_source_ip />* tag. This reduces false positives across our network environment. If you have deployed the OSSEC HIDS on a large network, often you will see multiple failed passwords during the course of a normal day. Restricting the composite rule to a single source IP address ensures that your rule will alert only if the same user unsuccessfully tries to authenticate five times in a row.

```
<rule id="100130" level="10" frequency="5" timeframe="600">
  <if_matched_sid>100124</if_matched_sid>
  <same_source_ip />
  <description>5 Failed passwords within 10 minutes</description>
</rule>
```

If you wanted your composite rule to alert on every authentication failure, instead of a specific OSSEC HIDS rule ID, you could replace the *<if_matched_sid></if_matched_sid>* tag with the *<if_matched_group></if_matched_group>* tag. This allows you to specify a category, such as *authentication_failure*, to search for authentication failures across your entire infrastructure.

```
<rule id="100130" level="10" frequency="5" timeframe="600">
  <if_matched_group>authentication_failure</if_matched_group>
  <same_source_ip />
  <description>5 Failed passwords within 10 minutes</description>
</rule>
```

In addition to *<if_matched_sid></if_matched_sid>* and *<if_matched_group></if_matched_group>* tags, we can also use the *<if_matched_regex></if_matched_regex>* tag to specify a regular expression to search through events as they are received.

```
<rule id="100130" level="10" frequency="5" timeframe="600">
<if_matched_regex>^Failed password</if_matched_regex>
<same_source_ip />
  <description>5 Failed passwords within 10 minutes</description>
</rule>
```

Working with Real World Examples

Because the OSSEC HIDS comes with more than 600 default rules, you might find that you do not need to create additional rules for your environment. You might, however, find that a certain rule doesn't fit your particular environment, so you must modify or extend the existing rule sets.

The first thing to note is that you should modify only the *local_rules.xml* file and not any of the other rules files. As stated earlier, if you modify these core OSSEC HIDS rules your changes will be lost when you upgrade. Also, please remember to only use OSSEC HIDS rule IDs 100,000 and above because these are reserved for user-defined rules.

Let's look at a few cases on how to use the rules.

Increasing the Severity Level of a Rule

Depending on your environment and alerting requirements you might decided that a particular OSSEC HIDS rule ID should have a higher severity level than the default. In the following example, it has been determined that invalid SSH logins are very important for your security team to monitor. You can change the severity of rule 5710, located within the *sshd_rules.xml* file by copying the rule definition into your *local_rules.xml* file.

Edit *the /var/ossec/rules/sshd_rules.xml* file and copy rule 5710:

```
# vi /var/ossec/rules/sshd_rules.xml
```

```
<rule id="5710" level="5">
  <if_sid>5700</if_sid>
  <match>illegal user|invalid user</match>
  <description>Attempt to login using a non-existent user</description>
  <group>invalid_login,</group>
</rule>
```

Paste rule 5710 to your *local_rules.xml* file and change the *level* tag from **5** to **10**. Also, add the *overwrite="yes"* option to the rule. Using the *overwrite* option instructs the OSSEC HIDS rule engine to use the local rule definition instead of the one found in the */var/ossec/rules/* directory.

```
# vi /var/ossec/rules/local_rules.xml
<rule id="5710" level="10" overwrite="yes">
  <if_sid>5700</if_sid>
  <match>illegal user|invalid user</match>
  <description>Attempt to login using a non-existent user</description>
  <group>invalid_login,</group>
  </rule>
```

Tuning Rule Frequency

Sometimes the frequency of the standard OSSEC HIDS rules is too small or large for your environment. To change the frequency of a rule, you can copy the standard rule to your *local_rules.xml* file and use the same *overwrite* attribute. In this example, we will increase the frequency of the rule that looks for *sshd* brute force attempts (5712) from **6** events to **15** events.

Edit *the /var/ossec/rules/sshd_rules.xml* file and copy rule 5712:

```
# vi /var/ossec/rules/sshd_rules.xml
<rule id="5712" level="10" frequency="6" timeframe="120" ignore="60">
  <if_matched_sid>5710</if_matched_sid>
    <description>SSHD brute force trying to get access to </description>
    <description>the system.</description>
    <group>authentication_failures,</group>
  </rule>
```

Paste rule 5712 to your *local_rules.xml* file and change the *frequency* tag from **6** to **15**. Also, add the *overwrite="yes"* option to the rule.

```
# vi /var/ossec/rules/local_rules.xml
  <rule id="5712" level="10" frequency="15" timeframe="120" ignore="60"
overwrite="yes">
    <if_matched_sid>5710</if_matched_sid>
    <description>SSHD brute force trying to get access to </description>
    <description>the system.</description>
    <group>authentication_failures,</group>
  </rule>
```

Ignoring Rules

Sometimes a rule might be too noisy for your environment and might generate more alerts than required. You can ignore the rule completely or tune the existing rule to alert only if a particular patter is found within the event. For example, an OSSEC HIDS user recently sent the following alert to the OSSEC HIDS mailing list asking for help on how to tune it out:

```
OSSEC HIDS Notification.
2007 Nov 08 12:00:46
```

```
Received From: neo->/var/log/messages
Rule: 1002 fired (level 7) -> "Unknown problem somewhere in the system."
Portion of the log(s):

Nov 8 12:00:45 neo ntop[11016]: **WARNING** RRD:
rrd_update(/usr/local/var/ntop/rrd/interfaces/eth0/matrix/196.35.43.xxx/196.35.xx.
xxx/pkts.rrd) error: illegal attempt to update using time 1194516045 when last
update time is 1194516045 (minimum one second step)
```

The first action is to identify how you want to adjust the rule. One solution is to disable the rule completely by using the *<if_sid></if_sid>* tag and changing the severity to **0** (ignored). Whenever rule 1002 matches an event, rule 100301 will force the event to be ignored:

```
<rule id="100301" level="0">
  <if_sid>1002</if_sid>
  <description>Ignoring rule 1002.</description>
</rule>
```

However, completely disabling a rule is not always the best option. Using the previous example, it might be better to just ignore this specific *ntop* error that is causing the log. This ensures that other events continue to match against rule 1002. Using the *<program_name> </program_name>* tag we can specify the application that is generating the event. Also, the *<match></match>* tag can be used to identify the common **illegal attempt to update** message within this log:

```
<rule id="100302" level="0">
  <if_sid>1002</if_sid>
  <program_name>ntop</program_name>
  <match>illegal attempt to update</match>
  <description>Ignoring rule 1002.</description>
</rule>
```

Ignoring IP Addresses

A common problem with security scanners is that they tend to generate an exceptional amount of alerts within the OSSEC HIDS. If you want to ignore a specific IP address completely, such as an internal vulnerability scanner, you can create a new rule to change the severity level to **0** for events with the source IP addresses specified using the *<srcip></srcip>* tags. You can also use the *<if_level></if_level>* tag, which tests all the alerts above the specified severity. In the following example, every alert with *level* if **4** or above, and a source IP address of 192.168.2.1 or 192.168.2.2, will be ignored.

```
<rule id="100303" level="0">
  <if_level>4</if_level>
  <srcip>192.168.2.1</srcip>
```

```
  <srcip>192.168.2.2</srcip>
  <description>Ignoring rule any level above 4 from ip X.</description>
</rule>
```

Correlating Multiple Snort Alerts

The OSSEC HIDS is widely used to monitor Snort IDS alerts. You can correlate multiple Snort events using an atomic and a composite rule. Let's say you want to see a higher severity alert if the Snort IDs 1:1002, 1:1003, and 1:1004 are seen from the same source IP address. The first thing you need to do is to create a local rule looking for them. Using the *<if_sid> </if_sid>* tag you can specify that you want to use the OSSEC HIDS rule that parses IDS events. You can specify that the events must be decoded as Snort events by using the *<decoded_as></decoded_as>* tag. To look for specific Snort IDs you can use the *<id></id>* tag and the pipe (|) character to logically *OR* our IDs.

```
<rule id="100415" level="6">
  <if_sid>20101</if_sid>
  <decoded_as>snort</decoded_as>
  <id>1:1002|1:1003|1:1004</id>
  <description>Watched snort ids</description>
</rule>
```

With your atomic rule created, you must create a composite rule looking for **5** of these events within **180** seconds. Using the *frequency* option you can specify that **5** events are required to create an alert from this rule. The *timeframe* option allows you to specify the **180** second time window to search within. The *<if_matched_sid></if_matched_sid>* tag uses your previously created atomic rule and the *<same_source_ip />* tag specifies that you want to create the alert only if the events are seen from the same source IP address.

```
<rule id="100416" frequency="5" level="10" timeframe="180">
  <if_matched_sid>100415</if_matched_sid>
  <same_source_ip />
  <description>Multiple snort alerts with the watched ids</description>
</rule>
```

Ignoring Identity Change Events

Sometimes the amount of file changes from the *syscheck* daemon might be more than you require in your environment or perhaps you want to create some additional alerts from them by ignoring or correlating some events. Because the default syscheck alerts are under the *syscheck* group, our basic rule always contains the following:

```
<rule id="100501" level="7">
  <if_group>syscheck</if_group>
</rule>
```

As you can see from the following alert, the filename that changed is always contained in single quotes:

```
** Alert 1199273862.1538: mail - ossec,syscheck,
2008 Jan 02 07:37:42 copacabana->syscheck
Rule: 550 (level 7) -> 'Integrity checksum changed.'
Src IP: (none)
User: (none)
Integrity checksum changed for: '/usr/bin/groups'
Size changed from '1931' to '1934'
Old md5sum was: 'b37f687b322e9fe7b0ee50408dde8770'
New md5sum is : 'd8b83bcbdf9f4f0474f6ad04fb0683da'
Old sha1sum was: 'caff65849b5547e5bc2bb665b97a7c5e12e16e9f'
New sha1sum is : 'b7683926118cf253a51fc29a33e61987a3a85fd9'
```

If you want to create a rule to ignore any change on the groups binary, you have to create a new rule with the *level* option set to **0** to ignore the event. Using the *<match></match>* tag you can exclude the */usr/bin/groups* file by specifying the **for: '/usr/bin/groups'** match string from the event.

```
<rule id="100501" level="0">
  <if_group>syscheck</if_group>
  <match>for: '/usr/bin/groups'</match>
  <description>Ignoring /bin/groups change.</description>
</rule>
```

NOTE

You do not have to escape (\) the single quote characters (') within the *<match></match>* tag.

If you want to ignore any change on the **C:\temp** directory of a Windows system, you could change your *<match></match>* tag to look for the **for: 'C:\temp** match string from the event.

```
<rule id="100501" level="0">
  <if_group>syscheck</if_group>
  <match>for: 'C:\temp</match>
  <description>Ignoring C:temp changes.</description>
</rule>
```

You can also go further and alert with a higher severity on any Windows executable file changes from your Windows systems by using the *<hostname></hostname>* tag and matching on them using the *<regex></regex>* tag to look for a string followed by the **.exe** file extension.

```
<rule id="100501" level="10">
  <if_group>syscheck</if_group>
  <regex>for: '\S+.exe'</regex>
  <hostname>winxp1|win20031</hostname>
  <description>Alerting on .exe changes from winxp1 and win20031.</description>
</rule>
```

TIP

Remember, you can logically *OR* multiple values within the rule tags using the pipe (|) character.

Writing Decoders/Rules for Custom Applications

The OSSEC HIDS comes with hundreds of default decoders and rules. Often, however, you will have custom applications and custom events to parse that do not have prebuilt rules and decoders. To solve that problem you must write the rules and decoders yourself.

Deciding What Information to Extract

The first thing that we need to do is to collect sample logs from your application. Remember, the more log samples you have, the more accurate your decoders and rules will be.

TIP

Some product vendors provide listings of all the possible events that their application can generate. It is strongly suggested that you consult your vendor documentation as part of your research phase.

In our example we have an application that is able to generate the following four events:

```
2007/28/Dec 17:45:10 Fakeinc: Failed password for user test, IP: 1.2.3.4 .
2007/28/Dec 17:45:21 Fakeinc: Accepted password for user test2, IP: 1.2.3.3 .
```

```
2007/28/Dec 17:45:35 Fakeinc: Application is shutting down: Internal error.
2007/28/Dec 17:45:47 Fakeinc: DEBUG: Received OK.
```

We need to categorize them, select the information we want to extract, and determine their severity before we start with the rules and decoders. Table 4.14 shows the information you might want to extract for each of the preceding log messages.

With the events categorized, we can start creating the decoders.

Table 4.14 Information to Extract

Log Message	Information to Extract
2007/28/Dec 17:45:10 Fakeinc: Failed password for user test, IP: 1.2.3.4.	Extract source IP (*srcip*) and user (*user*) information. Define as an *Authentication Failure (level 7) event.* Alert on multiple failed passwords *(level 10).*
2007/28/Dec 17:45:21 Fakeinc: Accepted password for user test2, IP: 1.2.3.3.	Extract source IP (*srcip*) and user (*user*) information. Define as an *Authentication Success (level 3)* event.
2007/28/Dec 17:45:35 Fakeinc: Application is shutting down: Internal error.	Nothing to extract. Define as an *Internal Error -> Alert ASAP (level 10).*
2007/28/Dec 17:45:47 Fakeinc: DEBUG: Received OK.	Nothing to extract. Define as a *Debug Message (level 0).*

Creating the Decoders

Because the messages are well formatted, and we only need the source IP address and username from two of the messages, a single decoder can work for us.

We will start by creating a new decoder in the *decoder.xml* file called *fakeinc_custom*. We will also define a *<prematch></prematch>* tag looking for the date, time, and *fakeinc* tag in the log:

```
<decoder name="fakeinc_custom">
  <prematch>^\S+ \d\d:\d\d:\d\d Fakeinc: </prematch>
</decoder>
```

Once the *prematch* is established, we must create the regular expression to extract the IP address and user name. We also need to set the *offset* so that the part of the message that was already checked during the *prematch* is not read again by using the *after_prematch* option:

```
<regex offset="after_prematch">^\w+ password for user (\w+), IP: (\S+) </regex>
```

We also need to specify the order to tell the OSSEC HIDS what each field is that we are parsing out of the message. In this case the order is a username and a source IP address.

```
<order>user, srcip</order>
```

Our completed decoder is:

```
<!-- Final decoder for fakeinc custom application -->
<decoder name="fakeinc_custom">
  <prematch>^\S+ \d\d:\d\d:\d\d Fakeinc: </prematch>
  <regex offset="after_prematch">^\w+ password for user (\w+), IP:
(\S+) </regex>
  <order>user, srcip</order>
</decoder>
```

Now that we have our decoders created in the *decoder.xml* file we can proceed to the creation of the rules.

Creating the Rules

The first rule we must create is a parent rule that looks for every event that was decoded by the *fakeinc_custom* decoder. This saves a lot of processing power compared to having a custom rule for each event.

Using the *<rule></rule>* tag we can create a new rule in the user defined rule ID range.

```
<rule id="100102" level="0">
</rule>
```

Using the *<decoded_as></decoded_as>* tag we can specify the decoder name that we're looking for.

```
<decoded_as>fakeinc_custom</decoded_as>
```

We can also use the *<description></description>* tag to add a meaningful description to the rule.

```
<description>Parent rule for FakeInc custom</description>
```

Our completed rule is:

```
<rule id="100102" level="0">
  <decoded_as>fakeinc_custom</decoded_as>
  <description>Parent rule for FakeInc custom</description>
</rule>
```

Our next rules will all be dependent on the parent rule, *100102*, meaning that they will be called only if it matches. Using the *<if_sid></if_sid>* tag we can specify that this rule is a subrule of the parent rule specified.

We can use the following template for all subrules to ensure we reference the parent rule properly:

```
<rule id="10010x" level="y">
  <if_sid>100102</if_sid>
  <match>XX</match>
  <description>Fakeinc Custom: XX</description>
</rule>
```

Each subrule that we create must have a distinct rule ID. It is generally a good idea to use sequential subrule ID numbers to make it easier for someone else to understand your rule structure. We will create our first rule to look for failed login attempts by using the *<match></match>* tag. Within the tag we will look for the string **Failed**.

```
<rule id="100103" level="7">
  <if_sid>100102</if_sid>
  <match>^Failed</match>
  <description>Fakeinc Custom: Failed password</description>
</rule>
```

We will create our second rule to look for successful login attempts by using the *<match></match>* tag. Within the tag we will look for the string **Accepted**.

```
<rule id="100104" level="3">
  <if_sid>100102</if_sid>
  <match>^Accepted</match>
  <description>Fakeinc Custom: Accepted password</description>
</rule>
```

We will create our third rule to look for internal errors by using the *<match></match>* tag. Within the tag we will look for the string **Internal error**.

```
<rule id="100105" level="10">
  <if_sid>100102</if_sid>
  <match>Internal error</match>
  <description>Fakeinc Custom: Internal error</description>
</rule>
```

We do not need a rule for the *DEBUG* message, because we simply want to ignore it because it represents little value to us from a security or operations perspective. To finish, our last rule will be a composite one looking for multiple failed passwords:

```
<rule id="100106" level="10">
  <if_matched_sid>100103</if_matched_sid>
  <same_source_ip />
  <description>Fakeinc Custom: Multiple Failed passwords</description>
</rule>
```

Notice how we use *<if_matched_sid></if_matched_sid>* instead of *<if_sid>*</if_sid>. This is because this is a composite rule. A composite rule is a rule that looks for multiple events that match another existing rule. In the previous example we are looking for multiple events that match the 100103 rule ID. If you recall this rule was created to catch failed login attempts. We also need to make use of the *<same_source_ip />* tag to make sure that this rule will be triggered only if the events matched in rule ID 100103 are from the same source IP address.

Our completed rule is shown here:

```
<rule id="100102" level="0">
  <decoded_as>fakeinc_custom</decoded_as>
  <description>Parent rule for FakeInc custom</description>
</rule>

<rule id="100103" level="7">
  <if_sid>100102</if_sid>
  <match>^Failed</match>
  <description>Fakeinc Custom: Failed password</description>
</rule>

<rule id="100104" level="3">
  <if_sid>100102</if_sid>
  <match>^Accepted</match>
  <description>Fakeinc Custom: Accepted password</description>
</rule>

<rule id="100105" level="10">
  <if_sid>100102</if_sid>
  <match>Internal error</match>
  <description>Fakeinc Custom: Internal error</description>
</rule>

<rule id="100106" level="10">
  <if_matched_sid>100103</if_matched_sid>
  <same_source_ip />
  <description>Fakeinc Custom: Multiple Failed passwords</description>
</rule>
```

Monitoring the Log File

Now that we have our decoders and rules created we need to ensure that the application server, where the OSSESC HIDS agent is installed, is configured to monitor the applications log file. For example, if the log file is located in */var/log/fakeinc.log*, the following must be added to the agents *ossec.conf*:

```
<localfile>
  <location>/var/log/fakeinc.log</location>
  <log_format>syslog</log_format>
</localfile>
```

NOTE

Always restart the OSSEC HIDS after changing the *ossec.conf* configuration.

Summary

OSSEC HIDS rules are located within the *rules* directory of your OSSEC HIDS installation as an individual XML file. Each XML file is named similar to the type of event for which it checks. For example, all rules for the Cisco PIX firewall are located within the *pix_rules.xml* file. The OSSEC HIDS installation provides you with 43 rules for various applications and devices. Every rule has a unique ID that is assigned when it is first created. Each log type has a specific range of IDs assigned to ensure that OSSEC HIDS released decoders are not overwritten by mistake. The OSSEC HIDS team provides you with a dedicated range of IDs (100,000 to 119,999) to be used for user-created rules. During the upgrade process, the scripts overwrite all rules files, except the *local_rules.xml* file. If you need to tweak or tune a specific rule that is shipped with the OSSEC HIDS, the *local_rules.xml* can be used to override how the standard rule functions.

The OSSEC HIDS tries to decode and extract any relevant information from received events. The event is decoded in two parts, called predecoding and decoding. The process of predecoding is meant to extract only static information from well-known fields of an event. Information such as time, dates, hostnames, program names, and the log message is extracted during predecoding. The goal of decoding is to extract nonstatic information from the events that we can use in our rules later in the process. IP address information, usernames, URLs, and port information are some of the common fields that can be decoded from the event. All decoders are user configured in the decoder.xml file in the etc directory of your OSSEC HIDS installation.

After *predecoded* and *decoded* information is extracted, the rule-matching engine is called to verify if an alert should be created. The OSSEC HIDS evaluates the rules to see if the received event should be escalated to an alert or if it should be a part of a composite alert (with multiple events). There are two types of OSSEC HIDS rules; Atomic and Composite. Atomic rules are based on single events, without any correlation. For example, if you see an authentication failure, you can alert on that unique event. Composite rules are based on multiple events.

Because the OSSEC HIDS comes with more than 600 default rules, you might find that you do not need to create additional rules for your environment. You might, however, find that a certain rule doesn't fit your particular environment, so you must modify or extend the existing rule sets. You should modify the *local_rules.xml* file only to adjust how the default rules operate, because changes to the OSSEC HIDS supplied rules will be overwritten on upgrades. It is quite easy to increase the severity, change the frequency, and so on of existing rules by creating your own rules in the *local_rules.xml* file. You can also ignore specific IP addresses, rules, users, hosts, and such by tuning the rules for your environment.

The OSSEC HIDS comes with hundreds of default decoders and rules, but they might not be able to process the logs from your custom application or device. To create custom decoders and rules for your application you must first research the types of logs that your application or device can create. Often, product vendors provide listings of all the possible events that their application can generate. It is strongly suggested that you consult your vendor documentation as part of your research phase.

Solutions Fast Track

Introducing Rules

☑ Every rule is stored, in XML format, within the *rules* directory of your OSSEC HIDS installation.

☑ Rules contain decoders designed to extract data from the raw events, which allows the OSSEC HIDS to correlate disparate events from multiple sources.

☑ Every local rule should go in the *local_rules.xml* file located within the *rules* directory of your OSSEC HIDS installation.

Understanding the OSSEC HIDS Analysis Process

☑ As soon as an event is received, the OSSEC HIDS will try to decode and extract any relevant information from it.

☑ Decoding of the event is performed in two parts, called predecoding and decoding.

☑ After predecoded and decoded information is extracted, the rule-matching engine is called to verify if an alert should be created.

Predecoding Events

☑ The process of predecoding is meant to extract only static information from well-known fields of an event.

☑ Log messages that follow widely used protocols, like Syslog or the Apple System Log (ASL) formats, are processed during the predecoding phase.

☑ The information extracted during this phase is *time*, *dates*, *hostnames*, *program names*, and the *log message*.

Decoding Events

☑ The goal of decoding is to extract nonstatic information from the events that we can use in our rules later in the process.

- ☑ IP address information, usernames, URLs, and port information are some of the common fields that can be *decoded* from the event.
- ☑ All decoders are user configured in the *decoder.xml* file in the *etc* directory of your OSSEC HIDS installation.

Understanding Rules

- ☑ There are two types of OSSEC HIDS rules: Atomic, which are based on single events without any correlation; and Composite, which are based on multiple events.
- ☑ Each rule, or grouping of rules, must be defined within a <group></group> element.
- ☑ Composite rules provide you with tags to specify that certain parts of the received event must be the same.

Working with Real World Examples

- ☑ Certain rules might not fit your environment so you can modify or extend the existing rule sets to better suit your needs.
- ☑ You should modify the *local_rules.xml* file only to adjust how the default rules operate because changes to the OSSEC HIDS supplied rules will be overwritten on upgrades.
- ☑ Any user rule created to replace a preexisting OSSEC HIDS rule must contain the *overwrite="yes"* option within the rule.

Writing Decoders/Rules for Custom Applications

- ☑ The OSSEC HIDS comes with hundreds of default decoders and rules, but they might not be able to process the logs from your custom application or device.
- ☑ In order to create custom decoders and rules for your application you must first research the types of logs that your application or device can create.
- ☑ Some product vendors provide listings of all the possible events that their application can generate. It is strongly suggested that you consult your vendor documentation as part of your research phase.

Frequently Asked Questions

Q: Where are my rules stored?

A: All the rules are stored in the *rules* directory where you installed the OSSEC HIDS. This typically is located at */var/ossec/rules/*. Each rule is defined in a separate XML file and is named accordingly.

Q: Where should I put the rules that I create?

A: Any user-created rule should go into the *local_rules.xml* file within the *rules* directory of your OSSEC HIDS installation. This ensures that the standard package of rules functions as they are intended.

Q: When I upgrade my OSSEC HIDS will my local rules be overwritten?

A: During the upgrade process, the scripts overwrite all rules files, except the *local_rules.xml* file. If you need to tweak or tune a specific rule that is shipped with the OSSEC HIDS, the *local_rules.xml* can be used to override how the standard rule functions.

Q: How does an event flow through the OSSEC HIDS?

A: An event, received by the OSSEC HIDS, is subject to several processes. The first is the predecoding process, which extracts static information from the event. This is followed by the decoding process, which extracts nonstatic information from the event. The decoded event is then matched against the OSSEC HIDS rules and, if the rule determines an alert should be generated, an alert in the form of an e-mail message, active response, or log is created.

Q: What are the decoded fields that I can match against?

A: Fields such as *location*, *hostname*, *program_name*, *srcip*, *dstip*, *srcport*, *dstport*, *protocol*, for example, can all be decoded from the event.

Q: What information can I extract in the predecoding phase?

A: The information extracted during this phase is *time*, *dates*, *hostnames*, *program names*, and the *log message*.

Q: Can I decode usernames as well?

A: You can, but not during the predecoding phase. The decoding of user names is performed during the decoding phase.

Q: How can the OSSEC HIDS take logs from different log types and predecode them the same way?

A: Within the OSSEC HIDS every event is normalized in a way that the same rule can be written to match multiple message formats.

Q: What is a nonstatic field?

A: A nonstatic field is a field that is common across most logs but is not necessarily located in the same place in the event. For example, a successful authentication event from a Linux server would not have the *user* field in the same place in the message that a Nortel VPN Gateway device would.

Q: Where do I configure my decoders?

A: All decoders are user-configured in the *decoder.xml* file in the *etc* directory of your OSSEC HIDS installation. This typically is located in */var/ossec/etc/decoder.xml.*

Q: What tag do I use to identify a decoder in the *decoder.xml* file?

A: Each decoder is delimited by a *<decoder></decoder>* tag, where the name of the decoder is specified.

Q: What is the difference between Atomic and Composite rules?

A: There are two types of OSSEC HIDS rules: Atomic, which are based on single events without any correlation; and Composite, which are based on multiple events.

Q: What rule IDs should I use for my rules?

A: User-defined rules should range from 100,000 to 119,999. If you choose any other ID, it might collide with the official ones from the OSSEC HIDS project.

Q: How many rules can I use within a group?

A: There is no limit to the number of rules that you can include within a group. Keep in mind, however, that the purpose of the group is to combine *like* rules to make processing of events more efficient.

Q: How can I increase the severity of a preexisting OSSEC HIDS rule?

A: The recommended way to increase the severity of a preexisting OSSEC HIDS rule is to create an identical rule in your *local_rules.xml* file and change the *level* value to the required severity level.

Q: I have a couple of really noisy servers that I don't want the OSSEC HIDS to create alerts for. How can I hide these systems from my OSSEC HIDS?

A: You can ignore servers in your environment by creating a rule in your *local_rules.xml* file with a *level* of **0**. This tells the OSSEC HIDS to ignore any event that matches the contents of the rule. Within the rule you can use the *<srcip></srcip>* tag to list the source IP addresses to ignore.

Q: I don't control my organization's Snort IDS sensor so I cannot tune out individual Snort IDs. Can the OSSEC HIDS ignore specific Snort IDs if I don't want them to create alerts?

A: You can create a rule in your *local_rules.xml* file to ignore Snort IDs using the *<if_sid></if_sid>* tag to select the rule that parses Snort IDS events, the *<decoded_as></decoded_as>* tag to check logs decoded as Snort events, and the *<id></id>* tag to specify as many Snort IDs as you would like to ignore.

Q: Why doesn't the OSSEC HIDS have decoders or rulesfor "Application [XYZ]"?

A: The OSSEC HIDS comes with hundreds of default decoders and rules but they might not be able to process the logs from your custom application or device. Because the OSSEC HIDS team cannot possibly create rules for every device or application we do provide you with the ability to create your own decoders and rules so that you can process the events.

Q: How do I know what information to extract from my application or device logs?

A: This information is entirely up to the capabilities of your application or device and your needs. The logs that your application or device can generate will dictate what kind of information you can bring into the OSSEC HIDS. Once you know the format and possible event types you can decide how much, or how little, information from the events you need.

Q: I have my decoders and rules created for my applications log but I'm not seeing any events from my OSSEC HIDS agent. What have I missed?

A: You must ensure that you have configured your OSSEC HIDS agent to monitor the log file for which you have created the decoders and rules. Also remember to restart your OSSEC HIDS after making changes to the *ossec.conf* file on the agent.

Chapter 5

System Integrity Check and Rootkit Detection

Solutions in this chapter:

- Understanding System Integrity Check
- Tuning syscheck
- Detecting Rootkits and Enforcing/Monitoring Policies

☑ Summary

☑ Solutions Fast Track

☑ Frequently Asked Questions

Introduction

Throughout the morning, Marty supervised Antoine's team and answered any questions they had about their newly created rules. By the time lunch arrived, Antoine was confident that he and his team had a firm understanding of how to create decoders and rules. As the team ate lunch, Marty noticed that they were all discussing how easy it was to create the rules, how it was going to save them time, and how they wish they had a tool like this before. Marty smiled and thought how perfect this was. Marty knew that there was no sense bringing a tool into the organization if the team that needed to use it did not find it useful. "So what do you think?" Marty asked Antoine. "Well Marty," Antoine responded. "It looks like you've found a great application to handle the messages from the various systems. Good work." Marty blushed. "All in a day's work, my friend." Marty winked. "Wait until you see the integrity and rootkit detection capabilities."

When all finished their lunch, checked their emails, and refilled their coffee cups, they returned to their seats ready to learn about the integrity checking and rootkit detection capabilities of the OSSEC HIDS. Marty revisited the recent breach that was the catalyst for bringing the OSSEC HIDS to everyone's attention. He made sure not to lay blame on any individual or team, but rather on the lack of protection and foresight that resulted in the embarrassing breach. "I think we can all agree that hindsight is 20/20 and foresight is a little cloudier," Marty said jokingly. "The OSSEC HIDS has the capability to record a cryptographic checksum of any file we specify on a deployed system. This allows us to keep tabs on exactly which files are installed on any of our systems." Marty took a gulp of coffee. "Also, the OSSEC HIDS records the changes in checksums over time. So, if a remote user somehow skirts around applying the latest update we can compare his file checksum to the checksum of the update." Alex, one of Antoine's team members, raised his hand. Marty pointed at Alex, indicating that he could ask the question.

"What about files that change all the time as a result of regular system operations?" asked Alex. "Is there any way to exclude certain files from being checked for changes?" Marty nodded. "You can explicitly include or exclude any file from being checked. Could you imagine if we created alerts every time some file in /proc changed on one of our servers?" The team laughed because they knew that files in /proc were dynamically generated at boot time and frequently updated when accessing information from the system's kernel. "I think we'd be chasing down alerts until the end of time if anything in that directory was being monitored for changes," laughed Alex. "Hey Antoine, we're going to need about 50 more people on the team if this is a requirement," joked Lucas, another member of Antoine's team.

"How about the rootkit detection capabilities?" asked Lucas. "Well," said Marty. "You get what you pay for, and for the cost of *free* you get a heck of a lot." Everyone smiled. "It does application-level rootkit detection using signature definitions," continued Marty. "And kernel-level rootkit detection using system call comparisons." Marty could tell by looking around the room that they were all anxious to get their feet wet. "Well, enough talking," said Marty. "Let's get our hands dirty. The best way to understand something is to tinker with it."

NOTE

This chapter is not an exhaustive chapter on what a rootkit, Trojan, or backdoor *is*, but rather how the OSSEC HIDS handles such malware.

Understanding System Integrity Check (syscheck)

File integrity checking is an essential part of all HIDS technologies and is typically performed by comparing the cryptographic checksum of a known *good* file against the checksum of the file after it has been modified. The OSSEC HIDS looks for changes in the MD5/SHA1 checksums of designated files on the system and registry keys within the Windows registry. The OSSEC HIDS agent scans the system every few hours, or at an interval you specify, and it sends the checksums of the monitored files and registry keys to the OSSEC HIDS server. The server stores the checksums and looks for modifications by comparing the newly received checksums against the historical checksum values of that file or registry key. An alert is sent if anything changes.

Notes from the Underground…

Using OSSEC HIDS with Hardened Systems

The OSSEC HIDS provides a great deal of power and flexibility for gleaning information about the security status of your network. This is especially true of the OSSEC HIDS server installations where many of the alerts and logs are stored. This information would be invaluable to any attacker seeking to know as much as possible about your network and the potential weak points. Installation of a rootkit or Trojan on the OSSEC HIDS server system could be a deadly blow to your network defense.

The OSSEC HIDS is able to play a role in defending the system on which it is hosted. However, as with virtually any intrusion detection software, it can only notify you during or after the attack has already happened. It is vital that an OSSEC HIDS server be one of the best-defended systems in the network. The operating system must help defend the OSSEC HIDS installation so the OSSEC HIDS can in turn help defend the network.

Continued

The specific techniques for hardening vary from one operating system to another. The primary concept to remember is that anything that opens access to the system is potentially an exploitable entry point into your system. Additionally, an attacker gaining access to other systems on the network might appear to be using a trusted system and therefore more easily gain access to the OSSEC HIDS. For the OSSEC HIDS to be effective in defending systems on the network, it must be as well defended against "friendly" systems as it is against the rest of the world.

Some guidelines to remember for OSSEC HIDS server operating system hardening:

- The system must be dedicated to the OSSEC HIDS server and provide no other services to the network.
- Unnecessary software must never be installed on the server.
- All non-OSSEC HIDS ports must be blocked.
- If SSH access is required to the system, it must be restricted to other secure hosts.
- If used, the WUI must only be accessible from other secured hosts.
- The OSSEC HIDS server system must not be part of the main network authentication domain.
- All documented techniques for hardening the chosen operating system must be followed before installing the OSSEC HIDS.

These suggestions are all intended as preventative measures to reduce the risk of unauthorized access. They also make rootkit and Trojan installation extremely difficult even during a major incursion into your network.

There are many resources available for system hardening. Thankfully, the OSSEC HIDS server does not run on Windows platforms so system hardening is not complicated. Here are some starting points for Linux system hardening:

www.securityfocus.com/infocus/1539
www.ibm.com/developerworks/linux/library/l-seclnx1.html
http://bastille-linux.sourceforge.net/

File integrity checking also ensures that malicious applications do not replace critical system files with modified copies. Malicious applications, when installed, typically leave some remnant or digital fingerprint on the system because of the installation process. These fingerprints are the cornerstones of the entire computer forensic analysis industry. Malicious applications, commonly referred to with the blanket designation of *malware*, attempt to circumvent the normal operation of your operating system. Rootkits are prime examples of malware that behave in this fashion. User-mode rootkits are often designed to copy modified system executables, which include backdoor and other malicious capabilities, to a target system. If installed successfully, the digital fingerprint of the modified files will change.

NOTE

If the application you use to verify cryptographic checksums, such as the *md5sum* utility, is overwritten with a malicious copy, it becomes a trivial task to hide changes in checksums. Remember, if you have the TV remote, you control what the people get to watch.

To configure the integrity-checking component of the OSSEC HIDS, named *syscheck*, you must first decide what you want to monitor. By default, the OSSEC HIDS checks the */etc*, */usr/bin*, */usr /sbin*, */bin*, and */sbin* directories on Unix, Linux, and BSD systems, and the *C:\Windows\System32* directory on Windows. All syscheck configuration parameters are found within the *<syscheck></syscheck>* tag of the ossec.conf file. The *<directories></directories>* tag allows us to specify the directories on the local file system to monitor. The default syscheck directory-monitoring configuration for Linux, Unix, and BSD systems is:

```
<syscheck>
   <directories check_all="yes">/etc,/usr/bin,/usr/sbin</directories>
   <directories check_all="yes">/bin,/sbin</directories>
</syscheck>
```

The default syscheck directory-monitoring configuration for Windows systems is:

```
<syscheck>
   <directories check_all="yes">%WINDIR%/system32</directories>
</syscheck>
```

NOTE

All queries are recursive, so only the directory must be specified. You do not need to specify all the files within the directory to monitor the directory contents.

The *<directories></directories>* tag allows you to include some additional check parameters to specify which syscheck attributes you want to monitor. Table 5.1 shows the additional *<directories></directories>* tag parameters.

Table 5.1 Additional Check Parameters

Check Parameter	Description
check_all	Perform all available integrity checks.
check_sum	Use MD5/SHA1 to check the integrity of files.
check_size	Check files for changes in size.
check_owner	Check files for ownership changes.
check_group	Check files for group ownership changes.
check_perm	Check files for permission changes.

To monitor the Windows registry keys, you can use the *<windows_registry></windows_registry>* tag. For example, to monitor the *HKEY_LOCAL_MACHINE\Software\Policies* software policy registry key, you configure your *<windows_registry></windows_registry>* tag as follows:

```
<syscheck>
<windows_registry>HKEY_LOCAL_MACHINE\Software\Policies</windows_registry>
</syscheck>
```

NOTE

On Windows systems, we can use system variables, including WINDIR, SYSDIR, and so on, to indicate directories.

After you specify which directories you want to monitor, you have the option to exclude files, directories, or registry keys from being checked for changes. Using the *<ignore></ignore>* tag, you can indicate which files and directories you want to exclude from the syscheck process. Similarly, the *<registry_ignore></registry_ignore>* tag can be used to exclude registry keys from the syscheck process.

For example, to ignore some log file directories on Windows, you could use the *<ignore></ignore>* tag:

```
<syscheck>
    <ignore>%WINDIR%/System32/LogFiles</ignore>
    <ignore>%WINDIR%/system32/wbem/Logs</ignore>
</syscheck>
```

NOTE

Directories containing files that are prone to change, such as log files, should generally be excluded from the syscheck process because they are expected to change as new entries are logged.

To ignore the *random-seed* file and the *messages* file on a Unix system, you could use the *<ignore></ignore>* tag:

```
<syscheck>
    <ignore>/etc/random-seed</ignore>
    <ignore>/var/log/messages</ignore>
</syscheck>
```

To ignore the registry key that stores the URL for your Internet Explorer start page, on a Windows system you could use the *<registry_ignore></registry_ignore>* tag:

```
<syscheck>
    <registry_ignore>HKEY_CURRENT_USER\Software\Microsoft\Internet Explorer\Main
    </registry_ignore>
</syscheck>
```

Another important option is the *<frequency></frequency>*tag, which specifies how often the OSSEC HIDS should scan the system for changes. The frequency is defined in seconds, with a minimum allowed time of one hour or 3600 seconds. The default syscheck configuration for a Linux, Unix, BSD system with the default 6-hour frequency set is:

```
<syscheck>
    <!-- Frequency that syscheck is executed - default to every 6 hours -->
    <frequency>21600</frequency>

    <!-- Directories to check (perform all possible verifications) -->
    <directories check_all="yes">/etc,/usr/bin,/usr/sbin</directories>
    <directories check_all="yes">/bin,/sbin</directories>

    <!-- Files/directories to ignore -->
    <ignore>/etc/mtab</ignore>
    <ignore>/etc/mnttab</ignore>
    <ignore>/etc/hosts.deny</ignore>
    <ignore>/etc/mail/statistics</ignore>
    <ignore>/etc/random-seed</ignore>
    <ignore>/etc/adjtime</ignore>
    <ignore>/etc/httpd/logs</ignore>
```

```
    <ignore>/etc/utmpx</ignore>
    <ignore>/etc/wtmpx</ignore>
</syscheck>
```

The integrity-checking configuration is local to the system on which it is running. If you configure an *<ignore></ignore>* tag on one agent, it is only going to ignore the file or directory on the local system. If configured on the server side, the *<ignore></ignore>* tag is checked against all agents and the server. Conversely, anything you ignore on the server is ignored on all agents.

The main syscheck configuration is very simple and does not allow granular configurations, such as ignoring one file for a group of agents or raising the alert level for a specific directory. You can configure granular options within the OSSEC HIDS rules as discussed in Chapter 4.

NOTE

Every alert from the OSSEC HIDS is the result of a carefully crafted rule. This powerful rule engine allows you to combine the log analysis, integrity checking, rootkit detection, and policy monitoring capabilities of the OSSEC HIDS in easy to use action alerts.

Tuning syscheck

An untuned system is similar to an untuned guitar; it will play music, but sound horrible. The same can be said about an untuned syscheck configuration; it will work, but the generated alerts will be a noisy mess. To get the most out of your OSSEC HIDS syscheck configuration, you must spend the time tuning it to the systems where the OSSEC HIDS will be deployed.

Working with syscheck Rules

If you recall from Chapter 4, the *<if_group></if_group>* tag allows you to create a new rule, or modify an existing rule, to depend on additional groups as part of your alert criteria. All syscheck alerts are located within the **syscheck** group. Any local rules you create to alert on file, directory, or registry key changes require the *<if_group>syscheck</if_group>* definition as follows:

```
<rule id="100501" level="7">
   <if_group>syscheck</if_group>
</rule>
```

The generated syscheck alerts always include the old checksum values and new checksum values for the monitored file. A change to the */usr/bin/groups* file might appear in your OSSEC HIDS logs as:

```
** Alert 1199273862.1538: mail - ossec,syscheck,
2008 Jan 02 07:37:42 copacabana->syscheck
Rule: 550 (level 7) -> 'Integrity checksum changed.'
Src IP: (none)
User: (none)
Integrity checksum changed for:'/usr/bin/groups'
Size changed from '1931' to '1934'
Old md5sum was: 'b37f687b322e9fe7b0ee50408dde8770'
New md5sum is : 'd8b83bcbdf9f4f0474f6ad04fb0683da'
Old sha1sum was: 'caff65849b5547e5bc2bb665b97a7c5e12e16e9f'
New sha1sum is : 'b7683926118cf253a51fc29a33e61987a3a85fd9'
```

NOTE

The modified file or registry key is always shown within single ('...') quotes, so your regular expressions within your rules should always be mindful of these patterns.

Ignoring Specific Directories

Using the previous example, if you want to ignore the */etc/www/logs* directory, you use your basic rule and add a *<match></match>* tag looking for the directory. You could use the entire *Integrity checksum changed for: '/usr/bin/groups'* string within your *<match></match>* tag, but the *Integrity checksum changed* string is a common occurrence within all syscheck events. Instead, you can simply use the *for: '/etc/www/logs* string:

```
<rule id="100611" level="0">
   <if_group>syscheck</if_group>
   <match>for: '/etc/www/logs</match>
   <description>Ignoring /etc/www/logs change.</description>
</rule>
```

Similarly, on a Windows system, if you want to ignore any change to files within the *C:\System32\Logs* directory, you can use match on the *for: 'C:\System32\Logs* string:

```
<rule id="100612" level="0">
   <if_group>syscheck</if_group>
   <match>for: 'C:\System32\Logs</match>
   <description>Ignoring Logs changes.</description>
</rule>
```

To restrict the rule further, you can specify which OSSEC HIDS agent events should be ignored using the *<hostname></hostname>* tag. For example, if you wanted to ignore the *C:\System32\Logs* directory on *agent1*, *agent2*, and *agent3* you can create your match rule as follows:

```
<rule id="100613" level="0">
    <if_group>syscheck</if_group>
    <match>for: 'C:\System32\Logs</match>
    <hostname>agent1|agent2|agent3</hostname>
    <description>Ignoring Logs changes.</description>
</rule>
```

Increasing the Alert Severity for Important Files

Imagine that your company has a few critical files that, if modified, should have an associated high severity alert generated. Let's say that these sensitive files are stored in the *C:\Docs* directory on the *central-2k* and *main-db* agents. These sensitive files are Microsoft Word document files that have the *.doc* file extension.

Using the *level* option in the *<rule></rule>* tag allows you to specify the severity of the alert. The *<if_group></if_group>* tag can make your rule dependant on the *syscheck* group. The *<match></match>* tag can be used to match the *for: 'C:\Docs* string within the syscheck event. The *<regex></regex>* tag can be used to search the syscheck event for any string that contains any Microsoft Word document with a *.doc* file extension. The *<hostname></hostname>* tag can be used to specify the two servers in question: *central-2k* and *main-db*. Finally, you can use the *<description></description>* tag to provide a meaningful description of the generated alert. The completed rule is:

```
<rule id="100614" level="10">
    <if_group>syscheck</if_group>
    <match>for: 'C:\Docs</match>
    <regex>for: '\S+.doc'</regex>
    <hostname>central-2k|main-db</hostname>
    <description>Important docs changed.</description>
</rule>
```

Increasing the Severity for Changes During the Weekend

Another situation that might require a higher severity alert is when sensitive files change outside of regular business hours. The *level* option can be used within the *<rule></rule>* tag to specify the increased severity of the alert. By using the *<if_sid></if_sid>* tag, you can have your new rule depend on the processing already performed in your previous rule (100614). As you have previously seen, the *<weekday></weekday>* tag can be used to indicate which day of the week the rule alerts on. Because you want to look for file changes during the weekend, you can use the **weekend** value to match any access on Saturday or Sunday. The *<description>* *</description>* tag can be used to provide a meaningful description of the new weekend alert. The completed rule is:

```
<rule id="100615" level="12">
   <if_sid>100614</if_sid>
   <weekday>weekend</weekday>
   <description>Important docs changed during the weekend.</description>
</rule>
```

Configuring Custom Syscheck Monitoring

To conclude our syscheck configuration, let's look at a custom configuration for a few systems in our *fakeinc.com* company. First, in our Unix systems we want to monitor the */opt/fakeinc* directory, which contains the data from our custom *fakeinc* accounting software. We also want to generate an alert if any of our Apache HTTP server pages, located in the */var/www/htdocs* directory, are changed. On our Windows systems, which run the client portion of the *fakeinc* accounting software, we want to look at the *C:\fakeinc* directory for changes, but ignore the *C:\fakeinc\temp* directory that contains constantly changing temporary files. We also want the checks to be executed every day so we must change the syscheck frequency to 86400 seconds.

On the Unix server, our syscheck configuration would appear as follows:

```
<syscheck>
   <frequency>86400</frequency>
   <directories check_all="yes">/opt/fakeinc,/var/www/htdocs</directories>
</syscheck>
```

For our Windows systems, we would add the following to the agent syscheck configuration:

```
<syscheck>
   <frequency>86400</frequency>
   <directories check_all="yes">C:\fakeinc</directories>
   <ignore>C:\fakeinc\temp</ignore>
</syscheck>
```

NOTE

Remember to always restart the OSSEC HIDS when finished modifying the *ossec.conf* file.

In addition, we want to generate a high severity alert if any changes are seen for the */opt/fakeinc/conf* and */var/www/htdocs* directories. Adding the following rule to the server creates an alert with a severity of 10 if any files changed within the directories:

```
<rule id="100617" level="10">
   <if_group>syscheck</if_group>
   <match>for: '/var/www/htdocs|for: '/opt/fakeinc/conf</match>
   <description>High severity alerts for syscheck changes.</description>
</rule>
```

Detecting Rootkits and Enforcing/Monitoring Policies

In addition to the log analysis and integrity checking capabilities previously discussed, the OSSEC HIDS *rootcheck* process performs rootkit detection on Linux, Unix, and BSD systems. It also performs policy monitoring/enforcement on Windows, Linux, Unix, and BSD systems. Rootkit detection on Linux, Unix, and BSD systems finds application-level rootkits through signature definitions and kernel-level rootkits using system call comparisons. Anomaly based checks are also performed to ensure that the system is operating as anticipated.

Policy monitoring/enforcement is the process of verifying that all systems conform to a set of pre-defined policies surrounding configuration settings and approved application usage. For example, perhaps your organization does not allow the installation or use of Mozilla Firefox and dictates that only Microsoft Internet Explorer can be used. The moment one of your users installs Mozilla Firefox, he is in violation of the organization's acceptable use policy.

Both the policy monitoring and rootkit detection capabilities are configured on the OSSEC HIDS server and pushed down to all OSSEC HIDS agents. The *<rootcheck></rootcheck>* tag is used to define all rootcheck configurations. Table 5.2 shows all available configuration options.

Table 5.2 Rootcheck Configuration Options

Configuration Option	Description
Frequency	Indicates how often the check runs, in seconds. The default is 36000.
Disabled	Enables or disables rootcheck. If not specified, the default value is *no*. To disable the rootcheck, use the *yes* option.
rootkit_files	Contains the Unix-based application level rootkit signatures. The default location is */var/ossec/etc/shared/rootkit_files.txt*.

Continued

Table 5.2 Continued. Rootcheck Configuration Options

Configuration Option	Description
rootkit_trojans	Contains the Unix-based application level Trojan signatures. The default location is */var/ossec/etc/shared/rootkit_trojans.txt*.
system_audit	Contains the audit (policy monitoring) settings for Linux, Unix, and BSD systems. The default location is */var/ossec/etc/shared/system_audit_rcl.txt*.
windows_audit	Contains the audit (policy monitoring) settings for Windows systems. The default location is *C:\Program Files\ossec-agent\shared\win_audit_rcl.txt*.
windows_apps	Contains the application enforcement settings for Windows systems. The default location is *C:\Program Files\ossec-agent\shared\win_applications_rcl.txt*.
windows_malware	Contains a list of malware applications that should not be installed (including spyware, adware, or anything against the acceptable use policy of the organization). The default location is *C:\Program Files\ossec-agent\shared\win_audit_rcl.txt*.

Most of these values, with the exception of the *frequency* option, should not be changed unless you want to modify configuration file locations or user-defined option files. For example, to change the frequency of the rootcheck scans from the default 10 hours (36000 seconds), the *<frequency></frequency>* tag can be modified as follows:

```
<rootcheck>
    <frequency>86400</frequency>
<rootkit_files>/var/ossec/etc/shared/rootkit_files.txt</rootkit_files>
<rootkit_trojans>/var/ossec/etc/shared/rootkit_trojans.txt</rootkit_trojans>
</rootcheck>
```

Detecting Rootkits on Linux, Unix, and BSD

Rootkit detection using the OSSEC HIDS is a two-step process. First, the application-level detection is performed using two files: *rootkit_files.txt* and *rootkit_trojans.txt*. These files are stored in the */var/ossec/etc/shared/* directory on the OSSEC HIDS server. Any changes made to these files are observed by all OSSEC HIDS agents.

The second step of the process introduces the kernel-level checks. The kernel-level checks do not use any signatures and instead rely on anomaly detection technology to look for rootkits. The following tests are performed to detect kernel-level rootkits:

1. Attempt to use the *stats, fopen, opendir,* and *chdir* calls for each entry in the *rootkit_files* and *rootkit_trojans* files. All these methods are used because some kernel-level rootkits hide their files from some, but not all, system calls. If there are any discrepancies in the results, rootcheck will generate an alert.
2. Scan the */dev* directory looking for anomalies. The */dev* directory should only contain device-specific files such as the primary IDE hard disk (*/dev/hda*), the first floppy drive (*/dev/fd0*), or the kernel random number generators (*/dev/random* and */dev/urandom*). Any additional files, outside of the expected device-specific files, should be inspected because many rootkits use */dev* as a storage partition to hide files.
3. Scan the entire file system looking for unusual files and permissions. Files owned by *root* with write permissions for other user accounts, suid files, hidden directories, and files are all inspected.
4. Inspect all process IDs (PID), and use the *getsid, getpgid,* and *kill* system calls to find all running processes. If the PID is being used, but the *ps* command cannot see it, a kernel-level rootkit or a Trojan version of *ps* might be running. We also compare the output of *getsid, getpgid,* and *kill* system calls looking for discrepancies.
5. Look for the presence of hidden ports. We use *bind()* to check every TCP and UDP port on the system. If we cannot bind to the port because it is in use, but the *netstat* command does not show it, a rootkit might be installed and operating on the port.
6. Scan all network interfaces on the system with promiscuous (*promisc*) mode enabled. If the interface is in promiscuous mode, the output of the *ifconfig* command will show that. If not, we might have a rootkit installed.

WARNING

Solaris and recent versions of Linux do not show promiscuous mode using the *ifconfig* command. Remember this when installing your OSSEC HIDS agents.

7. Scan the entire system comparing the differences between the *stat* size and the files size when using the *fopen + read* calls. The number of nodes in each directory is also compared with the output of *opendir + readdir*. If any results do not match, you might have a rootkit installed.

Detecting Rootkits with Signatures

When creating your rules, know that every alert from rootcheck is located within the *rootcheck* group. Using the *<if_group></if_group>* tag you can create a rootcheck rule as follows:

```
<rule id="100701" level="7">
   <if_group>rootcheck</if_group>
</rule>
```

Every alert from rootcheck has a different format depending on the message. When you create your rootcheck rules, you must create each rule on a case-by-case basis. For example, you could create a rule to increase the severity of any rootcheck alert from a specific agent. Using the *level* option within the *<rule></rule>* tag, you can specify the new severity level. You can also use the *<hostname></hostname>* tag to specify that you only want to increase the severity of the rootcheck alerts from one agent *(web1)*. The rule would appear as follows:

```
<rule id="100702" level="12">
   <if_group>rootcheck</if_group>
   <hostname>web1</hostname>
   <description>Increasing the severity of rootcheck alerts from agent "web1"
   </description>
</rule>
```

Similarly, if you want to ignore the following alert regarding a hidden file within the */dev* directory:

```
** Alert 1200871690.8582: mail - ossec,rootcheck,
2008 Jan 19 19:28:10 copacabana->rootcheck
Rule: 510 (level 7) -> 'Host-based anomaly detection event (rootcheck).'
Src IP: (none)
User: (none)
File '/dev/.hid' present on /dev. Possible hidden file.
```

You can create a rule that decreases the severity to 0, using the *level* option within the *<rule></rule>* tag, causing the alert to be ignored:

```
<rule id="100703" level="0">
   <if_group>rootcheck</if_group>
   <hostname>web1</hostname>
   <description>Ignoring rootcheck alerts from agent "web1"</description>
</rule>
```

Notes from the Underground…

Linux, Unix, and BSD User-Mode Rootkits

User-mode rootkits are designed to replace critical files on the host operating system with modified versions that have the same base functionality. The modified files are developed to function the same as the originals, but conceal the modifications, such as backdoor and other stealth capabilities, from the unsuspecting target.

Programs commonly replaced by user-mode rootkits include:

- **crontab**—*cron* configuration file that schedules shell commands to run at defined instances
- **du**—disk usage command that reports the sizes files and directories on disk
- **find**—used to locate files on the system
- **ifconfig**—allows the operating system to set up network interfaces and allows the user to view information about the configured network interfaces
- **inetd**—server process that indicates which services are started at boot time
- **killall**—cancels all running processes, except those producing the *killall* process
- **login**—initiates sessions on the system for the specified user
- **ls**—lists the contents of a directory
- **lsof**—lists information about files opened by processes
- **netstat**—displays network connections (both incoming and outgoing), routing tables, and several network interface statistics
- **md5sum**—calculates and verifies the MD5 hashes of files
- **passwd**—sets and changes passwords for users
- **pidof**—identifies the PID of a running job
- **ps**—writes the current status of active processes and, if the -m flag is given, associated kernel threads to standard output
- **pstree**—shows the running processes in tree format
- **rshd**—server for the *rcp* and *rsh* programs providing remote execution facilities with authentication based on privileged port numbers

- **sshd**—the OpenSSH SSH daemon
- **slocate**—provides a secure way to index and quickly search for files on your system
- **su**—changes user credentials to those of the root user or to the specified user
- **syslogd**—reads and logs messages into a set of files described by the */etc/syslog.conf* configuration file
- **tcpd**—access control facility for Internet services
- **top**—produces a frequently updated list of processes with the associated CPU and memory utilization
- **xinetd**—secure replacement for *inetd*

Monitoring and Enforcing Policy

Policy enforcement is a relatively new feature included with the OSSEC HIDS that is extremely useful for large installations. It allows the OSSEC HIDS to control, from a single location, how a specific host is configured and which applications or services it should be running.

With the Windows/Unix policy monitoring functionality of the OSSEC HIDS, alerts can be generated for applications that are defined as being against the organizational acceptable use policy. The following example alerts show the detection of Skype and Yahoo instant messaging applications:

```
2007 Jul 22 17:42:57 Rule Id: 514 level: 2
Location: (winxp23423) 192.168.2.190->rootcheck
Windows application monitor event.
--
Application Found: Chat/IM - Yahoo.
2007 Jul 22 17:42:57 Rule Id: 514 level: 2
Location: (winxp23423) 192.168.2.190->rootcheck
Windows application monitor event.
--
Application Found: Chat/IM/VoIP - Skype.
```

Similarly, if a system is configured to allow Null sessions or allow the users to specify weak passwords, the corresponding compliance alerts appear as:

```
2007 Jul 23 13:44:54 Rule Id: 512 level: 3
Location: (winxp23423) 192.168.2.190->rootcheck
Windows Audit event.
--
Windows Audit: Null sessions allowed.
```

```
2007 Jul 23 13:44:54 Rule Id: 512 level: 3
Location: (winxp23423) 192.168.2.190->rootcheck
Windows Audit event.
--
Windows Audit: LM authentication allowed (weak passwords).
```

Configuration checks, usually the result of known vulnerabilities in common application or server configuration settings, generate an alert as follows:

```
2008 Jan 20 20:08:31 copacabana->rootcheck
Rule: 516 (level 3) -> 'System Audit event.'
--
System Audit: PHP - Register globals are enabled.
```

The policy monitoring and enforcement checks have the capability to check if a process is running or not, if a file is present, if the contents of a file contain a pattern, or if a Windows registry key contains a string or is present. On Linux, Unix, and BSD systems, the *system_audit* file is responsible for all policy monitoring and enforcement definitions. On Windows systems, the *windows_audit*, *windows_apps*, and *windows_malware* files are responsible for the policy monitoring and enforcement definitions.

The format of the files might look complicated at first, but are easy to understand and work with once you become more familiar with them. The following configuration format, described in Table 5.3, follows a standard layout that applies to all four policy files:

```
[Application/Check name] [any or all or and] [reference]
type:<entry name> <test> <value>;
```

Table 5.3 Policy Monitoring and Enforcement Configuration Format

Configuration Field	Description
[Application/Check name]	A user-defined value that indicates which application or check will show in the generated alert. Any text string can be entered.
[any or all or and]	Indicates how to match the entries; *any* or *all* of the defined entries. The *and* value can also be used to indicate that multiple files must be present.
[reference]	Indicates a reference to something associated with this alert, such as a CVE number or Web page. Any text string can be entered.
type	Specifies if you want to monitor a file or directory (*f*), process (*p*), or registry key (*r*).

Continued

Table 5.3 Continued. Policy Monitoring and Enforcement Configuration Format

Configuration Field	Description
	For example: *f:/etc/test;*
<entry name>	Indicates the file, directory, process, or registry key to be monitored.
<test>	An optional test to compare an entry or value as defined in the *<value>* field. The following tests can be performed: = equal (default) **r** OSSEC HIDS regular expressions > string compare *greater than* operator < string compare *less than* operator
<value>	An additional pattern to compare against within the defined *<entry name>*. For example: f:$php.ini -> r:^register_globals = On;
;	Indicates the end of the *type* definition.

As an example, to alert when the message shows the */etc/abc* file is present, you would have the entry:

```
[File /etc/abc is present] [any] []
f:/etc/abc;
```

You can use the *any* or *all* configuration field to specify if all or just one of the entries that follow should match for the alert. You can also use the *and* value to indicate the multiple values must be present. For example, if you want to alert if the files */etc/test* and */etc/test1* are present, the following configuration can be defined:

```
[Files /etc/test and /etc/test1 are present] [and] []
f:/etc/test;
f:/etc/test1;
```

Variables can also be specified at the beginning of the file, to avoid typing the same content repeatedly. For example, to indicate that the */var/www/conf/php.ini*, */etc/php5/apache2/php.ini*, and */etc/php.ini* files are referenced when the *php.ini* variable is called, you would define your variable as:

```
$php.ini=/var/www/conf/php.ini,/etc/php5/apache2/php.ini,/etc/php.ini;
```

For files, you can use a right-facing arrow (->) to look for a specific value in the file. You can use this variable in a rule to see if the *register_globals* value is set to *true* by using:

```
# PHP checks
[PHP - Register globals are enabled] [any] [http://www.ossec.net/wiki]
f:$php.ini -> r:^register_globals = On;
```

Notice that we used the right-facing arrow to tell the OSSEC HIDS to look at the content of the file. We also used the *r:* type to specify that it should use a regex check to look for the content, in this case any line starting with **register_globals = On**.

When specifying a Windows registry key for your *<entry name>*, you can use a right-facing arrow to look for a specific entry and use another right-facing arrow to look for the value. Multiple patterns can also be specified using double ampersands (&&) for separation.

To look for processes, you can use the *p* type and the *&&* option for multiple patterns. The exclamation mark (!) is used to negate a value. For example, the following entry looks for the process named *svchost.exe* and alerts if it is not running inside the *%WINDIR%\System32* directory:

```
[Possible Malware - Svchost running outside system32] [any] []
p:r:svchost.exe && !%WINDIR%\System32\svchost.exe;
```

You can do the same for the *inetinfo.exe* process by using the configuration:

```
[Possible Malware - Inetinfo running outside system32\inetsrv] [any] []
p:r:inetinfo.exe && !%WINDIR%\System32\inetsrv\inetinfo.exe;
```

Policy Monitoring Rules

Rules for the policy monitoring/enforcement capabilities are similar to the other rules seen previously. There is, however, no specific group for policy monitoring/enforcement rules within the OSSEC HIDS, so you will need to define the individual *id* and use the *<if_sid> </if_sid>* tag within your rules.

The default rules are:

- **512**—Windows Audit
- **513**—Windows Malware
- **514**—Windows Application
- **516**—Unix Audit

The template for all policy monitoring/enforcement rules should be defined similar to the rule:

```
<rule id="100710" level="3">
    <if_sid>512, 513, 514, 516</if_sid>
</rule>
```

By default, both the policy auditing and application checks are logged with a severity level of 3, so you will not receive any email alerts with the default configuration. If you want to receive email alerts for the Windows Audit events, you could add a local rule with a higher severity:

```
<rule id="100711" level="9">
   <if_sid>512</if_sid>
   <description>Windows Audit event.</description>
   <group>rootcheck,</group>
</rule>
```

As an alternative, you can use the *<options></options>* tag and specify the *alert_by_email* option:

```
<rule id="100712" level="2">
   <if_sid>514</if_sid>
   <options>alert_by_email</options>
   <description>Windows application monitor event.</description>
   <group>rootcheck,</group>
</rule>
```

The Rootcheck Queue

The rootcheck queue is where every rootcheck entry is stored for each agent. It is located within the */var/ossec/queue/rootcheck* directory in a file named after the agent. The rootcheck file for the server is simply called *rootcheck*.

For example, to look for all applications found by the *winhome* agent, you can search through the related agent file:

```
# cd /var/ossec/queue/rootcheck
# cat *winhome*|grep "Application Found"
!1185284872!1185209094 Application Found: Chat/IM/VoIP - Skype.
!1185284872!1185209094 Application Found: Chat/IM - Yahoo.
!1185284872!1185209094 Application Found: Chat/IM - MSN. Reference:
http://www.msn.com.
```

To see which agents have reported the *Chat/IM* applications, you can search through all agent files for the *Chat* keyword:

```
# cd /var/ossec/queue/rootcheck
# grep "Application Found" * | grep Chat
(win64-1) 192.168.2.0->rootcheck:!1185305126!1185148006 Application Found:
Chat/IM - MSN. Reference: http://www.msn.com .
(winhome) 192.168.2.190->rootcheck:!1185284872!1185209094 Application Found:
Chat/IM/VoIP - Skype.
(winhome) 192.168.2.190->rootcheck:!1185284872!1185209094 Application Found:
Chat/IM - Yahoo.
```

```
(winhome) 192.168.2.190->rootcheck:!1185284872!1185209094 Application Found: Chat/
IM - MSN. Reference: http://www.msn.com .
```

To list all rootcheck events for one agent, you could do the following:

```
# cd /var/ossec/queue/rootcheck
# cat rootcheck
!1200874108!1193167503 Starting rootcheck scan.
!1200872667!1193167511 File '/var/log/ntop/access.log' is owned by root and has
written permissions to anyone.
```

Note that every line has two date entries: the first is the last time this event was alerted, and the second is the first time the event was reported.

Summary

The OSSEC HIDS looks for changes in the MD5/SHA1 checksums of designated files on the system and registry keys within the Windows registry using the *syscheck* process. The server stores and looks for modifications to the checksums by comparing the newly received checksums against the historical checksum values of the file or registry key. An alert is sent if anything changes.

Malicious applications, when installed, typically leave some remnant or digital fingerprint on the system as a result of the installation process. Malicious applications, commonly referred to with the blanket designation *malware*, attempt to circumvent the normal operation of your operating system. Rootkits are prime examples of malware that behave in this fashion. User-mode rootkits are often designed to copy modified system executables, which include backdoor and other malicious capabilities, to a target system. If installed successfully, the digital fingerprint of the modified files will change.

By default, the OSSEC HIDS checks the */etc*, */usr/bin*, */usr/*sbin, */bin*, and */sbin* directories on Unix, Linux, and BSD systems, and the *C:\Windows\System32* directory on Windows. All syscheck configuration parameters are found within the *<syscheck></syscheck>* tag of the *ossec.conf* file.

All syscheck alerts are located within the *syscheck* group. Any local rules you create to alert on file, directory, or registry key changes require the *<if_group>syscheck</if_group>* definition. The generated syscheck alerts always include the old checksum values and new checksum values for the monitored file.

Rootkit detection on Linux, Unix, and BSD systems finds application-level rootkits through signature definitions and kernel-level rootkits using system call comparisons. Policy monitoring/ enforcement is the process of verifying that all systems conform to a set of pre-defined policies surrounding configuration settings and approved application usage. Both the policy monitoring and rootkit detection capabilities are configured on the OSSEC HIDS server and pushed down to all OSSEC HIDS agents.

Solutions Fast Track

Understanding System Integrity Check

☑ The OSSEC HIDS agent scans the system every few hours, or at an interval you specify, and sends the checksums of the monitored files and registry keys to the OSSEC HIDS server.

☑ The server stores and looks for modifications to the checksums by comparing the newly received checksums against the historical checksum values of the file or registry key.

☑ By default, the OSSEC HIDS checks *the /etc, /usr/bin, /usr/sbin, /bin*, and */sbin* directories on Unix, Linux, and BSD systems, and the *C:\Windows\System32* directory on Windows.

Tuning syscheck

- ☑ To get the most out of your OSSEC HIDS syscheck configuration, you must tune it to the systems where it will be deployed.
- ☑ All syscheck alerts are located within the *syscheck* group. Any local rules you create to alert on file, directory, or registry key changes require the *<if_group>syscheck </if_group>* definition.
- ☑ The generated syscheck alerts always include the old checksum values and new checksum values for the monitored file.

Detecting Rootkits and Enforcing/Monitoring Policies

- ☑ OSSEC HIDS rootkit detection on Linux, Unix, and BSD systems finds application-level rootkits through signature definitions and kernel-level rootkits using system call comparisons.
- ☑ Policy monitoring/enforcement is the process of verifying that all systems conform to a set of pre-defined policies surrounding configuration settings and approved application usage.
- ☑ Both the policy monitoring and rootkit detection capabilities are configured on the OSSEC HIDS server and pushed down to all OSSEC HIDS agents.

Frequently Asked Questions

Q: Do I really need to install the OSSEC HIDS on a secure server?

A: The short answer is *yes*. If you cannot trust the integrity of the system files prior to the installation of the OSSEC HIDS, how can you possibly trust the integrity of the files after?

Q: How does the OSSEC HIDS verify the integrity of files?

A: The OSSEC HIDS server stores and looks for modifications to the checksums received from the OSSEC HIDS agents. Comparing the newly received checksums against the historical values of the file or registry key accomplishes this, and an alert is sent if anything changes.

Q: Which directories does the syscheck component check by default?

A: The OSSEC HIDS checks the */etc*, */usr/*bin, */usr/sbin*, */bin*, and */sbin* directories on Unix, Linux, and BSD systems, and the *C:\Windows\System32* directory on Windows.

Q: I'm using a Windows system. Can I use system variables such as %WINDIR% so I don't have to type the full directory path?

A: Yes, on Windows systems you can use system variables such as %WINDIR%, %SYSDIR%, and so on to indicate directories.

Q: Why do I need to tune my syscheck configuration?

A: To get the most out of your syscheck configuration, you must tune your deployment for the systems being monitored. Perhaps you don't like the OSSEC HIDS monitoring one of the default files, or you feel that the default configuration doesn't cover enough files. This is all part of your tuning exercise and is different for everyone and nearly every system on which the OSSEC HIDS solution is deployed.

Q: What if I want syscheck to ignore a particular alert?

A: Using the *<match></match>* tag you can search for patterns within the generated syscheck alerts and set the severity level of the alert to 0. This causes the alert to be ignored by the rest of the OSSEC HIDS processes.

Q: My OSSEC HIDS agent is deployed on a file server that contains many sensitive files. Can I create a rule that looks for changes to files on the server?

A: Yes. Using a combination of the *<match></match>* tag or *<regex></regex>* tag to find the related syscheck message for those documents, and the *<hostname></hostname>* tag to identify the agent, you can generate alerts for file changes on your server.

Q: How does the OSSEC HIDS detect application-level rootkits on Linux, Unix, or BSD systems? What about kernel-level rootkits?

A: Rootkit detection on Linux, Unix, and BSD systems finds application-level rootkits through signature definitions and kernel-level rootkits using system call comparisons.

Q: Can the OSSEC HIDS detect rootkits on Windows systems?

A: At the time of this writing, the OSSEC HIDS did not have the capability to detect Windows rootkits. This is, however, on the roadmap for a future release.

Q: Can I generate alerts if certain applications are found running on a host?

A: Yes, with the Windows/Unix policy monitoring functionality of the OSSEC HIDS, alerts can be generated for applications that are defined as against the organizational acceptable use policy.

Q: Is there a single place I can go to check for all applications found by a particular agent?

A: The */var/ossec/queue/rootcheck/* directory contains a rootcheck file for each agent. You can use a utility such as *grep* to look through the specific agent's rootcheck file for the "Application Found" string. A full list will be printed to your terminal window.

Chapter 6

Active Response

Solutions in this chapter:

- Introducing Active Response
- Examining Active Response
- Creating a Simple Response
- Configuring a Response with Timeout

☑ Summary

☑ Solutions Fast Track

☑ Frequently Asked Questions

Introduction

At the end of the meeting, Marty and Antoine walked together toward the elevator. "I don't suppose there is any way the OSSEC HIDS could tell our network security infrastructure to block attackers if specific criteria are met?" asked Antoine. "Actually," smiled Marty. "It can. Why don't I set up another session so we can talk about this with some of the network guys?" Antoine nodded. "Just let me know when and where." Marty nodded. "No problem. I'll coordinate through Simran and see who I need to invite." Marty looked at his watch, 5:30 P.M. He knew that Simran would still be around because she is typically one of the last people to leave the building. Simran was sipping tea when Marty flew around the corner into her office. "Hey boss!" Marty said, startling Simran. "What did I tell you about that, Marty?" Simran said. "The last time you startled me like that I spilled my coffee all over my laptop." Marty chuckled to himself. "Sorry boss, I just wanted to let you know that everything went well today." Marty sat down in Simran's guest chair. "Well, why don't you sit down then?" Simran said, rolling her eyes. "Thanks," said Marty, oblivious to Simran's sarcasm. "One thing did come up, though. Antoine asked if the OSSEC HIDS had any active response capabilities." Marty paused, waiting for Simran to acknowledge his last statement. "You're going to make me ask, aren't you?" asked Simran. Marty smiled. "Alright, Marty," Simran asked reluctantly. "Does it have the capability to communicate with other devices to have them add an ACL to block the traffic?" Marty shifted excitedly in his seat. "You bet it does!" exclaimed Marty. "You can write any script or application and have it called from a rule. The cool thing is that the people behind the OSSEC HIDS even provide some samples to get you going." Simran smiled, thinking that she had never worked with anyone who was so excited by security tools and concepts. "Why don't you talk with David and see if you can arrange another meeting with his and Antoine's teams?" suggested Simran. "Great minds think alike, boss," said Marty. "I just wanted to check with you to make sure that was copasetic."

The next day, Marty walked over to David's office, knocked on the door, and waited for David to acknowledge him. "What happened?" asked David as he looked up from his laptop. "Nothing," said Marty. "Why do you always expect the worst when I come around?" David rolled his eyes and smiled. "I think you know why, Marty. The day you come to my office informing me that I've won the lottery, I promise I'll welcome you with open arms the following day." Marty laughed. "You've got yourself a deal. The reason I dropped by is that in my meeting yesterday with Antoine's team, he asked me about some of the active response capabilities of the OSSEC HIDS." Marty took a sip of his coffee. "I was wondering if you could lend me Ming, Mark, and Sergei for another meeting to hash this all out." David checked the group calendar. "Sure, they're all free this afternoon," said David. "Just send them a meeting request."

The meeting room was full. Antoine made sure the same people from the previous session were present from his team. The addition of the three operations people also ensured that there wasn't a free seat in the room. Marty began his overview of the active response capabilities of the OSSEC HIDS and provided some sample code he had written to interface with a few of the deployed network devices in the lab. He proceeded to demo his script by creating a sample rule that looked for multiple failed authentication attempts to one of the lab servers. His alert, when trigged by the successive failures, created an alert that called his script. The script sent a command to create an ACL rule on the router between the offending host and the server. Marty tried to connect again to prove that his script was working as designed and, with Ming's help, checked the running configuration on the router. Everyone in the room was impressed and smiled at Marty.

"Well I don't know about you guys," said Marty. "But, I think this might help us out."

Introducing Active Response

Automated remediation to security violations and threats is a powerful means for containing damage and reducing risk. You use remediation to block specific hosts and/or services so that a detected violation can be stopped or contained and controlled. The violation does not necessarily have to take the form of an attack; it might be a policy violation or simply an unauthorized access. A remediation solution performs actions or alters configurations to prevent a violator access to services or networks.

Notes from the Underground...

Automated Remediation

Automated systems to contain attacks, worms, or policy violations are becoming increasingly popular in corporate networks. The techniques vary, but the common theme is that the network must react reflexively to perceived attacks. To remediate these perceived attacks, you can use several types of automated responses to proactively slow down or block the offender. By slowing down these attacks, you provide network, systems, and security personnel time to analyze the threat and determine if a more complete response is needed.

Remedial actions will often be one of the following:

- **Firewall block or drop** This action is the simplest way to deny access to a host or service. Depending on the information available about the violation, this might block an IP address entirely or it might block access to specific services (port numbers).
- **Quarantine** This action is characterized by restricting a host network access to an isolated network segment. Typically, this is performed during host

Continued

authorization for a virtual private networking (VPN) solution or a network access control (NAC) solution. Often, however, a host previously granted access might be later quarantined based on new violations. The general objective with a *quarantine* action is to redirect the host to a network subnet where services are available to remedy the violation. If a host does not meet the required patch level, a dedicated patch server on the *quarantine* subnet might be available to provide the patches. After it is remedied, the host might then be allowed access to the entire network. *Quarantine* subnets are also a valuable resource for investigating worm and automated attackers against your network. Honeypots can be configured on the *quarantine* subnet, emulating your production servers, to see how the attacker interacts with the servers. This information provides valuable ammunition when it comes time to tune the rules of your security devices throughout your network.

- **Traffic shaping or throttling** This action is generally only useful for worm, denial of service (DoS), and distributed denial of service (DDoS) attacks where it might not be desirable to block a service entirely. You would, however, want to slow things down to prevent a complete network outage.
- **Account lockout** This action is used if a violation can be attributed to a specific user; that user's authorization to use network services or access to a host might be revoked by locking or disabling his login.

Consider these remedial actions when deciding which types of responses will work best for your network. If, for example, you have NAC equipment in use, it might be very easy to quarantine a host. The OSSEC HIDS provides blocking responses, which provide a good starting point for creating your own responses.

The OSSEC HIDS uses the term *active response* to refer to its solution for automated remediation. Active response allows a scripted action to be performed whenever a rule is matched in your OSSEC HIDS rule set. There can be any number of responses attached to any of the configured rules. Therefore, active response is part of rule writing, but deserves some special attention. The impact of incorrectly implemented rules and responses can be dangerous and can even allow a clever attacker to use your rules against you.

Packaged with the OSSEC HIDS installation is a collection of active response scripts you are free to use in your environment. The firewall-drop active response script is provided as an optional parameter during the OSSEC HIDS installation. Firewall block or drop responses are generally the most common forms of remediation used in security products. Firewalls are the simplest form of access control and most have a command-line interface, which allows for scripting responses. Because the OSSEC HIDS is host-based, it is possible to use the host firewall, sometimes referred to as a *packet filter*, to block internal and external attackers. Active responses can be passed important information from the rule-match, such as source

IP address or username, to be used in applying the response. The response is an executable script and therefore any remedy action can be used. This, of course, depends entirely on the type of enforcement services or products available to interact with the OSSEC HIDS.

Examining Active Response

The OSSEC HIDS active response scripts are found in the *active-response/bin/* directory where the OSSEC HIDS is installed; for example, the */var/ossec/active-response/bin/* directory. The active response scripts packaged with the OSSEC HIDS are all shell scripts and include:

- **disable-account.sh** Disables an account for logins on most Unix-like operating systems.
- **host-deny.sh** Adds hosts to the */etc/hosts.deny* file used by *tcpwrappers*. This is only useful for services with *tcpwrappers* enabled.
- **route-null.sh** Adds an IP address to the reject or blackhole list. This is similar to *firewall-drop.sh*, except it is only useful on hosts that forward packets between networks, such as a router, and it does not use the packet filtering code in the kernel.
- **firewall-drop.sh** A universal firewall response script that should work with common Linux/Unix operating systems.
- **ipfw_mac.sh** A firewall-drop response script created for the Mac OS X firewall.
- **ipfw.sh** A firewall-drop response script created for *ipfw*, the FreeBSD IP packet filter.
- **pf.sh** A firewall-drop response script created for pf, the BSD licensed stateful packet filter.

NOTE

If the *firewall-drop.sh* script does not work on your operating system, consider using *ipfw_mac.sh*, *ipfw.sh*, or *pf.sh* as alternatives or frameworks to create your own firewall-drop script.

These shells are written to perform *blocking* or *prevent* actions, typically by changing configuration using IP addresses or usernames. Considerable care has been taken with these executable programs to ensure they do only what is intended. Poorly written scripts might be *trick-able* by truly clever attackers, which is why you should always test your scripts before using them on production OSSEC HIDS deployments.

The executables are run as the *root* user and therefore can be made to perform virtually any action an administrator is capable of. Having this level of access allows you to create responses that can change firewall rules, manipulate routing, disable user accounts, adjust Address Resolution Protocol (ARP) tables, and much more.

Command

A *command* must be defined so your OSSEC HIDS scripts can be referenced by your rules to perform a particular active response. Any script can be used as long as it is designed to accept parameters from the command line of the system where the script is located. All OSSEC HIDS commands must be located in the *active-response/bin* directory along with the other active response commands. Active response commands are specified in the *ossec.conf* file, typically located in the */var/ossec/etc/* directory, using an easy to follow command script. For example, a *command* named *host-deny* can be created to use the *host-deny.sh* script. This script has the capability to take in the provided source IP address and provides a mechanism to timeout after a period of time. This example can be enabled as a *command* using:

```
<command>
  <name>host-deny</name>
  <executable>host-deny.sh</executable>
  <expect>srcip</expect>
  <timeout_allowed>yes</timeout_allowed>
</command>
```

Several tags can be used to enhance the functionality of an OSSEC HIDS command. Table 6.1 lists the available XML tags.

Table 6.1 Command Values

Tags	Possible Values	Description
<name></name>	Any name you want to use to define the rule. For example: <name>host-deny</name>	Used to reference the rule from other sections of the configuration—specifically when you assign a response to a rule.
<executable> </executable>	Name of the script or binary to execute. For example: <executable>host-deny. sh</executable>	The name of the script or binary that will carry out the response. It must exist in */var/ossec/ active-response/bin*.

Continued

Table 6.1 Continued. Command Values

Tags	Possible Values	Description
<expect></expect>	Variables to be handed to the script or binary executable. For example: <expect>srcip</expect> <expect>user</expect>	A comma-separated list of variables to be handed to the command line of the executable. The variables are passed in the order specified here. There are only two variables currently available in the OSSEC HIDS: *srcip* and *user*. The *srcip* variable allows you to pass a source IP address to your executable. The *user* variable allows you to pass a username to your executable.
<timeout_allowed></timeout_allowed>	*yes* or *no* For example: <timeout_allowed> yes </timeout_allowed>	This is either *yes* or no. If *yes*, the response will timeout allowing an automated expiry of the response condition. If *yes*, the executable must be written to handle undoing its actions.

WARNING

When writing a command that is able to timeout, take steps to ensure that it can only *undo* the changes it has specifically made. For example, firewall rules might be added by other administrators, processes, or devices, so your *command* must be able to distinguish configuration changes it has added from others. This way, you ensure that you only remove the changes your script has made.

Active Response

Binding a command to one or more rules, or to a specific severity level, creates an active response. The *command* will be executed for any event matching the given rules or for any event matching the given severity level. In the active response definition, you must also specify the location where the command will be executed. Rules might be executed locally, on the server, or on all agents. This adds to the flexibility and the risk of active response.

The active response configuration section looks like:

```
<active-response>
  <disabled>no</disabled>
  <command>host-deny</command>
  <location>local</location>
  <agent_id>001</agent_id>
  <level>6</level>
  <rules_id>444,458</rules_id>
  <rules_group>webserver</rules_group>
  <timeout>600</timeout>
</active-response>
```

The XML tags used to specify the *active-response* are show in Table 6.2.

Table 6.2 *<active_response>*</active_response> Values

Tags	Possible Values	Description
<disabled></disabled>	*yes* or *no* For example: <disabled>no</disabled>	If set to *yes*, the response is disabled. If the tag is set to *no*, or not defined, the response is enabled.
<command></command>	Must reference a previously defined command. For example: <command>host-deny </command>	The name of the command to be used in the response. This must match an already created command. See the **Command** section in this chapter for more information.
<location></location>	One of the following: ■ local ■ server ■ defined-agent ■ all	Defines where the command is executed. To execute the command on the agent that reported the rule-matching events, use the *local* location.

Continued

Table 6.2 Continued. *<active_response>*</active_response> Values

Tags	Possible Values	Description
	For example: <location>local </location> <location>defined-agent </location>	To execute the command on the OSSEC HIDS server only, use the *server* location. To execute the command on designated agents, use the *defined-agent* location. To execute the command on all agents, use the *all* location.
<agent_id></agent_id>	A numeric identification number of your OSSEC HIDS agent when it was created on the OSSEC HIDS server. For example: <agent_id>001 </agent_id>	Only used if the location is *defined-agent*. This is the numeric ID of the OSSEC HIDS agent on which the command will be executed.
<level></level>	A numeric value of the severity. For example: <level>6</level>	The command is executed for any rule match where the rule is of this severity or higher.
<rules_id>444</rules_id>	A numeric rule ID number. For example: <rules_id>444</rules_id> <rules_id>444,458 </rules_id>	The command is executed for any event matching one of these rule IDs. Multiple rule IDs can be defined as a comma-separated list of rule IDs.
<rules_group> </rules_group>	Alphanumeric group names. For example: <rules_group>webserver </rules_group>	The command is executed for any event matching a rule in one of these groups. Multiple group names can be defined as a comma-separated list of rule group names.
<timeout></timeout>	A numeric value. For example: <timeout>600</timeout>	The duration, in seconds, for the timeout of this response.

TIP

When planning for active response, begin with the more general cases by assigning responses to rule-groups or levels. As you refine your rules, you can also add responses for specific rule IDs. This strategy allows active response to be refined over time.

Tying It Together

An OSSEC HIDS active response is the combination of an executable program or script, a *command* definition, an *active-response* definition, and the OSSEC HIDS rules. This flexible mapping allows for powerful automated remediation of security violations. The ability to create custom commands using any programming language also means integration is possible with any number of devices or services that are used to restrict or prevent access.

Tools & Traps...

Helping Your Attacker

A danger in automating responses to events is that an attacker might discover a combination of responses that disrupts your normal network operation. In some cases, it might even be possible for an attacker to use your rules and responses to gain access to the network.

For this reason, OSSEC HIDS includes some features in active response to reduce some of the risks. One feature is a timeout on responses, which is used to ensure that the response action is not permanent. If communication is disrupted through a firewall-drop response, the timeout will ensure that service resumes within minutes while still affecting the attacker.

The ability to select an agent to perform the response is also useful in reducing risk. Using specific agents to perform firewall-drop responses only on dedicated firewalls is one example of limiting the scope of responses. Consider carefully the techniques for limiting the risks associated with responses.

Creating a Simple Response

One of the simplest possible responses is to send an email with a warning about the user or IP address that triggered the rule match. We will create such an email response using a shell script, define the command, and then bind the command to a rule.

The Executable

Create a script in */var/ossec/active-response/bin* and call it *mail-notify.sh*. Add the following lines:

```
#!/bin/sh
# Adds an IP to the /etc/hosts.deny file
# Requirements: working local SMTP relay (example: sendmail)
# Expect: user, srcip

ACTION=$1
USER=$2
IP=$3

MAIL_SUBJECT="OSSEC HIDS Response"
MAIL_ADDRESS="ossec_user@domain.tld"
MAIL_CMD=mail -s "$MAIL_SUBJECT" $MAIL_ADDRESS
MAIL_BODY="This is an automated response. $ACTION restriction for
$USER at $IP"

echo "$MAIL_BODY" | $MAIL_CMD
```

TIP

Note the comment block at the top of the scripts that come with the OSSEC HIDS. There is no requirement to form your comments in the same way. However, the samples provide a good convention to follow when writing your own scripts.

The comments at the top of the script indicate the purpose and requirements for the script. This script will expect both the user and the IP address parameters and then add these to the email message. Because the command is identical for both *add* and *delete* actions, there is no need for the script to remember previous actions. More complex responses often require this sort of memory to process *delete* actions for previous *add* actions when the response times out.

Tools & Traps...

Working with Vendor Products

Many organizations secure their networks using a combination of vendor equipment, making it difficult to centrally manage all active response actions. For example, the management solution for *Vendor A* might not be able to add, remove, or change actions deployed to the network solution for *Vendor B*, and vice versa. Nearly all network and security platforms allow for some method of remote access for configuration and maintenance tasks. Most of these provide a mechanism for the remote addition or removal of configuration settings to assist administrators with equipment in remote locations.

Many network administrators have created their own scripts to help them manage the ACL rules throughout their environment. Furthermore, some vendors provide an application programming interface (API) and sample code to explain how your scripts could interact with their devices.

However, sometimes the methods for interacting with the vendor device are not well documented or sample code is not available. In this case, you will have you create your own scripts. The Perl scripting language is the preferred language for such tools because it provides you with the flexibility of a shell script with the power of a programming language. Before starting your own script, it might be a good idea to search the Comprehensive Perl Archive Network (CPAN) search site at http://search.cpan.org/ to see if someone has already scripted what you need.

If Perl is not your scripting language of choice, consider using Ruby, Python, or another language you are more familiar with. If the script can run on the platform it is located on, then the OSSEC HIDS can call it to perform the required action.

You can also send an email to the OSSEC HIDS mailing list and ask your peers if anyone has ever developed a script to address your need. Because the OSSEC HIDS community is a large and open community, you might find that someone has exactly the script you are looking for already completed.

The Command

Next, you must define the command in *ossec.conf*, remembering that we must give it a meaningful name and specify the parameters it will take. For this case, set timeout to *no* because this response is stateless.

Add the following to the *<command></command>* section of your *ossec.conf*:

```
<command>
  <name>mail-notify</name>
```

```
  <executable>mail-notify.sh</executable>
  <expect>user,srcip</expect>
  <timeout_allowed>no</timeout_allowed>
</command>
```

TIP

This command definition follows the practice of giving the command a name that is similar to the executable name. This is a good practice to follow because it makes reading the configuration easier and makes maintenance work easier for everyone.

Again, the executable value is simply the name of the script without any extra path information. Because this command is able to make use of username (*user*) and source IP (*srcip*) address, we include both within the *<expect></expect>* tag. Timeout is not allowed, however, because sending email is not an action that can be undone.

The Response

Now, let's assume you want to be emailed for each SSH related event. The simplest approach is to create an active response that acts each time a rule in the *sshd* group is matched and executes the command on the server. Add the following to the *<active-response></active-response>* section of your *ossec.conf* file:

```
<active-response>
  <disabled>no</disabled>
  <command>mail-notify</command>
  <location>server</location>
  <rules_group>sshd</rules_group>
</active-response>
```

Because the command for this response sends an email, it makes the most sense to execute on one host only; for example, the server. Executing the script on multiple agents results in your personal mail bomb. This is an important point when planning your responses; consider which location is best for the response.

WARNING

Make certain that the resources that must not be blocked or removed from service are properly defined within the *<white_list></white_list>* tags in your *ossec.conf* file. This will make it safer to use the *all* location without creating your own DoS attack.

Configuring a Response with Timeout

The previous example was almost trivial in that it performed a simple command and did not require any special timeout processing. The *host-deny.sh* script that comes with the OSSEC HIDS installation provides an example of a more complex situation. To respond to the *delete* action, the script has to be able to find the previous *add* and undo it.

Host-Deny Command

Look at the command definition for *host-deny* from the *ossec.conf* file:

```
<command>
  <name>host-deny</name>
  <executable>host-deny.sh</executable>
  <expect>srcip</expect>
  <timeout_allowed>yes</timeout_allowed>
</command>
```

Because the script works only on IP addresses, *srcip* is the expected parameter. Because the *host-deny.sh* script can undo its actions, a timeout is allowed. As you noticed with the *mail-notify.sh* script, the first parameter the OSSEC HIDS passes to the script is the action, which can be *add* or *delete*. When the action is triggered, the script is called with *add*; if and when there is a timeout, the script is called with *delete*.

Host-Deny Response

By default, the *host-deny* command is used in a response for any rule match with severity level >= 6 and only on the agent that generated the event.

```
<active-response>
  <!-- This response is going to execute the host-deny
     - command for every event that fires a rule with
     - level (severity) >= 6.
     - The IP is going to be blocked for 600 seconds.
    -->
  <command>host-deny</command>
  <location>local</location>
  <level>6</level>
  <timeout>600</timeout>
</active-response>
```

For very severe rule matches it could be reasonable for you to deny access across your entire network by simply changing the location from *local* to *all*. In that case, whenever a rule of severity *6* or greater is matched, the source IP address is automatically denied SSH access to all agent hosts for five minutes.

Summary

Active response combines the power of the command line with mapping to rules. The ability to select which agents perform the response actions allows for flexible response scenarios to rapidly contain and restrict attacker activities. Any form of automated response comes with a risk that it can be used against you. The OSSEC HIDS provides some features in active response to reduce the risks, such as timeouts and defined locations for command execution.

With careful planning, active response can quickly respond to security events faster than an administrator can. This feature is a significant part of the OSSEC HIDS value.

Solutions Fast Track

Introducing Active Response

☑ The objective with remediation is to block specific hosts and/or services so a detected violation can be stopped or contained and controlled.

☑ A remediation solution performs actions or alters configurations to prevent a violator access to services or networks.

☑ Active responses can be passed important information from the rule-match, such as source IP address or username, to be used in applying the response.

Examining Active Response

☑ The active response scripts packaged with the OSSEC HIDS are shell scripts.

☑ A *command* must be defined so your OSSEC HIDS scripts can be referenced by your rules to perform a particular active response.

☑ Binding a *command* to one or more rules or to a specific severity level creates an active response.

☑ An OSSEC HIDS active response is the combination of an executable program or script, a *command* definition, an *active-response* definition, and of course, an OSSEC HIDS rule.

Creating a Simple Response

☑ One of the simplest possible responses is to send an email with a warning about the user or IP address that triggered the rule match.

☑ The *executable*, required to perform the action, must be created and placed on the agent or server where you want it to be executed from.

- ☑ The *command* must be defined in the *ossec.conf* file, remembering that we must give it a meaningful name and specify the parameters it will take.
- ☑ The *response* must be defined in the *ossec.conf* file using the *<active-response> </active-response>* tag.

Configuring a Response with Timeout

- ☑ The *host-deny.sh* script that comes with the OSSEC HIDS installation provides an example of a script with the capability to remove its previously implemented action.
- ☑ The *command* must be created using the *<timeout_allowed></timeout_allowed>* tag to indicate that the script allows the action to be removed after a period of time.
- ☑ The *response* must be created using the *<timeout></timeout>* tag with the desired timeout for the action in seconds.

Frequently Asked Questions

Q: What is the benefit of using automated remediation?

A: The business world has become a 24/7/365 operation. Attackers do not execute their attacks at a time that conveniently fits into your schedule. As such, mechanisms to thwart attackers must be installed to reduce the need of having analysts watching the network for obvious attacks 24 hours a day.

Q: What are some common remediation actions?

A: There are several well-known, and heavily used, remediation types available. The most commonly used types are using a firewall ACL to block/drop the offending traffic, quarantining a host from your network by directing the traffic to another subnet, shaping or throttling the traffic to reduce its impact, and removing access rights for a particular account.

Q: Can I use the active response capabilities of the OSSEC HIDS to interact with a host, or can I only interface with network appliances?

A: You can use the active response capabilities of the OSSEC HIDS to interact with any device, application, or system your script is developed to interface with. You are only limited by your imagination. For example, there is nothing stopping you from creating a script to *ssh* to a host and tell it to shut down if certain messages match your created rule. Although the practicality of this approach could be disputed, the reasoning behind it is entirely up to you.

Q: I've tried the *firewall-drop.sh* script, but it is not working properly. What do I do?

A: Several other firewall scripts come with the OSSEC HIDS. Depending on your type of host firewall, you might have to use one of them or even write your own.

Q: Where do I create my active response commands?

A: All active response commands must be created in your *ossec.conf* configuration file.

Q: Can I remove a deployed action after a period of time?

A: Yes, using the *<timeout_allowed></timeout_allowed>* tag in your command configuration and the *<timeout></timeout>* tag in your active-response configuration, you can set your *command* timeout after the configured amount of time.

Q: Do I need to add comments at the top of my script?

A: No, but it is generally a good practice to do so. This ensures that the next person who must update your script knows what it was designed to do.

Q: I must create a script to interface with a vendor's firewall solution. Is there anywhere I can get the script?

A: If you cannot find the script that addresses your requirements, you might have to create your own. Start by researching your vendor documentation to see if there is an API or sample code available to interface with the product. Also, try searching the Internet to see if someone has already completed the script and has posted the source code.

Q: Can you create a script for me?

A: You can send an email to the OSSEC HIDS mailing list and ask your peers if any of them has ever developed a script to address your need. Because the OSSEC HIDS community is a large and open community, you might find that someone has exactly the script you are looking for already completed.

Q: What is the difference between a *stateful* and a *stateless* command?

A: A *stateful* command has the capability to remove the applied action after a period of time. A *stateless command* does not.

Q: What tag do I need to use to tell the *command* that it needs to be stateful?

A: The *<timeout_allowed></timeout_allowed>* tag must be used to identify your *command* as one that is stateful.

Q: When using the *<timeout></timeout>* tag in my response, what measurement of time is used?

A: The *<timeout></timeout>* tag expects the time you configure to be in seconds.

Chapter 7

Using the OSSEC Web User Interface

Solutions in this chapter:

- Introducing the OSSEC HIDS WUI
- Identifying WUI Pre-installation Considerations
- Downloading the WUI
- Installing and Configuring the WUI
- Describing the WUI Components

☑ Summary

☑ Solutions Fast Track

☑ Frequently Asked Questions

Introduction

The next morning, Antoine and Marty waited on the main floor for the elevator to arrive. "Good morning," Marty nodded at Antoine. "Good morning," Antoine replied. "You do realize," Antoine said in a sly tone, "that we never did cover the Web User Interface." Marty's eyes went big in shock. "*Doh!*" said Marty. "I knew we forgot something. Are you guys available for a quick meeting this morning?" The elevator chimed and the door opened. Antoine stepped in, turned around, and smiled at Marty. "It's already booked," said Antoine as he looked at his watch. "You've got about 15 minutes to check your email and fill up your coffee. We'll meet you back in the big meeting room." Marty chuckled to himself. "I guess it's a good thing I know what I'm talking about," Marty exclaimed. "Alright, I'll see you guys there."

After Marty checked his email, cleared out his usual 20 or so spam emails, and filled his coffee he packed up his laptop and headed toward the meeting room. As he passed Simran's office, she shouted out to him. "Where are you in such a rush to get to this early in the morning?" asked Simran. "I forgot to cover the WUI," replied Marty. "It shouldn't take longer than an hour or so." Simran smiled. "I spoke with Antoine yesterday and arranged for some of the good coffee to be brought up from the cafeteria for your meeting." Marty set his cup down on Simran's desk. "Well I guess I don't have to drink this sludge, then. I'll drop by when I'm done." Simran stared at the coffee cup. "You better be back for this cup, Marty. If you don't, I'm chucking it in the garbage," Simran said as Marty continued on his way.

"Alright," Marty said as he made his way toward the good coffee. "We're going to make this short and sweet because this is probably one of the easiest to use Web interfaces on the planet." Marty poured his coffee and walked over to the head of the table. He began by providing an overview of the installation. He showed everyone how to install the WUI, using one of the lab OSSEC HIDS servers for his demonstration. Marty let the group install the WUI on the other two servers so they could get a feel for how easy it was to install. After the installation, Marty walked them through the various screens, detailing the purpose of each as he went. "Wow," exclaimed Antoine. "This is very intuitive…for a change." Marty laughed. "Ya, it's not often that you can install and master a product inside of 15 minutes these days." Within the hour, everyone on the team had a firm understanding of how to use the WUI to perform system monitoring and investigatory tasks.

Marty stopped by Simran's office on the way back to his desk. "Well boss," Marty said. "I think we're right where we need to be. The operations and incident teams know how to install, configure, and tune the OSSEC HIDS." Marty paused and took a sip from his coffee cup. "I guess all we need now is the green light to get it installed." Simran looked up from her laptop. "Well Marty," Simran said with a smile. "I've got good news. Your project kicks off tomorrow." Marty looked at Simran. "My project?" Simran nodded. "You didn't think I was going to let just anyone head this deployment, did you?" Simran took a sip from her own coffee cup. "Plus, it'll be good practice for when I move you into my old position, pending management approval of course." Marty's eyes went wide. "Really?" Marty said, almost spitting his coffee out. "Wow, thanks Boss." Simran shook her head. "No Marty, thank you. We couldn't have done this without you. You did a good job finding us a tool that was easy to use, didn't impact our budget, and impressed everyone." Simran's phone chimed. "Got to go, board meeting." Marty stepped aside to let Simran pass. "Oh Marty," Simran said as she walked away. "Don't forget your coffee cup. It's not your office yet." Marty smiled as he grabbed his cup and headed back to his smaller, temporary office.

Introducing the OSSEC HIDS WUI

Not everyone is comfortable combing through log files at the command line or running complex SQL queries against a database to retrieve stored data. Wouldn't it be easier if there were a web-based interface that allowed you to run reports against the collected OSSEC HIDS information? Wouldn't it also be easier for large teams of incident handlers and security analysts to have a tool available to perform detailed forensic analysis on collected events and alerts?

Few people, especially those in management positions, enjoy looking at raw data when there is an easy-to-use alternative. The OSSEC HIDS Web User Interface (WUI) provides a Web-based interface that performs the statistical analysis and correlation of data for you.

NOTE

The authors are not suggesting that looking at raw data isn't valuable as part of the incident handling or forensic analysis process, but rather present the WUI as an additional tool to help perform some of the legwork for you.

The main dashboard page gives you a 10,000-foot view into what is happening throughout your OSSEC HIDS deployment. A powerful search engine is available to help you investigate the collected OSSEC HIDS events and alerts. All file integrity changes are recorded, and a powerful interface allows you to view the changes to the file over time. Finally, a powerful statistics engine allows you to aggregate all collected events and alerts to give you a statistical view of what is happening on your network.

Throughout this chapter, we will explore the WUI for your OSSEC HIDS server.

Identifying WUI Pre-installation Considerations

The WUI was designed to run on an OSSEC HIDS local or server type installation. Typical deployments have the WUI installed on a server type installation. As the need grows for the collection of alerts from multiple agents, the WUI becomes an invaluable tool to help visualize all the generated alerts.

NOTE

The WUI cannot be installed on an agent, because all collected alerts are sent back to an OSSEC HIDS server for processing.

The WUI is supported on all Linux, Unix, and BSD operating systems provided that the operating system is capable of running:

- **OSSEC HIDS version 0.9-3 and later**
- **Apache HTTP Server** The Apache HTTP Server Project is a collaborative software development effort aimed at creating a robust, commercial-grade, feature-full, and freely available source code implementation of an HTTP (Web) server. More information about the Apache HTTP Server Project can be found at the project's Web site (www.apache.org).

NOTE

At the time of this writing, there were no capabilities in the WUI to handle individual user accounts. This is currently a roadmap item for future development. However, because we are using the Apache HTTP server, we can leverage *.htaccess* files allowing us to specify user access to the directory where the WUI is installed. This is covered in more detail later in this chapter.

- **PHP 4.1 and later** PHP is a widely used, general-purpose scripting language that is especially suited for Web development and can be embedded into HTML. More information about PHP can be found at the project's Web site (www.php.net).

WARNING

When PHP is installed on your server, you must ensure that you do not disable POSIX support. POSIX support is enabled by default on most installations. More information about POSIX support can be found at www.php.net/posix.

Downloading the WUI

Now that you know about the dependencies the WUI requires, we can download the WUI installation package from the OSSEC HIDS Web site. You can always find the latest released, beta, and alpha versions of the WUI software at www.ossec.net/files/ui/.

The easiest way to obtain the WUI installation file is to use the *wget* utility from your Linux, Unix, or BSD system that houses your OSSEC HIDS server. We must download the WUI package, the checksum file, and the signature file using the following commands:

```
$ wget http://www.ossec.net/files/ui/ossec-wui-0.3.tar.gz
$ wget http://www.ossec.net/files/ui/ossec-wui-0.3-checksum.txt
$ wget http://www.ossec.net/files/ui/ossec-wui-0.3.tar.gz.sig
```

Now that we have the files, we must verify that the files have not been altered or corrupted during the download by running the following commands:

```
$ md5 ossec-wui-0.3.tar.gz
MD5 (ossec-wui-0.3.tar.gz) = 45abaaf0e460ad38caa6932b69511cd7

$ sha1 ossec-wui-0.3.tar.gz
SHA1 (ossec-wui-0.3.tar.gz) = 70198da3932f597d3b5632dc4d87637922bd8ad8

$ gpg --verify ossec-wui-0.3.tar.gz.sig ossec-wui-0.3.tar.gz
gpg: Signature made Tue Mar 27 23:51:15 2007 ADT using RSA key ID 6B30327E
gpg: Good signature from "Daniel B. Cid (Ossec development) <dcid@ossec.net>"
Primary key fingerprint: 86C6 D33B C52E 19BF DDAE 57EB 4E57 14E2 6B30 327E
```

NOTE

At the time of this writing, the WUI version 0.3 was still an alpha release; therefore, the preceding fingerprint and hash information might not reflect the current available release.

If the file fails the preceding integrity checks, it is recommended that you attempt to re-download the file to your current system or download it to another system. If the problem persists, please contact the OSSEC development team.

TIP

The MD5 specification, RFC 1321, is available at www.ietf.org/rfc/rfc1321.txt, and the SHA-1 specification, RFC 3174, is available at www.faqs.org/rfcs/rfc3174.html.

Tools & Traps...

Using *md5deep* on Windows

If you prefer to verify the integrity of your downloaded archive on a Windows system, or on a system other than a standard Linux/Unix distribution, consider using *md5deep*. Jesse Kronblum wrote the *md5deep* utility while working as a Special Agent with the United States Air Force Office of Special Investigations (AFOSI). Kronblum still maintains the utility and, since its inception, it has become one of the most commonly used tools by incident handlers and forensic investigators. From the *md5deep* Web page:

md5deep is a cross-platform set of programs to compute MD5, SHA-1, SHA-256, Tiger, or Whirlpool message digests on an arbitrary number of files. md5deep is similar to the md5sum program found in the GNU Coreutils package, but has the following additional features:

- *Recursive operation—md5deep is able to recursive examine an entire directory tree. That is, compute the MD5 for every file in a directory and for every file in every subdirectory.*
- *Comparison mode—md5deep can accept a list of known hashes and compare them to a set of input files. The program can display either those input files that match the list of known hashes or those that do not match. Hashes sets can be drawn from Encase, the National Software Reference Library, iLook Investigator, Hashkeeper, md5sum, BSD md5, and other generic hash generating programs. Users are welcome to add functionality to read other formats too!*
- *Time estimation—md5deep can produce a time estimate when it's processing very large files.*
- *Piecewise hashing—Hash input files in arbitrary sized blocks.*
- *File type mode—md5deep can process only files of a certain type, such as regular files, block devices, etc.*

The *md5sum* utility is supported on the following operating systems:

- Microsoft Windows (Vista, XP, 2003, 2000, NT)
- Cygwin
- Linux
- FreeBSD, OpenBSD, and NetBSD
- Mac OS X

- OpenSolaris
- HP/UX

The *md5deep* utility is available as a free download from the project page located at http://md5deep.sourceforge.net/and, at the time of this writing, the latest stable version was 2.0.1.

Installing and Configuring the WUI

With the WUI installation package downloaded and verified, we can now look to the installation and configuration of the WUI. The first thing we must do is extract the downloaded WUI package to a directory. To extract the archive to the current directory we can use the *tar* command:

```
$ tar -zxvf ossec-wui-0.3.tar.gz
```

Tools & Traps...

Extracting the OSSEC HIDS Archive

The WUI installation archive contains the entire file set required to install, configure, and run the WUI. When you extract the archive using the *tar* utility, a full list of extracted files is displayed:

```
$ tar -zxvf ossec-wui-0.3.tar.gz
ossec-wui
ossec-wui/css
ossec-wui/css/images
ossec-wui/css/images/arrow.gif
ossec-wui/css/images/favicon.ico
ossec-wui/css/images/hr_tag_sep.gif
ossec-wui/css/images/hr_title_sep.gif
ossec-wui/css/images/pagebg.gif
ossec-wui/css/cal.css
ossec-wui/css/css.css
```

Continued

```
ossec-wui/img
ossec-wui/img/191×81.jpg
ossec-wui/img/background.png
ossec-wui/img/calendar.gif
ossec-wui/img/donate.gif
ossec-wui/img/ossecLogo.png
ossec-wui/CONTRIB
ossec-wui/LICENSE
ossec-wui/README
ossec-wui/README.search
ossec-wui/index.php
ossec-wui/ossec_conf.php
ossec-wui/setup.sh
ossec-wui/js
ossec-wui/js/calendar-en.js
ossec-wui/js/calendar-setup.js
ossec-wui/js/calendar.js
ossec-wui/js/hide.js
ossec-wui/lib
ossec-wui/lib/os_lib_agent.php
ossec-wui/lib/os_lib_alerts.php
ossec-wui/lib/os_lib_firewall.php
ossec-wui/lib/os_lib_handle.php
ossec-wui/lib/os_lib_mapping.php
ossec-wui/lib/os_lib_stats.php
ossec-wui/lib/os_lib_syscheck.php
ossec-wui/lib/os_lib_util.php
ossec-wui/lib/ossec_categories.php
ossec-wui/lib/ossec_formats.php
ossec-wui/site
ossec-wui/site/footer.html
ossec-wui/site/header.html
ossec-wui/site/help.php
ossec-wui/site/main.php
ossec-wui/site/search-misc.php
ossec-wui/site/search.php
```

```
ossec-wui/site/searchfw.php
ossec-wui/site/stats.php
ossec-wui/site/syscheck.php
ossec-wui/site/user_mapping.php
```

The WUI archive has several folders that contain specialized files for operation. The *css* directory contains all the cascading style sheets (CSS) used to give the WUI its look and design. The *img* directory contains all the images used within the interface. The *js* directory contains the JavaScript code used within the interface. The *lib* directory contains all the code used by the various pages within the WUI because some pages reuse the same functions.

Next, we must move the WUI files to a directory your Web server can access:

```
$ sudo su -
# mv ossec-wui* /var/www/
```

NOTE

At the Linux, Unix, and BSD command-line interface (CLI) prompt, a standard user account is denoted by the *$* character, and the root (administrator) user account is denoted by the # character.

This command moves the ossec-wui directory from the current location to the /var/www/ directory, which is the root Web directory on the server in this example.

NOTE

Depending on the rights of your user account, you might have to use the *sudo* command to temporarily grant your account root-level privileges to copy to your system's Web directory. Alternately, you can log in as the root user or use *sudo su* - to switch to the root user account.

We must now change into the ossec-wui directory and execute the setup using the following commands:

```
# cd /var/www/ossec-wui/
# ./setup.sh
```

```
Setting up ossec ui...
Username: Joe
New password:
Re-type new password:
Adding password for user Joe
Setup completed successfully.
```

The installation prompts for a username to associate with the WUI installation. You are also prompted to provide and confirm a password.

NOTE

The user is added to the default *.htaccess* file located in the *ossec-wui* directory. The *.htaccess* file is discussed in more detail later in this chapter.

NOTE

The password does not appear when you type.

For the WUI to function properly, we must add your Web server user to the *ossec* group. The Web server user is typically *apache*, *www*, *www-data*, or *nobody* depending on your operating system and how you installed the Apache HTTP Server. To add the Web server user, use the *usermod* command as follows:

```
# usermod -G ossec www
```

If you prefer to add the user to the group manually, locate the *ossec* group in your */etc/group* file and change it from:

```
ossec:x:1001:
```

to:

```
ossec:x:1001:www
```

NOTE

You specify the Web server user in the etc/group file based on your operating system.

For our WUI installation to run statistics and generate reports properly, we must adjust the permissions on the */tmp* directory. The */tmp* directory is used store temporary files during the normal operation of the WUI. To change the permissions, you must do the following:

```
# chmod 770 tmp/
# chgrp www tmp/
```

Finally, we must restart the Apache HTTP server for our changes to take effect. There are several ways to restart Apache, but you should be able to restart it with one of the following commands:

```
# /etc/init.d/httpd restart
```

or:

```
# service httpd restart
```

or:

```
# apachectl restart
```

After the Apache HTTP server restarts, you should be able to access the WUI from your browser by entering the IP address of your OSSEC HIDS server and the path to the ossec-wui directory in the address bar. For example, if the IP address of our OSSEC HIDS server is *192.168.200.150* and the WUI was installed in the *ossec-wui* directory, we can input the following into our browser address bar: http://192.168.200.150/ossec-wui/

Advanced Installation Topics

The previous steps detail how to configure the WUI in the most basic and commonly implemented form. There are situations where you might want to spend more time securing and optimizing your WUI installation by configuring multi-user access, enabling SSL, and optimizing PHP.

Using *.htaccess* for Multi-User Access

To add more user accounts to your WUI console, you can use the *.htaccess* file. Included with the WUI is a modified copy of the *.htaccess* and *.htpasswd* files. The *.htaccess* file contains the basic user configuration settings and some protection to prevent malicious users from accessing your configuration files and any scripts you might have created. The stock *.htaccess* file that comes with the WUI looks like this:

```
# cat .htaccess
AuthUserFile /var/www/ossec-wui/.htpasswd
AuthName "Restricted Access"
Require valid-user
AuthType Basic
<Files *.sh>
```

```
deny from all
</Files>
<Files ossec_conf.php>
deny from all
</Files>
<Files .*>
deny from all
</Files>
```

The *AuthUserFile* directive is used to declare where the associated *.htpasswd* file is located. The stock configuration points to the password file that is in the *ossec-wui* directory, but you can move it to wherever you'd like. The *AuthName* directive can be changed to whatever suits your needs. The *Require valid-user* and *AuthTypeBasic* directives should not be modified for authentication to work properly.

To prevent the download of key files, the OSSEC HIDS team has prevented the download of any custom shell scripts you might have created (*.sh), the download of your WUI configuration file (*ossec_conf.php*), and hidden files (.*). You can add more protection as you see fit. Please use the following guide as a reference for modifying the *.htaccess* file: http://httpd.apache.org/docs/2.2/howto/htaccess.html.

Tools & Traps...

Modifying Your Apache Configuration

Sometimes, configuring your *.htaccess* file isn't enough to enable the functionality of the file. If this is the first time you are configuring the Apache HTTP server, you must make some modifications to the Apache configuration file.

The first thing we must do is identify which configuration file your Apache HTTP server is using. The fastest way to determine the configuration file is to check the *DistrosDefaultLayout* page at the Apache.org Wiki. This page explains where each distribution configuration file resides. This page is located at *http://wiki.apache.org/httpd/DistrosDefaultLayout*.

When you know which configuration file to modify, you must open and add some information to it. For the purpose of this example, we will assume that */etc/apache2/apache2.conf* is the name of your Apache configuration file.

With the apache2.conf file open, browse through the configuration file until you see the first *<Directory>* declaration. Under the last *</Directory>* closing tag, add:

```
<Directory "/var/www/ossec-wui">
  AllowOverride AuthConfig Limit
  Order allow,deny
  Allow from all
</Directory>
```

The *<Directory "/var/www/ossec-wui">* directive tells the Apache HTTP server the location of the Web directory for configuration. The directive is closed with the *</Directory>* tag, and all options within the tags are associated with that Web directory.

The *Order* directive is configured so that we will allow explicitly allowed clients and deny everyone else. Any clients matched by both allow and deny are denied.

The *Allow* directive allows access from any IP address. You can restrict the *Allow* directive by specifying IP ranges or hostnames.

Save the configuration file and restart the Apache HTTP server using the restart command for your particular distribution. The following list provides you with the most common commands for restarting the Apache HTTP server:

Apache 2.2 default layout (when building from source):

```
/usr/local/apache2/bin/apachectl restart
```

Debian, Ubuntu with Apache2:

```
/etc/init.d/apache2 restart
```

Fedora Core, CentOS, Red Hat Enterprise Linux:

```
/sbin/service httpd
```

Mac OS X:

```
apachectl restart
```

FreeBSD 6.1 with Apache 2.2:

```
/usr/local/etc/rc.d/apache22.sh restart
```

If your distribution does not have one of the commands listed here, check the *DistrosDefaultLayout* page at http://wiki.apache.org/httpd/DistrosDefaultLayout.

If you look at the *.htpasswd* file located in the *ossec-wui* directory, you will notice that the user we created during the installation is listed:

```
# cat .htpasswd
Joe:LHY.bIPCr1pP6
```

NOTE

The password is stored in an md5 encrypted hash.

To add more users, use the *htpasswd* command as follows:

```
# htpasswd -m /var/www/ossec-wui/.htpasswd Bob
New password:
Re-type new password:
Adding password for user Bob
```

NOTE

The password does not appear when you type.

You can repeat the *htpasswd* command as many times as you want to add more users to the system. To verify which users have already been added, you can check the *.htpasswd* file:

```
# cat .htpasswd
Joe:LHY.bIPCr1pP6
Andrew:$apr1$1L1Zs/..$YvHgKSV74eh.5DZSxKigf/
Bob:$apr1$SrCT2...$KOi7LiCNmrWxmc2DfRfqs.
```

Enabling SSL Access

To secure your WUI, you can configure your Apache HTTP server to encrypt your WUI session. These instructions are primarily intended to work for Apache 2.x on Ubuntu 7.10. Most Debian-based operating systems will also work with these instructions, but for others you may need to consult the distribution specific forums or documentation. Some operating system distributions may have a different layout for the Apache configuration files (e.g., */etc/httpd* instead of */etc/apache2*).

Unfortunately, the *apache2-ssl-certificate* utility found in previous Ubuntu versions is missing in release 7.10. We can, however, download and install it using the following commands:

NOTE

All steps need to be performed with the root user unless otherwise stated.

```
# wget http://launchpadlibrarian.net/7477840/apache2-ssl.tar.gz
# tar -xvzf apache2-ssl.tar.gz
# cp ./ssleay.cnf /usr/share/apache2/
# cp ./apache2-ssl-certificate /usr/sbin/
```

Create your self-signed certificate by running the apache2-ssl-certificate as follows:

TIP

The values chosen here reflect those of the OSSEC HIDS VMware image. You may provide your own values for Country, State, Locality, Org, Org Unit, and email address. The *server name* field should be the fully qualified domain name you will use in your URL to access the site.

```
# /usr/sbin/apache2-ssl-certificate -days 365
creating selfsigned certificate
replace it with one signed by a certification authority (CA)
enter your ServerName at the Common Name prompt
If you want your certificate to expire after x days call this program
with -days x
Generating a 1024 bit RSA private key
.++++++
..........................................++++++
writing new private key to '/etc/apache2/ssl/apache.pem'
```

You will be asked to enter information that will be incorporated into your certificate request. What you are about to enter is called a *distinguished name*, or a DN. There are quite a few fields, but you can leave some blank. For some fields there will be a default value. If you enter a period (.) and press **Enter**, the field will be left blank.

```
Country Name (2 letter code) [GB]:CA
State or Province Name (full name) [Some-State]:NB
Locality Name (eg, city) []:Moncton
Organization Name (eg, company; recommended) []:OSSEC
Organizational Unit Name (eg, section) []:OSSEC HIDS Book
server name (eg. ssl.domain.tld; required!!!) []:ossec-local.ossec.net
Email Address []:marty@localhost
```

Once complete, enable the SSL protocol for your Apache HTTP server:

```
# a2enmod ssl
```

Copy and link to the configuration for the SSL site:

```
# cp /etc/apache2/sites-available/default /etc/apache2/sites-available/ssl
# ln -s /etc/apache2/sites-available/ssl /etc/apache2/sites-enabled/ssl
```

Edit the default site, */etc/apache2/sites-available/default*, and change the first two lines of your configuration to use port 80. This can be done by adding *:80* to the virtual host directives:

```
# vi /etc/apache2/sites-available/default
NameVirtualHost *:80
<VirtualHost *:80>
```

Do the same for the SSL site using port *443*, but also add the directives for enabling SSL on the site:

```
# vi /etc/apache2/sites-available/ssl

NameVirtualHost *:443
<VirtualHost *:443>
  SSLEngine On
  SSLCertificateFile /etc/apache2/ssl/apache.pem
```

Ensure that your Apache HTTP server will listen to TCP port 443 by examining */etc/apache2/ports.conf*. You should see the following lines within the file:

```
# less /etc/apache2/ports.conf
Listen 80
<IfModule mod_ssl.c>
  Listen 443
</IfModule>
```

Before you can connect to your WUI using HTTPS, you must restart the Apache HTTP server using:

```
# /etc/init.d/apache2 restart
```

You should now be able to connect to your WUI using the **https** protocol, followed by the address of your WUI. For example, if you previously used *http://192.168.200.150/ossec-wui/* to access your WUI, it would now be located at *https://192.168.200.150/ossec-wui/*.

Optimizing PHP for Large OSSEC Deployments

If you have a large OSSEC HIDS installation, you might want to re-configure PHP to support longer lasting scripts and higher memory utilization. The following entries in your php.ini can be increased:

```
max_execution_time = 180
```

The *max_execution_time* sets the maximum time, in seconds, a script is allowed to run before the parser terminates it. Setting this time helps prevent poorly written scripts from tying up the server. The default time is 30 seconds. For more information on this variable, see the www.php.net/info Web site.

```
max_input_time = 180
```

The *max_input_time* sets the maximum time, in seconds, a script is allowed to parse input data, such as POST, GET, and file uploads. For more information on this variable, see the www.php.net/info Web site.

```
memory_limit = 30M
```

The *memory_limit* sets the maximum amount of memory, in bytes, a script is allowed to allocate. This limit helps prevent poorly written scripts from using all available memory on a server. To specify no memory limit, set the *memory_limit* variable to –1. For more information on this variable, see the www.php.net/ini.core Web site.

NOTE

The PHP configuration remains unchanged until the Web server is restarted.

Describing the WUI Components

The WUI has several tabs, each of which serves a specific purpose.

- **Main** The main dashboard page of the WUI.
- **Search** Allows you to search through collected OSSEC HIDS alerts.
- **Integrity Checking** Allows you to search through collected OSSEC HIDS syscheck alerts.
- **Stats** Displays statistics about the collected OSSEC HIDS alerts.
- **About** Displays license and copyright information about the OSSEC HIDS and the WUI.

Throughout this section, we will discuss each component in detail to provide you with a look into the importance of each tab within the WUI.

Main

The Main tab is a dashboard for everything that is being reported to your OSSEC HIDS server. It allows anyone with valid WUI credentials to see what is happening in your OSSEC HIDS deployment. The Main tab details three sections, each with a specific purpose:

- Available agents
- Latest modified files
- Latest events

Available Agents

All configured agents are shown in the Available agents section on the Main tab. The agent name and associated IP address is displayed for each agent. If the agent is inactive or unable to connect to the OSSEC HIDS server, the word *Inactive* is displayed beside the agent name.

Clicking on the agent shows you more detailed information about the host where the OSSEC HIDS agent is installed. Figure 7.1 shows the detailed information associated with each agent.

Figure 7.1 Available Agents

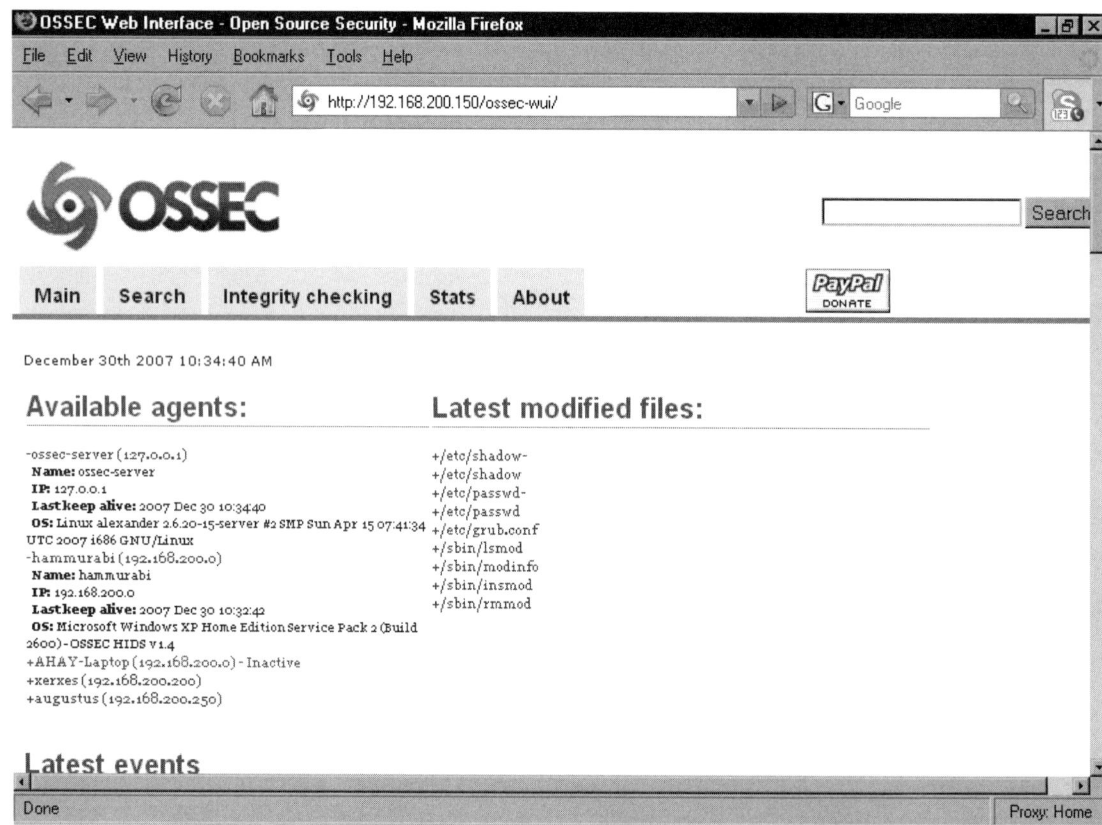

Table 7.1 describes the possible values that might be seen in the agent details.

Table 7.1 Available Agents

Value	Description
Name:	The name of your OSSEC HIDS agent. The agent name is defined when configuring the agents on your OSSEC HIDS server. For example: Name: hammurabi See Chapter 2 for more information on configuring OSSEC HIDS agents.
IP:	The IP address associated with your OSSEC HIDS agent. This might not be the physical IP address of your OSSEC HIDS agent, but it is what you entered when you configured your agent on the OSSEC HIDS server. For example: IP: 192.168.200.250 For example: IP: 192.168.200.0 See Chapter 2 for more information on configuring OSSEC HIDS agents.
Last keep alive:	The date and time stamp of the last keep-alive packet received from your OSSEC HIDS agent. For example: Last keep alive: 2007 Nov 21 23:39:29
OS:	The operating system information and OSSEC HIDS agent version. For example: OS: Microsoft Windows XP Home Edition Service Pack 2 (Build 2600)—OSSEC HIDS v1.4 For example: OS: Darwin AHAY-Laptop.local 9.1.0 Darwin Kernel Version 9.1.0: Wed Oct 31 17:46:22 PDT 2007; root:xnu-1228.0.2~1/RELEASE_I386 i386—OSSEC HIDS v1.4 For example: OS: Linux xerxes 2.6.20-15-server #2 SMP Sun Apr 15 07:41:34 UTC 2007 i686—OSSEC HIDS v1.4

Latest Modified Files

The Latest modified files section shows a complete listing of the latest modified files for all agents. Each modified file is listed under the date the syscheck service reported the change to the OSSEC HIDS server. As seen in Figure 7.2, when you click on the modified file, the details for the file are displayed.

NOTE

The number of modified files depends on the number of agents you have configured. This is determined by the *agent_count + 4* equation, where *agent_count* is the number of agents you have configured.

If you have 10 agents, it will only show the last 14 modified files. Similarly, if you only have one agent, it will only show the last five modified files. The *agent_count + 4* equation is in place to ensure that the UI remains organized as additional agents are configured.

Figure 7.2 Latest Modified Files

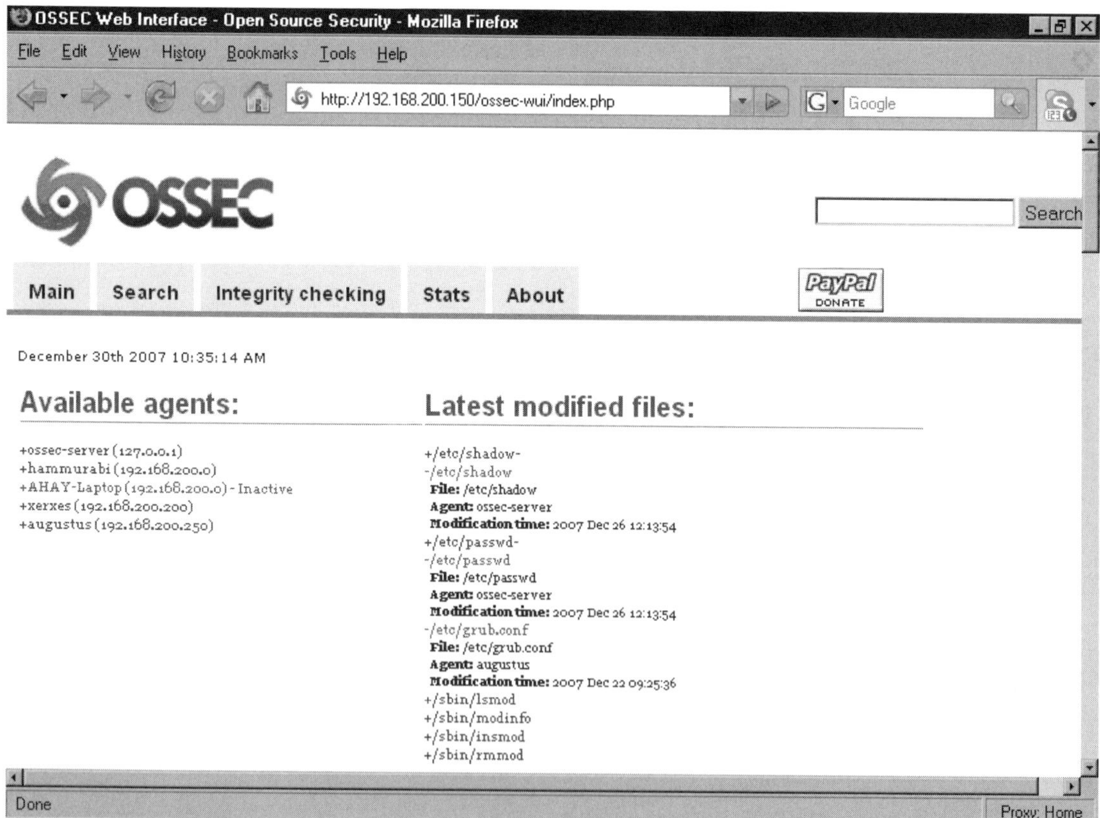

Table 7.2 describes the possible values that may be seen within the modified files details.

Table 7.2 Latest Modified Files

Value	Description
File:	The name of the modified file. If your OSSEC HIDS agent is installed on a Linux, Unix, or BSD operating system, you will see the full path and filename for the modified file. If your OSSEC HIDS agent is installed on a Windows operating system, you might see a mixture of Windows registry keys and filenames, depending on the reported modifications. For example: File: C:\WINDOWS/system32/inetsrv/MetaBase.bin For example: File: HKEY_LOCAL_MACHINE\Software\Microsoft\Windows NT\CurrentVersion\WPAEvents For example: File: /usr/bin/syslinux
Agent:	The OSSEC HIDS agent that reported the syscheck change. If the modification is reported for a specific file, only the agent name is displayed. If a Windows registry modification is reported by the syscheck service, the words *Windows registry* appear beside the agent name. For example: Agent: hammurabi Windows registry For example: Agent: augustus The agent name is defined when configuring your agents on the OSSEC HIDS server. See Chapter 2 for more information on configuring OSSEC HIDS agents.
Modification time:	The date and time stamp that the OSSEC HIDS agent reported the modification. For example: Modification time: 2007 Nov 25 07:00:59

Latest Events

The Latest events section shows the latest events reported by your OSSEC HIDS agents to your OSSEC HIDS server. Each event record contains the information listed in Table 7.3.

Table 7.3 Latest Events

Value	Description
Date	The date and time stamp of the event recorded by your OSSEC HIDS agent. The date and time stamp are displayed at the beginning of every event. For example: 2007 Dec 09 09:24:26
Rule Id:	The associated OSSEC HIDS rule that generated the event. Each Rule Id has a link to information about the rule. Clicking on the Rule Id number will bring you to the rule specific information page on the OSSEC Web site. For example: Rule Id: 20101
Level:	The log level for the OSSEC HIDS event. The level values range from 0 to 12. For example: level: 6
Location:	The OSSEC HIDS agent that reported the event and the monitored file where the event was logged, or the associated process involved in the event. For example: Location: (xerxes) 192.168.200.200->ossec For example: Location: (augustus) 192.168.200.250->/var/log/snort/alert
Description	A summary description of the event reported. For example: Login session closed. For example: Unknown problem somewhere in the system. For example: IDS event.

Figure 7.3 shows examples of the different messages you might see in the Latest events table.

Figure 7.3 Latest Events

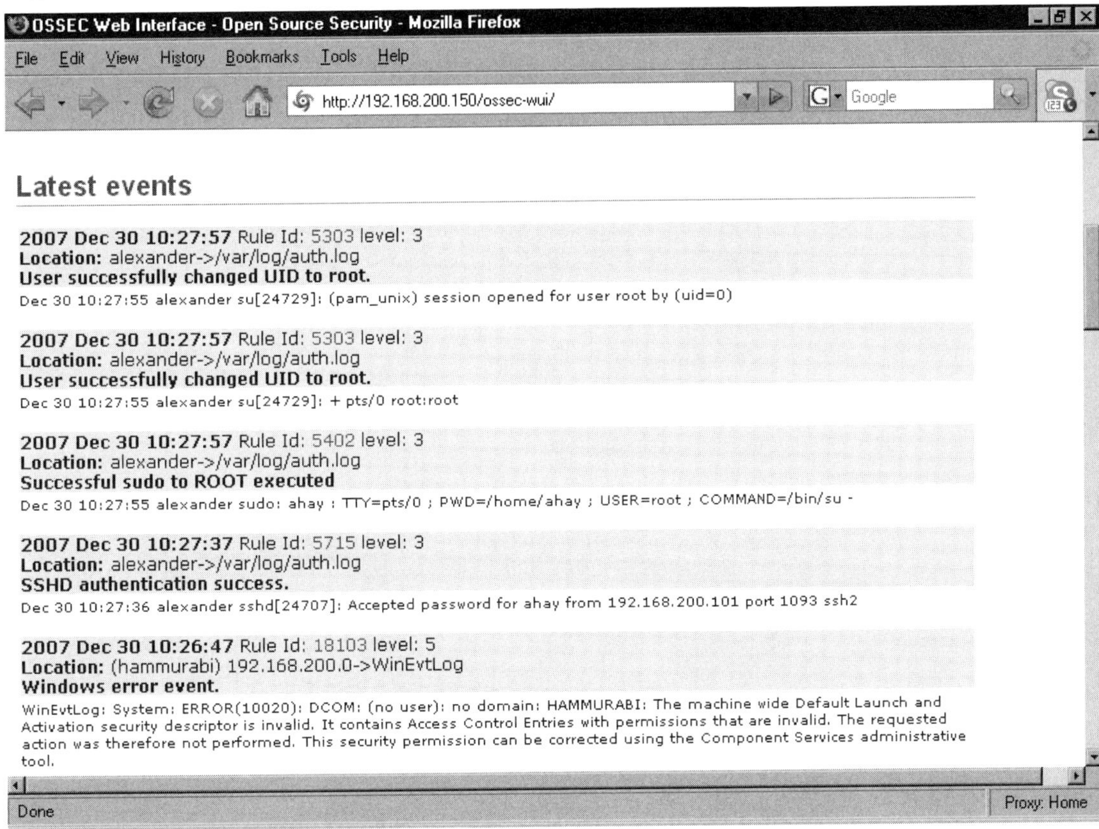

Search

The WUI provides a powerful search engine, which allows you to filter on specific criteria and watch the results of your search in real time or perform historical analysis on stored event data.

The Search tab is divided into three sections, each with a specific purpose:

- Alert search options
- Results
- Alert list (appears after a search is executed)

Alert Search Options

The Alert search options section of the Search tab allows you to specify your search criteria for the alerts you want to view. This powerful search engine allows you to specify a date and time range for the archived alerts you require. If you want to view your alerts in real time, you can select **Real time monitoring** and select your filter criteria accordingly. Table 7.4 explains the various Alert search options that you can use in your queries.

Table 7.4 Alert Search Options

Value	Description
Date Range	The 'From:' and 'To:' date/time ranges available for your queries. The Date selector icon provides a calendar interface to specify the date and time you want to set as your filter. Figure 7.4 shows the Date selector interface. Date and time can also be entered manually in the format: [YYYY-MM-DD HH:MM] For example: 2007-12-09 07:39
Real time monitoring	View alerts in real time instead of performing archived alert searches for specific date and time ranges. All available filters can still be applied to assist in your monitoring of alerts.
Minimum level:	Shows the minimum alert levels to filter on. The available options are All, which displays all alerts, and a range of 15 down to 2. Selecting an alert level will show you all alerts that are of that alert level or higher. For example, if an alert level of 9 is selected, all alerts with a level from 9–15 are displayed.
Pattern:	Specify a pattern to match to in the generated alert. Simple pattern matching and Perl regular expressions can be used.
Srcip:	Filter on a specific source IP in the generated alert. Simple pattern matching, not using regular expressions, can be performed. For example, if you want to match a network, you can use *192.168.2.* to represent the entire 192.168.2.0/24 class C network range, or *172.16.* to represent the entire 172.16.0.0/16 class B network range.
Location:	Filter on a specific OSSEC HIDS agent. For example: alexander The agent name is defined when configuring your agents on your OSSEC HIDS server. See Chapter 2 for more information on configuring OSSEC HIDS agents.

Continued

Table 7.4 Continued. Alert Search Options

Value	Description
Max Alerts:	Specify the maximum number of alerts records to display in your search. The default value is 1000.
Category:	Specify a category to use as a filter. Available categories to include in your alert search are: All categories Reconnaissance ■ Connection Attempt ■ Web scan ■ Generic scan Authentication Control ■ Success ■ Failure ■ Invalid ■ Login denied ■ Multiple failures ■ User account added/changed/removed Attack/Misuse ■ Worm (Non targeted attack) ■ Exploit pattern ■ Invalid access ■ Spam ■ Multiple Spams ■ SQL Injection ■ Generic Attack ■ Rootkit detection ■ Virus detected

Continued

Table 7.4 Continued. Alert Search Options

Value	Description
	Access Control ■ Access denied ■ Access allowed ■ Access to Inexistent resource ■ Firewall Drop ■ Multiple firewall drops ■ Client mis-configuration ■ Client error Network Control ■ New host detected ■ Possible ARP spoof System Monitor ■ Service start ■ Service availability in Risk ■ System error ■ Shutdown ■ Logs removed ■ Invalid request ■ Promiscuous mode detected ■ Policy changed ■ Configuration changed ■ Integrity Checking ■ Low disk space ■ Time changed Policy Violation ■ Login time ■ Login day

Continued

Table 7.4 Continued. Alert Search Options

Value	Description
Log formats:	Specify a log format to use as a filter. Available log formats to include in your alert search are: All log formats Syslog (all) ■ Shd ■ Arpwatch ■ Ftpd ■ Pam Unix ■ Proftpd ■ Pure-ftpd ■ Vsftpd ■ Sendmail ■ Postfix ■ Imapd ■ Vpopmail ■ Spamd ■ Horde IMP ■ Smbd ■ NFS ■ Xinetd ■ Kernel ■ Su ■ Cron ■ Sudo ■ PPTP ■ Named ■ Firewall ■ Pix ■ Netscreen

Continued

Table 7.4 Continued. Alert Search Options

Value	Description
	Microsoft (all) ■ Windows ■ MS Ftp ■ Exchange Web logs (all) Squid (all) Security devices (all) ■ Cisco VPN ■ Symantec AV ■ NIDS
User:	Specify a user to filter on within your alert search. For example: root
Rule id:	Specify a particular rule ID to filter on within your alert search. For example: 5303

Figure 7.4 Alert Search Options: Date Selector

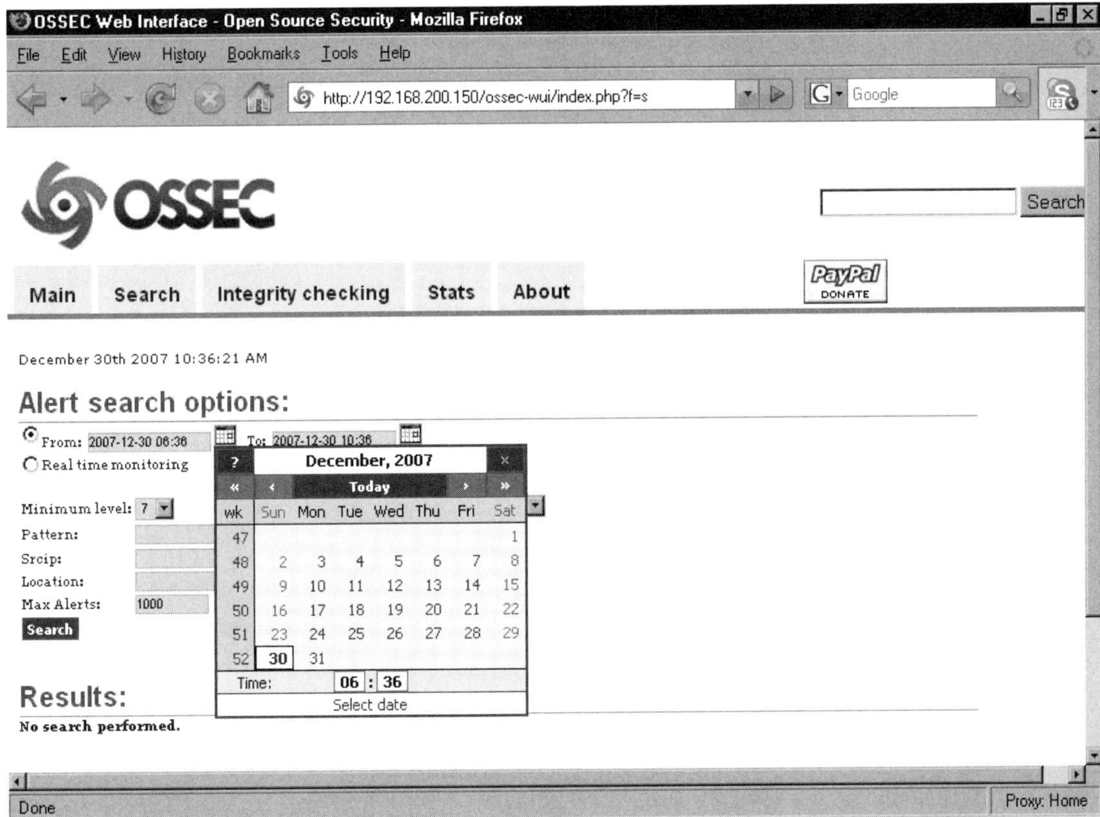

When you have completed configuring your alert search filter criteria, you must click the **Search** button to retrieve the alert records. Figure 7.5 shows the Alert Search Options tab with an example of some prepared filters.

Figure 7.5 Alert Search Options: Example Options

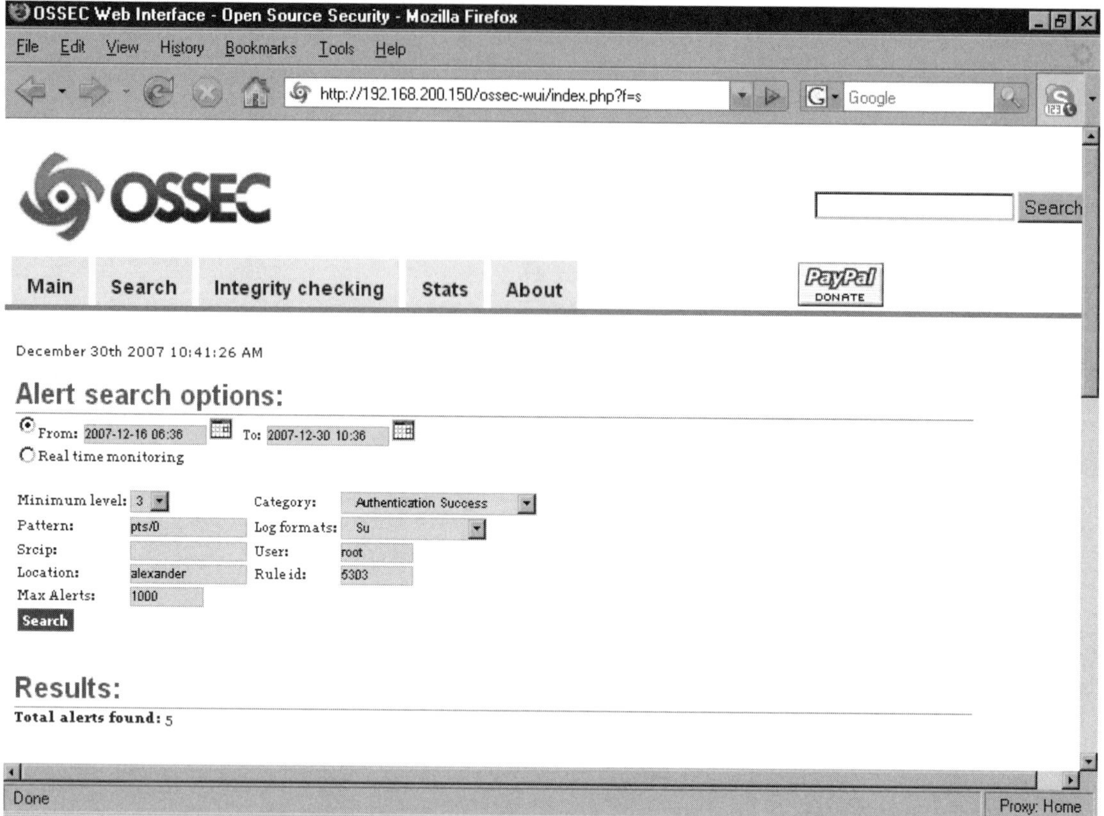

Results

The Results section shows you the results of your alert query based on the filters set in the Alert search options section. At the top of the Results section, you will see the total number of alerts found that match your search criteria.

The information is then displayed in three distinct groupings allowing you to view the breakdown of your results by:

- Severity
- Rules
- Src IP (source IP)

Each breakdown shows you the total number of alerts for each Severity, Rule, and Source IP address. Figure 7.6 shows the results of an example search and the expanded Severity, Rules, and Source IP headings.

Figure 7.6 Results: Severity/Rules/Src IP Breakdown

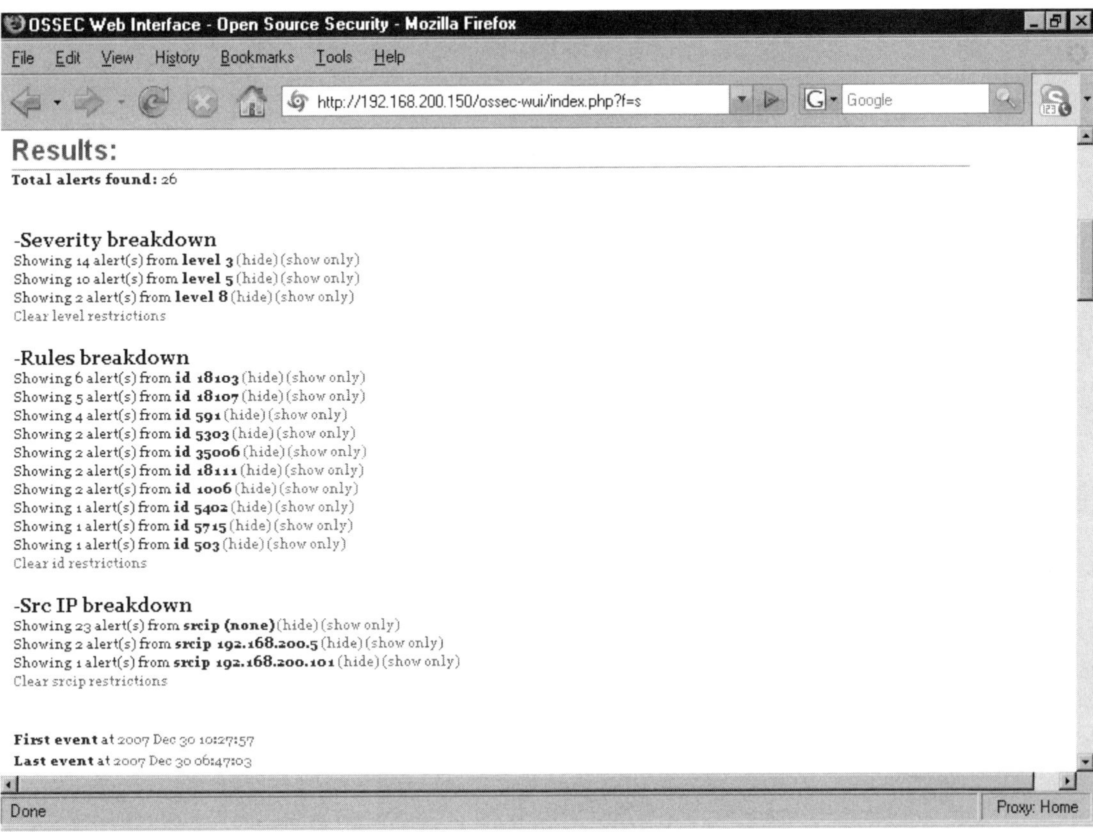

Within each grouping, you have the option to show or hide alerts of the selected type. Clicking the **red link** beside the entry sets the filter. If you want to include other entries in your new filter, you can click the **show** link beside the entry. To hide entries, click the **hide** link beside the entry. To clear your filters, click the **Clear restrictions**link within that group.

NOTE

Each group has a *Clear restrictions* link and each is named accordingly. To clear the restrictions within the Severity breakdown group, click the **Clear level restrictions** link. To clear the restrictions within the Rules breakdown group, click the **Clear id restrictions** link. To clear the restrictions within the Src IP breakdown group, click the **Clear srcip restrictions** link.

At the bottom of the Results section are links to the first and last events seen based on your current alert filters. These two links display the date and time stamp for each event. You are taken to the associated event in the Alert list when you click the link.

NOTE

The first and last event links will greatly assist you when trying to determine the duration of an incident based on the reported alerts.

Alert List

The Alert list displays the results of your search with the filters defined in the Alert search options and Results sections. Each event record contains the information listed in Table 7.5.

Table 7.5 Alert List

Value	Description
Date	The date and time stamp that your OSSEC HIDS agent recorded the event. The date and time stamp are displayed at the beginning of every event. For example: 2007 Dec 09 09:24:26
Rule Id:	The associated OSSEC HIDS rule that generated the event. Each Rule Id has a link to information about the rule. Clicking on the Rule Id number will bring you to the rule specific information page on the OSSEC Web site. For example: Rule Id: 20101
Level:	The log level for the OSSEC HIDS event. The level values range from 0 to 12. For example: level: 6
Location:	The OSSEC HIDS agent that reported the event and the monitored file where the event was logged, or the associated process involved in the event. For example: Location: (xerxes) 192.168.200.200->ossec For example: Location: (augustus) 192.168.200.250->/var/log/snort/alert

Continued

Table 7.5 Continued. Alert List

Value	Description
Description	A summary description of the event reported. For example: Login session closed. For example: Unknown problem somewhere in the system. For example: IDS event.

Figure 7.7 shows examples of the types of messages you might see in the Alert list table.

Figure 7.7 Alert List

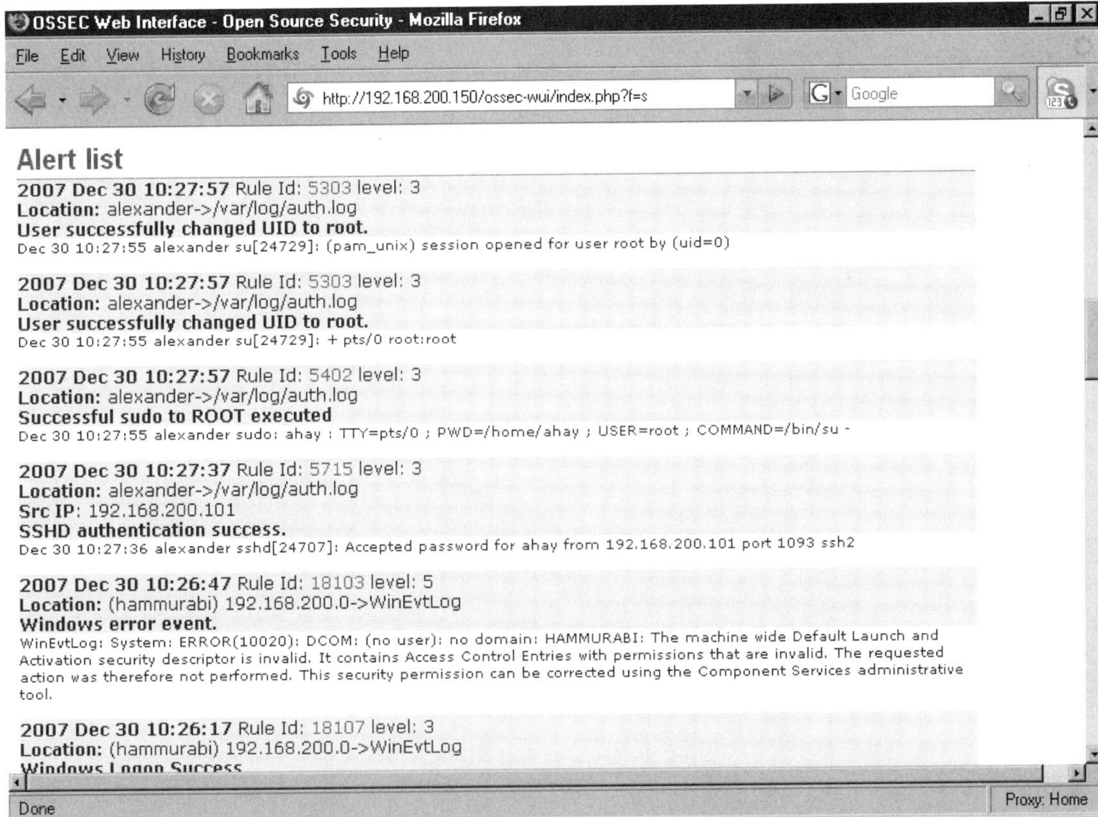

Integrity Checking

The Integrity checking tab provides two very important features of the WUI: a complete listing of the modified files for all agents, and a method for dumping the entire syscheck database for a particular agent.

Latest Modified Files (for All Agents)

The Latest modified files section shows a complete listing of the latest modified files for all agents. Each modified file is listed under the date that the syscheck service reported the change to the OSSEC HIDS server. As seen in Figure 7.8, when you click on the modified file the details for the file are displayed.

Figure 7.8 Latest Modified Files (for All Agents)

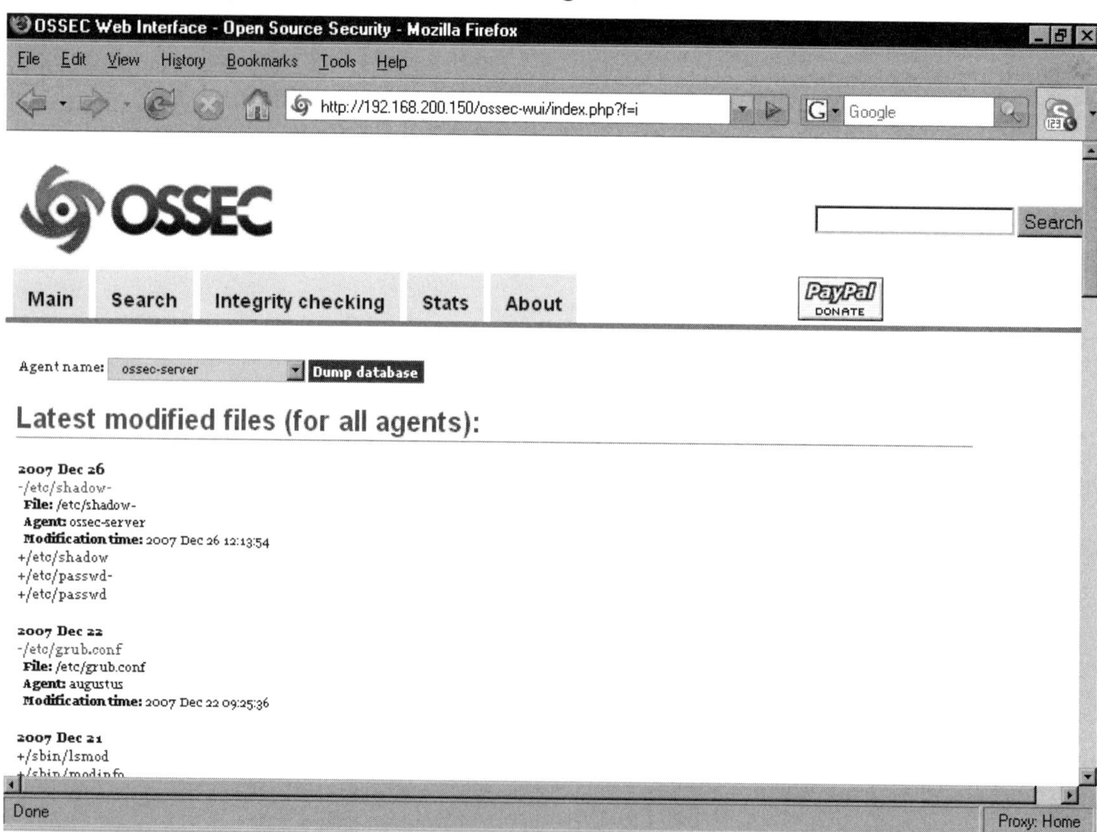

Table 7.6 describes the possible values that may be seen within the modified files details.

Table 7.6 Latest Modified Files (for All Agents)

Value	Description
File:	The name of the modified file. If your OSSEC HIDS agent is installed on a Linux, Unix, or BSD operating system, you will see the full path and filename for the modified file. If your OSSEC HIDS agent is installed on a Windows operating system, you might see a mixture of Windows registry keys and filenames, depending on the reported modifications. For example: File: C:\WINDOWS/system32/inetsrv/MetaBase.bin For example: File: HKEY_LOCAL_MACHINE\Software\Microsoft\Windows NT\CurrentVersion\ WPAEvents For example: File: /usr/bin/syslinux
Agent:	The OSSEC HIDS agent that reported the syscheck change. If the modification is reported for a specific file, only the agent name will be displayed. If a Windows registry modification is reported by the syscheck service, the words *Windows registry* appear next to the agent name. For example: Agent: hammurabi Windows registry For example: Agent: augustus *The agent name is defined when configuring your agents on your OSSEC HIDS server. See Chapter 2 for more information on configuring OSSEC HIDS agents.*
Modification time:	The date and time stamp that the modification was reported by the OSSEC HIDS agent. For example: Modification time: 2007 Nov 25 07:00:59

Dump Database

The Integrity checking tab allows you to specify a configured agent, as seen in Figure 7.9, and dump the entire contents of the syscheck database for that agent.

Figure 7.9 Dump Database

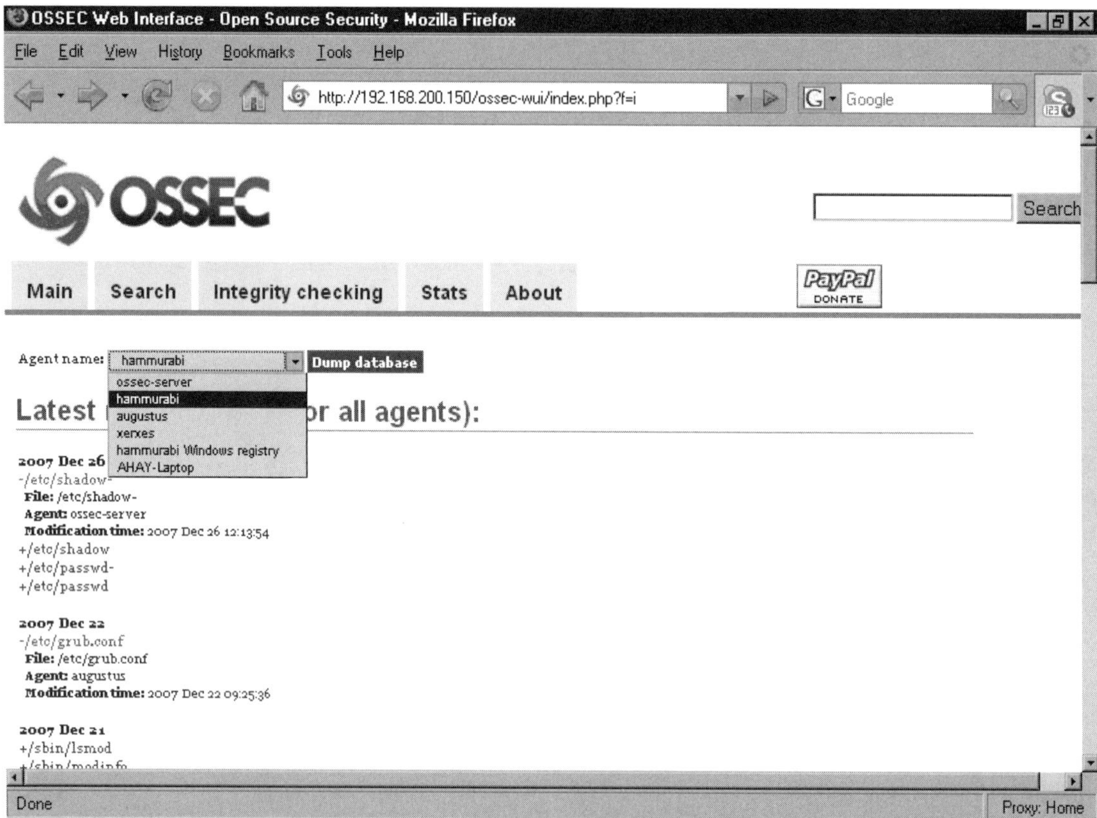

The Dump database function displays the latest modified files for the agent name specified in the Agent name drop-down list. This section, as shown in Figure 7.10, shows you the last five modified files and the date when the files were modified. Clicking any of the files brings you to the entry within the Integrity Checking database table.

Figure 7.10 Latest Modified Files

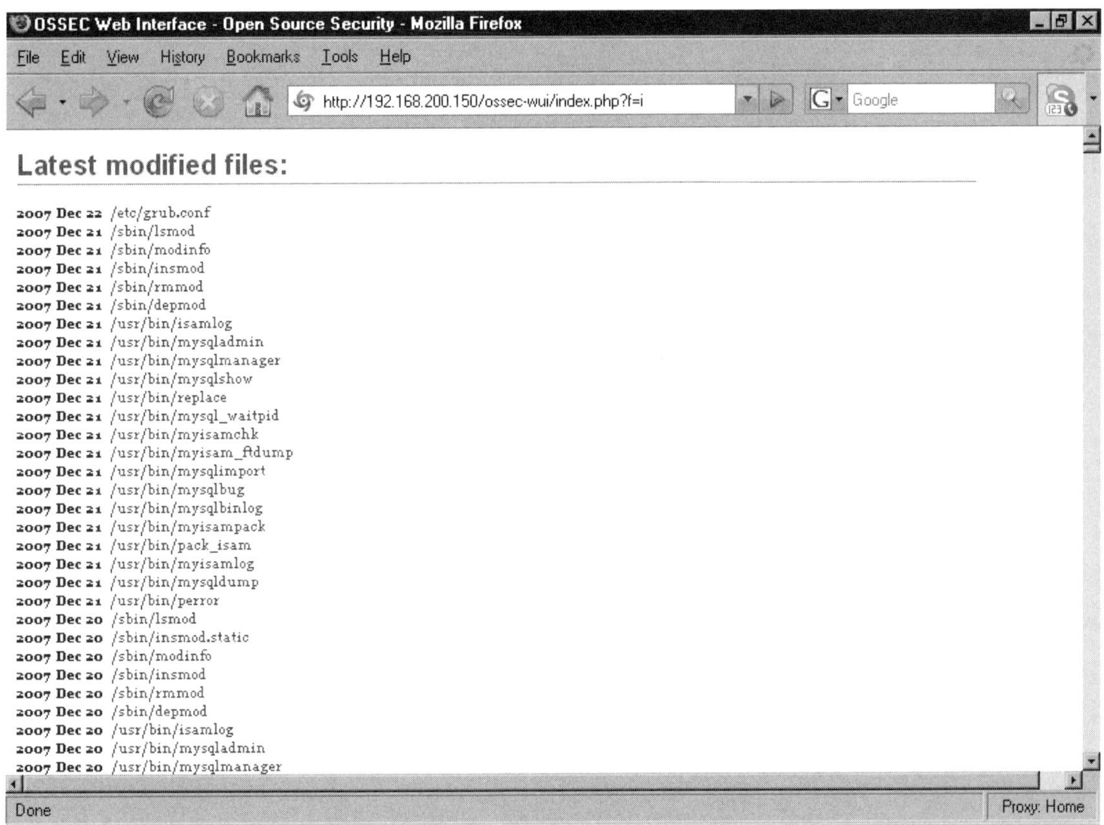

Under the *Latest modified files* section, the *Integrity Checking database* section provides a complete listing of all files or Windows registry keys the syscheck service has reported an integrity change for. Table 7.7 describes the possible values that might appear within the Integrity Checking database table if your agent is installed on a Linux, Unix, or BSD system.

Table 7.7 Integrity Checking Database (Linux/Unix/BSD Agent)

Value	Description
File name	The name of the file monitored by the syscheck process. If the checksum of the file has changed multiple times, the filename text will be red instead of the usual black. For example: /etc/group
Checksum	The md5 and sha1 checksum of the monitored file. If the file checksum has changed multiple times, the checksums are shown with an arrow (->) between them. This indicates the change from the old checksum to the new checksum. See Figure 7.11 for more details. For example: md5 3e478974b8009ac3747c958ee95324d3 sha1 15aa02d9a3bcc49d92e62b11a49e980d12b6e521 -> md5 232b0fce56f755cf8ba5f1f77593ab90 sha1 b8cef03337d35adb70a79c75606110391ae793fd -> md5 32a291da4bb1d3e99daa6e6f7a29de36 sha1 e90c3bcfbf7088961422cd1eee1a587ec0a7b751
Size	The size of the monitored file. If the file size has changed multiple times, it is shown with an arrow (->) indicating the new file size. See Figure 7.11 for more details. For example: 681 -> 705 -> 718

Figure 7.11 shows an example of the results seen within the Integrity Checking database for a Linux, Unix, or BSD agent.

Figure 7.11 Integrity Checking Database (Linux/Unix/BSD Agent)

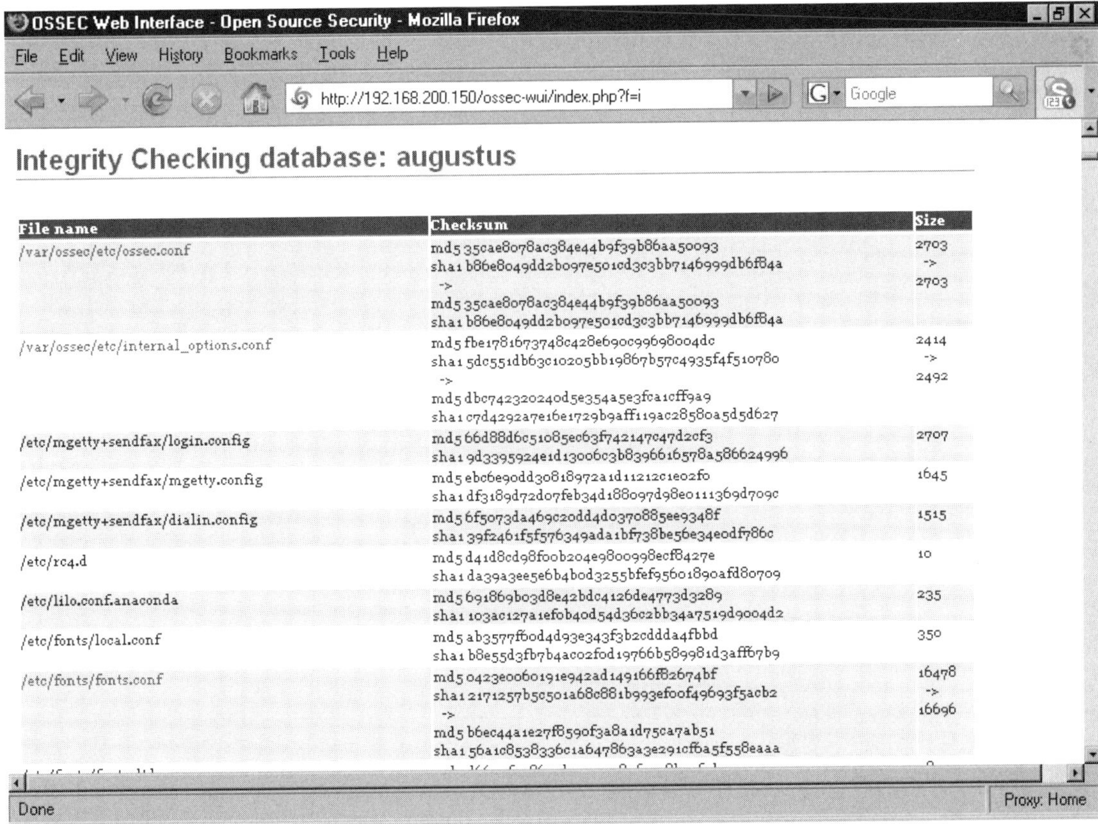

Table 7.8 describes the possible values that might be seen within the *Integrity Checking database* table if your agent is installed on a Windows system and you choose to dump the *Windows registry* database for that agent. As you can see in Figure 7.12, the Windows agent, *hammurabi*, has two entries: *hammurabi* and *hammurabi Windows registry*. This is because there is a separate Integrity Checking database for Windows files and another for Windows registry keys.

NOTE

The *Integrity Checking database* is the same for all operating system types. Only OSSEC HIDS agents on Windows systems will have two *Integrity Checking database* entries for each agent.

When dumping the Windows registry database for your agent, you might notice that the size column no longer appears. This is because the syscheck service is monitoring the Windows registry and not an individual file on the host.

Table 7.8 Integrity Checking Database (Windows Registry)

Value	Description
File name	The name of the Windows registry key monitored by the syscheck process. If the checksum of the registry key has changed multiple times, the file name text will be red instead of the usual black. For example: HKEY_LOCAL_MACHINE\Software\Policies\Adobe\Acrobat Reader\8.0\ FeatureLockdown\cDefaultExecMenuItems
Checksum	The md5 and sha1 checksum of the monitored Windows registry key. If the file size has changed multiple times, it is shown with an arrow (->) indicating the new file size. See Figure 7.12 for more details. For example: md5 420fdacae704f8cb65af8887493a51c6 sha1 056f3bffe8e66de08b942fd1d4072919b486185f

Figure 7.12 shows an example of the results seen within the Integrity Checking database for a Windows agent.

Figure 7.12 Integrity Checking Database (Windows Agent)

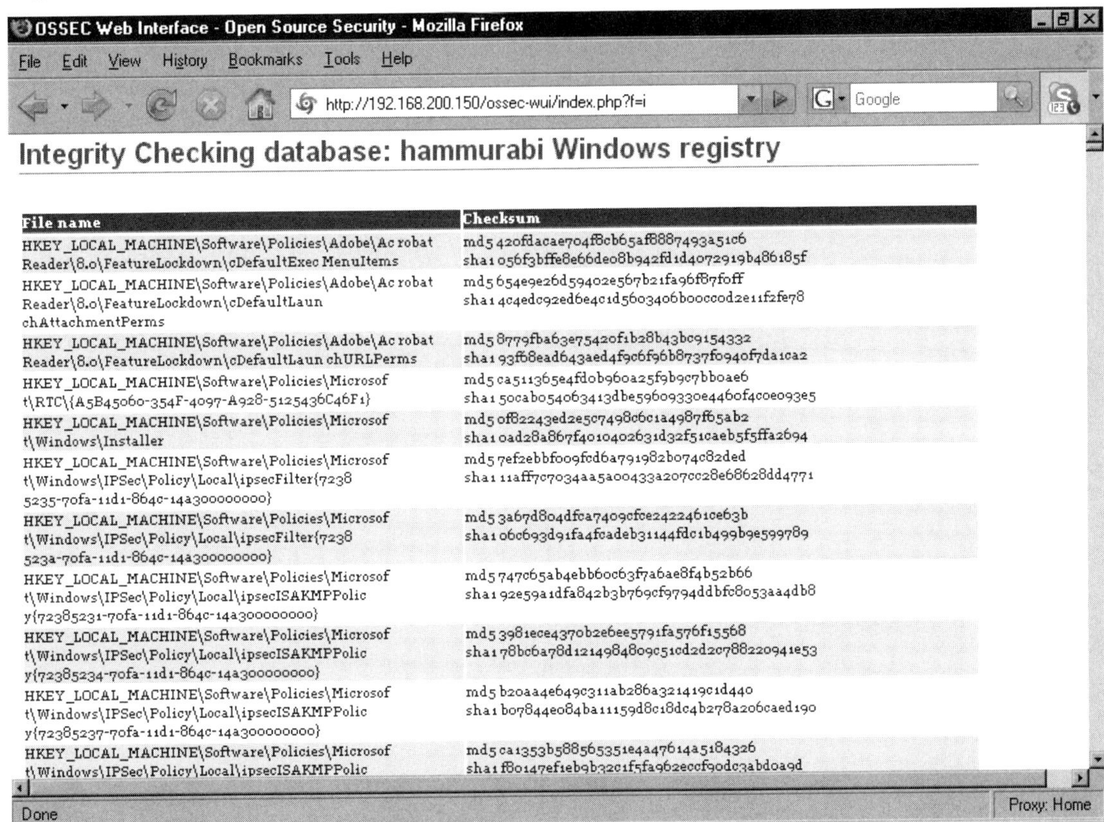

Stats

The WUI has a powerful statistical reporting engine that allows you to quickly display breakdowns of your OSSEC alerts, syscheck changes, and firewall alerts for any day, month, or year. This gives you the ability to pick a point in time and display the associated alerts generated by your agents and collected by your server.

Stats Options

A series of drop-down lists, across the top of the Stats tab, are provided that allow you to specify the day, month, and year for specific statistical intervals. As seen in Figure 7.13, the day, month, and year can be selected and the statistics can be requested by clicking the **Change Options** button.

Figure 7.13 Stats Options

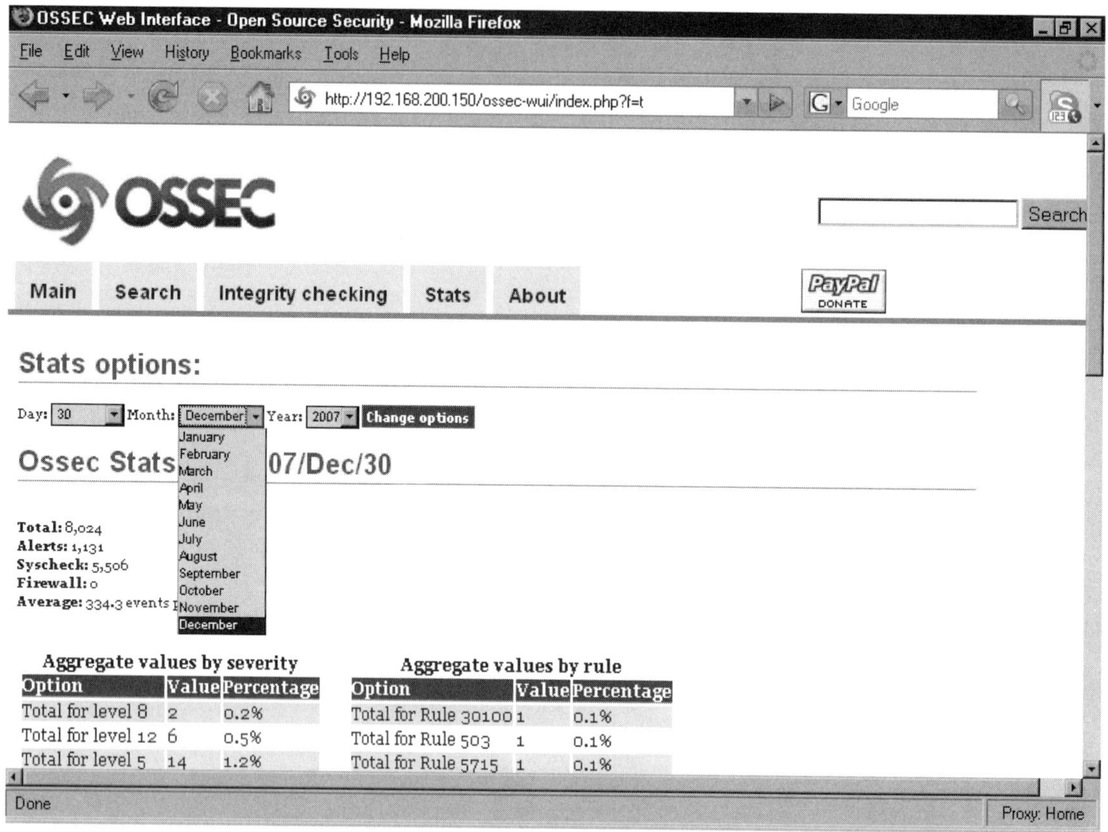

NOTE

If *All days* is selected from the Day drop-down list, a cumulative total for the month specified appears.

OSSEC Stats

The WUI is separated into three main reporting sections, each providing a different aggregate of your collected alerts:

- Aggregate values by severity
- Aggregate values by rule
- Total values per hour

OSSEC Stats Snapshot

A quick representation of statistics for the current day is displayed at the top of the screen. As seen in Figure 7.14, this snapshot provides you with a total of the recorded OSSC HIDS alerts, syscheck changes, and firewall alerts.

Figure 7.14 Total Stats

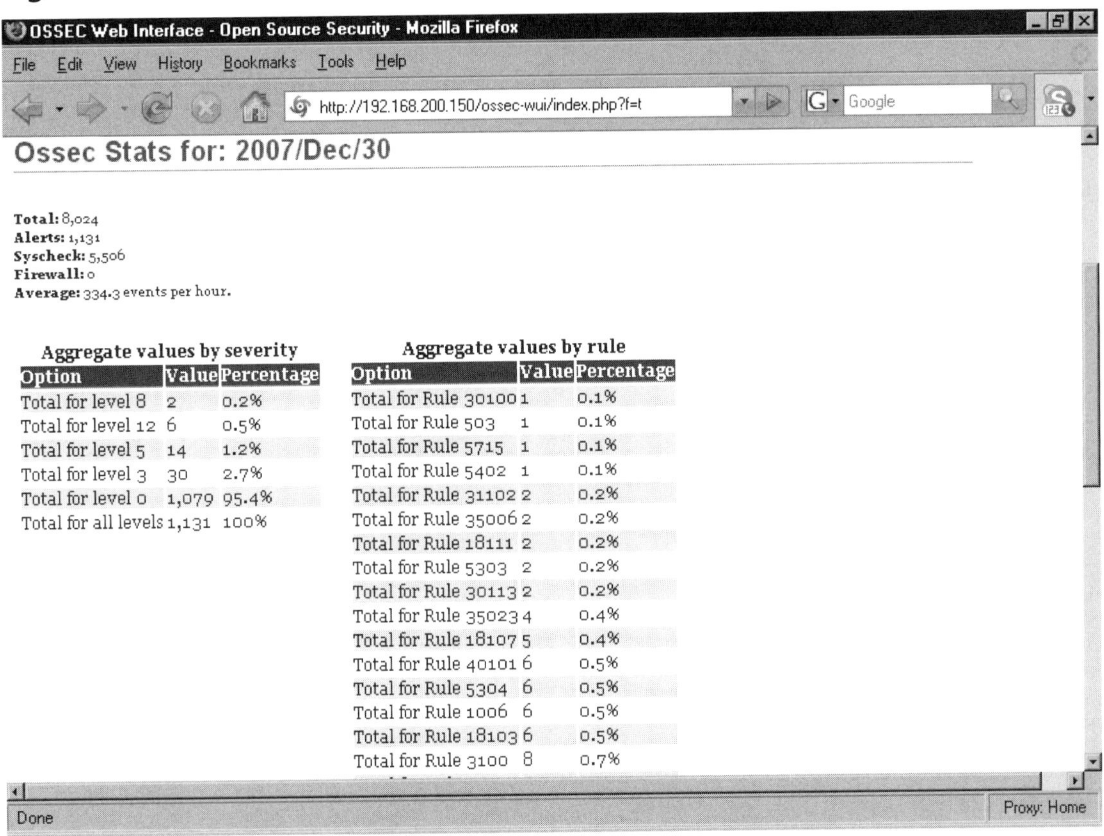

An *Average*, representing the events per hour rate, also appears. This average provides a good representation of the number of events per hour your OSSEC HIDS deployment is generating and processing. This becomes important if you are considering expanding your deployment and balancing alerts between multiple OSSEC HIDS servers.

Aggregate Values by Severity

Aggregating your results by severity shows you the total number of alerts broken down by the severity of the alert. Table 7.9 describes the possible values that might be seen within the Aggregate values by severity table.

Table 7.9 Aggregate Rules by Severity

Value	Description
Option	All alert severities recorded by the OSSEC HIDS. The level values range from 0 to 12, and only severities with an alert count greater than 0 are displayed. For example: Total for level 10
Value	The total number of alerts received with this severity type.
Percentage	The percentage breakdown of alert severities.

As seen in Figure 7.15, the alert severities most frequently seen appear near the bottom of the list, while the more infrequent alert severities are higher up on the list.

Aggregate Values by Rule

Aggregating your results by rules shows you the total number of alerts broken down by the rule that the alert was created by. Table 7.10 describes the possible values that might be seen within the Aggregate values by rule table.

Table 7.10 Aggregate Values by Rule

Value	Description
Option	All OSSEC HIDS alert rules recorded by the OSSEC HIDS. The rule values are configured within each OSSEC rule and only rules with an alert count greater than 0 will be displayed. For example: Total for Rule 35005
Value	The total number of alerts reported.
Percentage	The percentage breakdown of alert rules.

As seen in Figure 7.15, the alert rules most frequently seen appear near the bottom of the list, while the more infrequent alert rules are higher up on the list.

Total Values per Hour

Totaling your results per hour shows you the total number of alerts broken down by the hour that the alert was reported to the OSSEC HIDS. Table 7.11 describes the possible values that might be seen within the Total values per hour table.

Table 7.11 Total Values per Hour

Value	Description
Hour	The hour in which the alert was triggered. For example: Hour 9
Alerts	The number of OSSEC HIDS alerts recorded.
Alerts %	The percentage of OSSEC HIDS alerts reported.
Syscheck	The number of syscheck changes reported.
Syscheck %	The percentage of syscheck changes reported.
Firewall	The number of firewall alerts reported.
Firewall %	The percentage of firewall alerts reported.
Total	The total number of OSSEC HIDS alerts, syscheck changes, and firewall alerts reported.
Total %	The total percentage of OSSEC HIDS alerts, syscheck changes, and firewall alerts reported.

As seen in Figure 7.15, the alerts are sorted sequentially by time at the hour where the first alert is seen.

Figure 7.15 Total Values per Hour

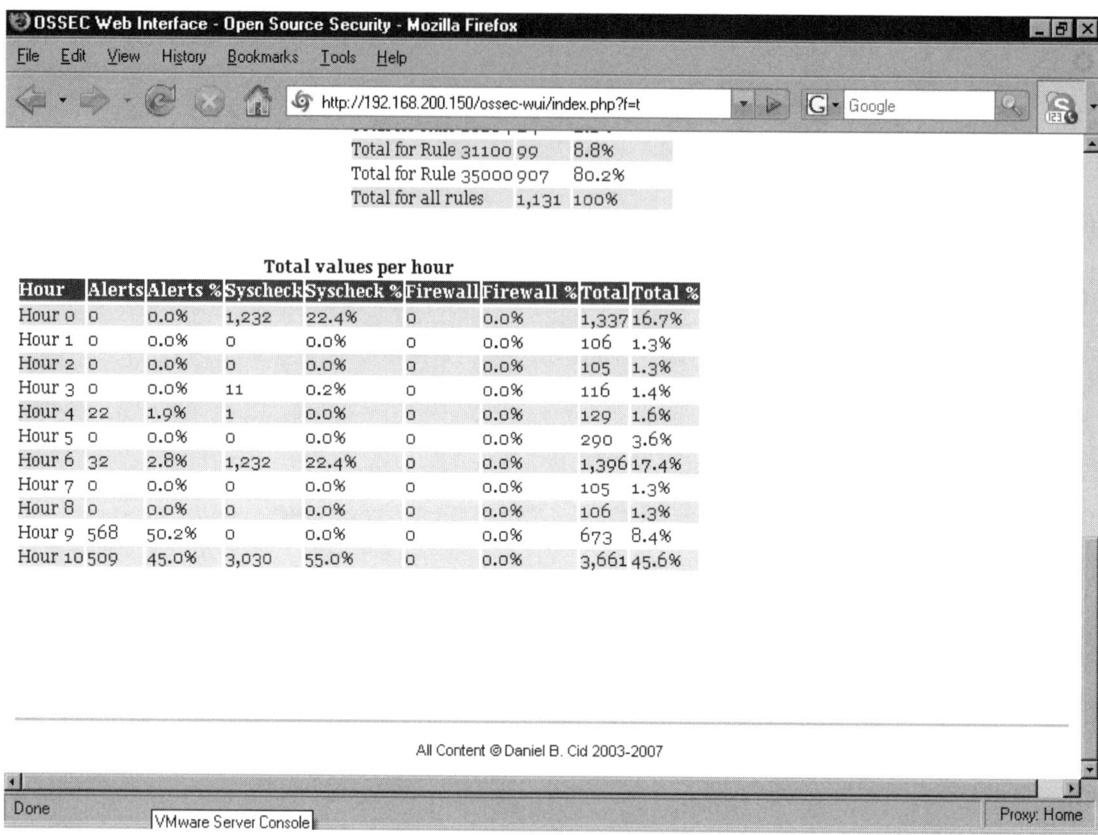

Hour	Alerts	Alerts %	Syscheck	Syscheck %	Firewall	Firewall %	Total	Total %
Hour 0	0	0.0%	1,232	22.4%	0	0.0%	1,337	16.7%
Hour 1	0	0.0%	0	0.0%	0	0.0%	106	1.3%
Hour 2	0	0.0%	0	0.0%	0	0.0%	105	1.3%
Hour 3	0	0.0%	11	0.2%	0	0.0%	116	1.4%
Hour 4	22	1.9%	1	0.0%	0	0.0%	129	1.6%
Hour 5	0	0.0%	0	0.0%	0	0.0%	290	3.6%
Hour 6	32	2.8%	1,232	22.4%	0	0.0%	1,396	17.4%
Hour 7	0	0.0%	0	0.0%	0	0.0%	105	1.3%
Hour 8	0	0.0%	0	0.0%	0	0.0%	106	1.3%
Hour 9	568	50.2%	0	0.0%	0	0.0%	673	8.4%
Hour 10	509	45.0%	3,030	55.0%	0	0.0%	3,661	45.6%

If you change the Day drop-down list to *All days* within the Stats options section, as seen in Figure 7.16, the Total values per hour table changes to a Total values per Day representation.

Figure 7.16 Total Values per Day

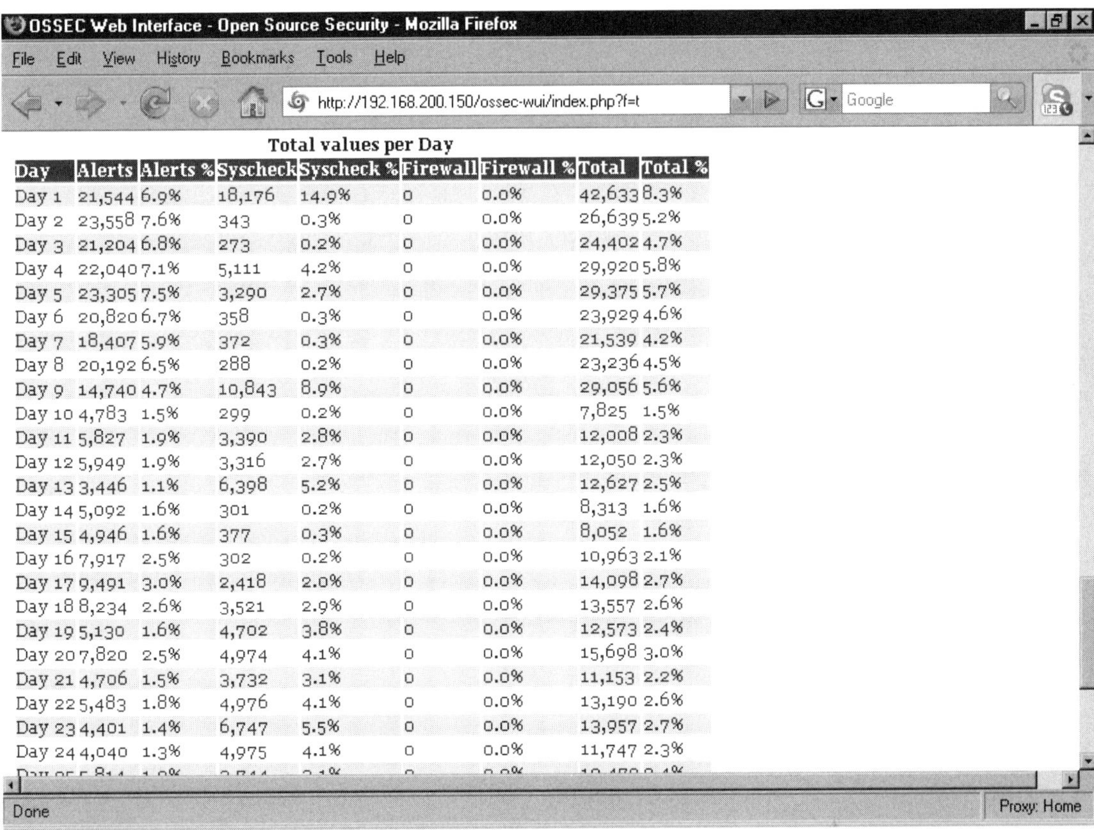

Total values per Day

Day	Alerts	Alerts %	Syscheck	Syscheck %	Firewall	Firewall %	Total	Total %
Day 1	21,544	6.9%	18,176	14.9%	0	0.0%	42,633	8.3%
Day 2	23,558	7.6%	343	0.3%	0	0.0%	26,639	5.2%
Day 3	21,204	6.8%	273	0.2%	0	0.0%	24,402	4.7%
Day 4	22,040	7.1%	5,111	4.2%	0	0.0%	29,920	5.8%
Day 5	23,305	7.5%	3,290	2.7%	0	0.0%	29,375	5.7%
Day 6	20,820	6.7%	358	0.3%	0	0.0%	23,929	4.6%
Day 7	18,407	5.9%	372	0.3%	0	0.0%	21,539	4.2%
Day 8	20,192	6.5%	288	0.2%	0	0.0%	23,236	4.5%
Day 9	14,740	4.7%	10,843	8.9%	0	0.0%	29,056	5.6%
Day 10	4,783	1.5%	299	0.2%	0	0.0%	7,825	1.5%
Day 11	5,827	1.9%	3,390	2.8%	0	0.0%	12,008	2.3%
Day 12	5,949	1.9%	3,316	2.7%	0	0.0%	12,050	2.3%
Day 13	3,446	1.1%	6,398	5.2%	0	0.0%	12,627	2.5%
Day 14	5,092	1.6%	301	0.2%	0	0.0%	8,313	1.6%
Day 15	4,946	1.6%	377	0.3%	0	0.0%	8,052	1.6%
Day 16	7,917	2.5%	302	0.2%	0	0.0%	10,963	2.1%
Day 17	9,491	3.0%	2,418	2.0%	0	0.0%	14,098	2.7%
Day 18	8,234	2.6%	3,521	2.9%	0	0.0%	13,557	2.6%
Day 19	5,130	1.6%	4,702	3.8%	0	0.0%	12,573	2.4%
Day 20	7,820	2.5%	4,974	4.1%	0	0.0%	15,698	3.0%
Day 21	4,706	1.5%	3,732	3.1%	0	0.0%	11,153	2.2%
Day 22	5,483	1.8%	4,976	4.1%	0	0.0%	13,190	2.6%
Day 23	4,401	1.4%	6,747	5.5%	0	0.0%	13,957	2.7%
Day 24	4,040	1.3%	4,975	4.1%	0	0.0%	11,747	2.3%

Table 7.12 describes the possible values that might be seen within the Total values per Day table.

Table 7.12 Total Values per Day

Value	Description
Day	The day of the selected month in which the alert was triggered. For example: Day 1
Alerts	The number of OSSEC HIDS alerts recorded.
Alerts %	The percentage of OSSEC HIDS alerts reported.
Syscheck	The number of syscheck changes reported.
Syscheck %	The percentage of syscheck changes reported.
Firewall	The number of firewall alerts reported.
Firewall %	The percentage of firewall alerts reported.
Total	The total number of OSSEC HIDS alerts, syscheck changes, and firewall alerts reported.
Total %	The total percentage of OSSEC HIDS alerts, syscheck changes, and firewall alerts reported.

About

The About tab of the WUI provides the copyright and license information for the WUI and the OSSEC HIDS. The license indicates that the OSSEC HIDS is free software and that it can redistributed and/or modified under the terms of the GNU General Public License (version 3). This license as published by the FSF—Free Software Foundation.

NOTE

The GNU General Public License Version 3 (GPLv3) is published by the Free Software Foundation (FSF). Information surrounding the GPLv3 can be found at the FSF Web site: www.fsf.org/licensing/licenses/gpl.html.

The About page, as seen in Figure 7.17, also indicates that the OSSEC HIDS is "*distributed in the hope that it will be useful, but WITHOUT ANY WARRANTY; without even the implied warranty of MERCHANTABILITY or FITNESS FOR A PARTICULAR PURPOSE.*" This is not to say that installing the OSSEC HIDS will harm your system. This is a commonly used clause in open source software projects used to indemnify the development team of any problems that might arise from using the OSSEC HIDS software.

Figure 7.17 About Page

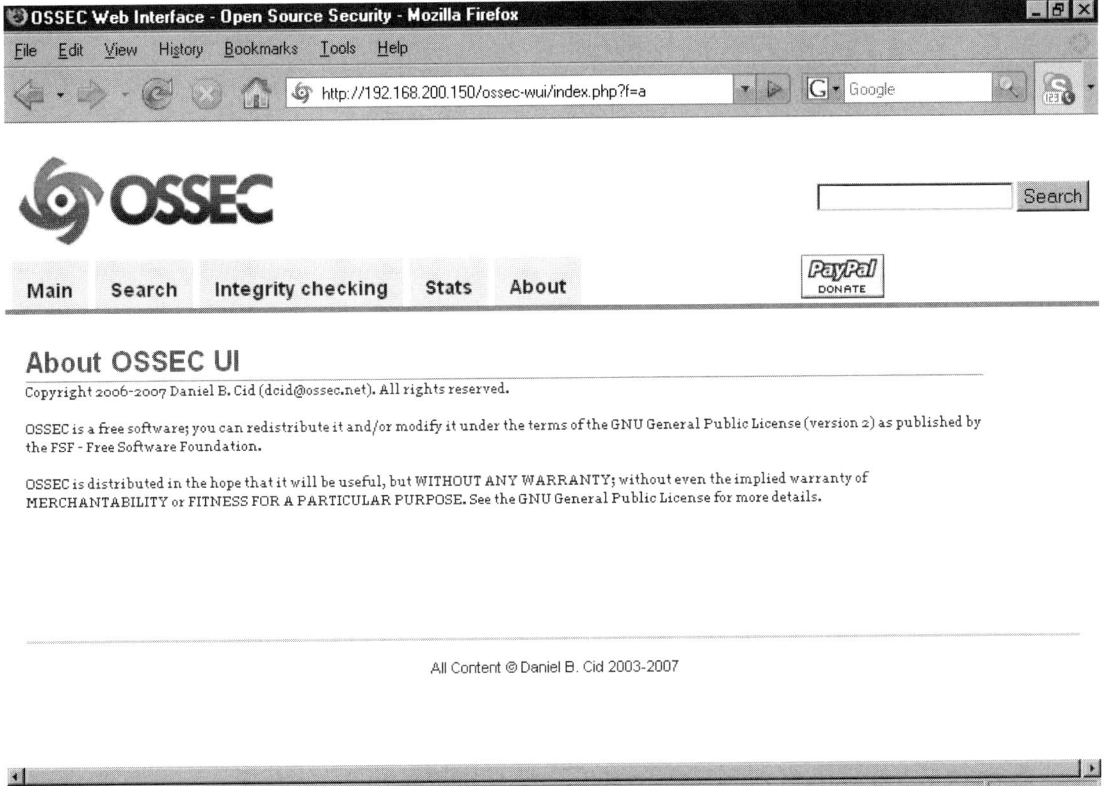

Summary

The OSSEC Web User Interface (WUI) was created to provide a visual representation of your collected OSSEC HIDS alerts in an easy-to-use Web page. From the WUI, an analyst can view all alerts and individual events related to an incident, review historical data to see if there are any similarities from previous incidents, and present management with recommendations on how to address the incident and prevent it from happening again in the future.

The WUI allows you to look into all aspects of the OSSEC HIDS. The Main page, which acts as a dashboard for your entire deployment, provides a listing of the latest modified files, latest events, and the current status of all OSSEC HIDS agents in your deployment.

Collected events and alerts are readily accessible using the powerful search capabilities of the tool. What this means is no more manual digging through log files with custom-made scripts to get at the data you need to address incidents.

Historical integrity information is stored for all OSSEC HIDS agents, allowing you to compare changes between files over the course of a week, month, year, or several years. This provides a window into the integrity of key files on all of your deployed OSSEC HIDS agents and allows you to see if a rootkit or malicious application has altered key system files without the user's knowledge.

OSSEC HIDS statistics can be viewed and aggregated by severity, rule numbers, and even the hour they occur to help you visualize what is happening on your network. This information can be used to determine your event rate and help you decide when to add additional hardware to your OSSEC HIDS deployment to help with the collection and processing of events.

Solutions Fast Track

Introducing the OSSEC HIDS WUI

☑ The OSSEC Web User Interface (WUI) was created to provide a visual representation of your collected OSSEC HIDS alerts in an easy-to-use Web page.

☑ Few people, especially those in management positions, enjoy looking at raw data when there is an easy-to-use alternative that performs the statistical analysis and correlation of data for them.

☑ There is a time and a place for combing through raw data, but the WUI provides an initial view into this collected information that may help alleviate some of the legwork during an incident.

Identifying WUI Pre-installation Considerations

☑ The WUI was designed to run on an OSSEC HIDS local or server type installation.

☑ The WUI cannot be installed on an agent because all collected alerts are sent back to an OSSEC HIDS server for processing.

☑ A multi-user WUI environment can be achieved by using the Apache HTTP server.htaccess files.

Downloading the WUI

☑ You can always find the latest released, beta, and alpha versions of the WUI software at the www.ossec.net/files/ui/ Web site.

☑ The integrity of the WUI files can be verified by comparing the provided checksum, from the OSSEC site, against the checksum of the downloaded archive, using tools to generate the cryptographic checksum of the downloaded files.

☑ If the file fails the integrity checks, it is recommended that you attempt to re-download the file to your current system or download it to another system.

Installing and Configuring the WUI

☑ The WUI installation archive contains the entire file set required to install, configure, and run the application.

☑ For the WUI to function properly, you must add your Web server user to the *ossec* group.

☑ If you have a large OSSEC HIDS installation, you might want to re-configure PHP to support longer lasting scripts and higher memory utilization.

Describing the WUI Components

☑ The Main tab is a dashboard for everything that is being reported to your OSSEC HIDS server.

☑ The WUI provides a powerful search engine, which allows you to filter on specific criteria and watch the results of your search in real time or perform historical analysis on stored event data.

☑ The Integrity checking tab provides you with two very important features of the WUI: a complete listing of the modified files for all agents, and a method for dumping the entire syscheck database for a particular agent.

☑ The WUI has a powerful statistical reporting engine that allows you to quickly display breakdowns of your OSSEC alerts, syscheck changes, and firewall alerts for any day, month, or year.

Frequently Asked Questions

Q: Does the file integrity checking only show all changes from when OSSEC HIDS is installed?

A: Yes, when the OSSEC HIDS is installed it performs an initial calculation of the files it is configured to monitor. Changes made prior to the installation of the OSSEC HIDS cannot be calculated.

Q: Can I export the stats to a spreadsheet?

A: At the time of this writing, the WUI was unable to export its data to another file. This is, however, on the roadmap for a future release.

Q: Does the search engine allow me to search through all events and alerts?

A: Yes, any events that are collected by the OSSEC HIDS server can be searched. Granular search options can also be used to track down the data you are looking for.

Q: Can I run the WUI with any Web browser?

A: The WUI will run with all of today's most popular browsers, including, but not limited to, Internet Explorer, Mozilla Firefox, Safari, and Opera.

Q: Are there any hardware requirements for the WUI?

A: No, there are no specific hardware requirements to run the WUI. If the OSSEC HIDS server can run on the platform you have selected, the WUI will more than likely run.

Q: Can I access the WUI remotely?

A: Yes, since the WUI is accessed using a Web browser, you can access the interface from any system connected to the network. You need to ensure that access to the OSSEC HIDS server from your system is configured to allow TCP port 80 or TCP 443 if using an HTTPS connection.

Q: How will I know if any of the downloaded installation files were corrupted or altered during the download?

A: Comparing the checksum and signature files from the OSSEC HIDS Web site to the cryptographic checksums of your downloaded files ensures that your files are the original, unaltered downloads.

Q: If I am having browser problems, is there an FTP site with the installation files that I can access?

A: Unfortunately, there is no public FTP site available to download the WUI. If you cannot download the file using the HTTP protocol, please send an email to the OSSEC HIDS mailing list and we will try our best to make arrangements for you.

Q: Should I install the alpha or beta versions of the WUI?

A: It is not recommended that you install the alpha or beta releases of the WUI in a production environment. You can, however, download the unreleased WUI and extract it in another Web server accessible directory to try it out. The new WUI instance will be able to reference all of the same information as your production WUI.

Q: Can I install the WUI on a Windows system?

A: No, the WUI needs to be installed on an OSSEC HIDS server, which cannot be installed on a Windows system.

Q: Is there a particular username that I should specify with the WUI installation?

A: It is recommended that your username is something that identifies you as an individual. If you plan to have multiple users access the WUI, you may want to decide on a common naming scheme, such as using the first initial of your first name and your surname (e.g., jsmith).

Q: Can I modify the *.htaccess* file to block other file type modifications?

A: Yes, you can modify the *.htaccess* file as you see fit. For more information on how to configure your *.htaccess* file, see the Apache HTTP server *howto* at http://httpd.apache.org/docs/2.2/howto/htaccess.html.

Q: Can I create as many users as I want?

A: You can create as many WUI users as you want.

Q: Are there any restrictions to username or password lengths?

A: Usernames and passwords are limited to 255 characters. Any password that is longer than 255 characters will be truncated to 255 characters.

Q: Are there any restrictions to username or password characters?

A: Usernames must not contain the colon, ":", character. Passwords can user any alphanumeric character available.

Q: If there is a connection problem with an agent and the server, will the available agents section on the Main tab provide any information?

A: If your OSSEC HIDS agent is unable to communicate with the server, the agent name will be displayed in red on the WUI dashboard. The agent name will also show "- Inactive" to inform you that the server is not receiving any communications from the agent.

Q: In the *Integrity checking* tab, does the WUI show the file extension for all file types?

A: Yes, the full filename and file extension are recorded within the OSSEC HIDS server. As such, the WUI displays the full filename when displaying the results to the screen.

Q: Are rule IDs static values created when the rules are created?

A: Yes, when you create a rule you must specify a unique rule ID. These rule IDs are associated with the generated alerts so you can easily find which rule triggered the alert.

Q: Since the software is open source, can I just copy it and incorporate it in my product?

A: The OSSEC HIDS software was licensed under the GPLv3 to protect the author while allowing anyone to freely use the software. The foundations of the GPL state that no users should be restricted by the software they use. There are also four freedoms that every user should have: to use the software for any purpose, to share the software with your friends and neighbors, to change the software to suit your needs, and to share the changes you make. Please verify that your intended use of the OSSEC HIDS does not violate the GPLv3 by checking the restrictions of the license: www.fsf.org/licensing/licenses/gpl.html.

Epilogue

After deploying the OSSEC HIDS, it appears that Simran's gamble paid off. The introduction of this new technology hasn't completely eliminated incidents throughout the organization, but it has significantly reduced the amount of time it takes to handle an incident. The OSSEC HIDS has helped Antoine's team detect and prevent several rootkit and malware installations over the past few months. Antoine's team, to reduce false positives, has also actively tuned the rules. In fact, the number of rootkits successfully installed is now less than 2% throughout the entire organization. David's team has made the installation of an OSSEC HIDS agent part of every new workstation, laptop, and server installation. This ensures that any system David's team installs has the proper versions of all files before the systems connect to the network. Alex, Ming, and Sergei have become so interested in the OSSEC HIDS that they have started contributing to the project with code, examples, and even help answer questions on the mailing list.

The senior management team is so impressed by the efficient and cost-saving solution that they have no issues promoting Marty to backfill Simran's old position. As the new CISO, Simran knows that there will be new and exciting challenges to face. She also knows that these challenges will be better met if she and her organization are properly prepared to handle them. The internal response has been so positive that Marty has been volunteered by Simran to present an overview of the OSSEC HIDS to all organizational partners. Because a big part of Simran's new security policy is that all firms dealing with the organization must prove the security of their systems, she believes Marty is the best person to talk about the organization's experiences. The OSSEC HIDS solution is simply one part of the organization's security infrastructure. Now it is up to Marty and his team to determine the next possible breach point.

Byung-Soon is still perfecting his craft and is getting better. The longer he can stay ahead of his targets, the more money he can make. He might retire some day, but right now, far too many organizations leave themselves wide open to his style of attacks. Checking his inbox, Byung-Soon notices a new email from one of his target clients, a major aerospace contractor responsible for supplying the United States with its newest line of fighter aircraft. Byung-Soon smiles and thinks to himself, "I love a challenge."

From the Authors

Even though the story, its characters, and the organizations involved in this book are fictional, the resulting breach is an unfortunate reality. Rootkits and covertly installed malware have become a primary concern over the last couple of years. There does not appear to be any end in sight for malicious attackers and their carefully created software. The only thing we can do as users, administrators, and business decision makers is surround ourselves with what we like to call the three Ps of security: *policies*, *professionals*, and *products*.

When properly positioned and implemented, products play a crucial role in your efforts to protect against known and unknown threats. Placing a product on your network to prevent a potential attack without first creating the policy and best practices for the product is foolhardy and quite possibly destined to fail before it touches your network. Similarly, if the professionals within your organization are not trained on the product you are implementing, you run the risk of introducing new breach points into your network.

We hope you enjoyed reading this book as much as we enjoyed writing it. Please check the OSSEC HIDS Web site for the latest version, sign up on the mailing list, and sleep better knowing that your system is more secure with the OSSEC HIDS installed.

—Andrew Hay, Rory Bray, and Daniel Cid

Appendix A

Log Data Mining

Solutions in this chapter:

- Introduction
- Data Mining Intro
- Log Mining Intro
- Log Mining Requirements
- What We Mine For?
- Deeper into Interesting
- Conclusion

Introduction

A vast majority of log analysis techniques required that an analyst know something specific about what he is looking for in the logs. For example, he might "scan" the server logs for "known bad" log (just as OSSEC does!) records that indicate attacks, exploits, server failures, or whatever other infraction of interest by using string matching or regular expressions. One can observe that it requires significant domain knowledge; in the preceding case, expertise in security and specific type of logs available for analysis on all stages of the log analysis process, from reviewing the data to running queries and searches all the way to interpreting the results to acting on the conclusions. In other words, you have to know what questions to ask before you get the answer you want—a tricky proposition at best. In addition, it requires an immense amount of patience to merely start the task, since one can be going through logs for a long time without finding the aberrant line or a group of lines; or, it might not even be there.

In this appendix, we describe methods for discovering interesting patterns in log files for security without specifically knowing what we look for and thus without the onerous "patience requirement" and the expensive "expertise requirements" on all analysis stages. We review some practical results of such methods, demonstrate the tools, and discuss how they can be used in various scenarios that occur in the process of maintaining security and availability of IT operation as well as assisting with compliance initiatives.

Since the techniques we will cover are similar in many regards to data mining, we need to step back and provide a brief data mining overview for those readers not familiar with it.

Data Mining Intro

We will start from a "dictionary," rather a Wikipedia, definition of *data mining* that can be found at http://en.wikipedia.org/wiki/Data_mining. It succinctly states, "Data mining, also known as knowledge-discovery in databases (KDD), is the practice of automatically searching large stores of data for patterns." Two other definitions found in Wikipedia will also be useful for our purposes: "The nontrivial extraction of implicit, previously unknown, and potentially useful information from data,"[1] and "The science of extracting useful information from large data sets or databases."[2] Yet another definition useful for our purposes is "An information extraction activity whose goal is to discover hidden facts contained in databases."

For those with an affinity for less technical definitions, MSN EnCarta defines *data mining* as "search for hidden information: the locating of previously unknown patterns and relationships within data using a database application" (http://encarta.msn.com/dictionary_1861602675/data_mining.html).[3]

Notice what is in common among those:

- Data mining (further DM for brevity) deals with a pool of data, possibly very large.
- Such data exists on a computer system in machine-readable format (such as a relational database system); in other words, it is structured data.[4]
- Available data might lead us to some interesting conclusion, but, then again, it might not.
- There is some useful outcome we are trying to get to, which requires searching or otherwise analyzing the data.

Structuring the DM using the preceding items reveals definite similarities between it and log analysis. We have a large pool of log records and we need to understand what the computer systems are trying to tell us by producing those logs. What they are trying to say is sometimes on the surface, but in other cases is hidden within a deluge of meaningless or irrelevant information. Thus, likeness between log analysis and DM leads us to believe that DM can be useful for our challenge at hand: making sense of logs.

Let's dive a bit deeper into data mining. The realm of data mining covers a broad range of scientific methods, software applications, and usage scenarios. Here we try to show you the parts of data mining related to security log analysis. Consequentially, DM finds uses in many areas of business, from retail to fraud analysis and risk management.

In general, there are two broad types of data mining methods: predictive and descriptive. While everybody will rush to try to peek into the future by using predictive DM, descriptive is just as useful since it can reveal the hidden truths applicable to past and present, a no mean feat in itself. Descriptive DM also serves to describe data sets in an informative way, thus almost "explaining" what is going on. Predictive DM, on the other hand, allows making forecasts about the not-yet-available data based on whatever is already here.

Since DM finds so many uses in retail, our illustrative DM examples—before we move to mining the logs—will be from that area. Descriptive DM may reveal what else you have likely bought if you just purchased a car CD player (for example, disks, cable kit, speakers), thus allowing the store to position them closer to the player. On the other hand, predictive DM might help the store to figure out what you will buy next (or when you will go broke from buying too much already).

Individual DM techniques are numerous. Table A.1 lists some that find common use.

Table A.1 DM Techniques

Type	Technique	Example
Descriptive	Clustering	Group people with common hobbies
Descriptive	Association Rule Discovery	Discover what parameters in data are associated with other
Descriptive	Frequent Item sets Discovery	Finding what objects occur in groups
Descriptive	Sequential Pattern Discovery	Finding what objects occur in a specific sequence
Predictive	Classification	Sorting the data bits into classes
Predictive	Regression	Predicting the behavior of a data set, similar to the one being mined
Predictive	Deviation Detection	Discovering whether the data points actually fit the profile, mined previously

The data mining process is often described as having the following steps:

1. **Acquiring subject matter expertise** in the area the data relates to. It is essential to "know what you are doing" in data mining, as much as (or more than) in other areas. DM tools do not "perform magic" and will likely not produce the results unless the user understands the data to be mined.[5]
2. **Defining the goal** is an obvious but critical step. While explorative techniques are known, we still need to know why we want to collect, prepare, and mine the data, and what will be done with the results.
3. Planning for collection and then **collecting data**. This sets the foundation for future DM endeavors. Data also has a nasty tendency to grow beyond control, as we observed with audit log data.
4. **Data preprocessing and cleaning** are often needed for the DM process to be effective or even to happen at all. Sometimes, DM experts estimate that this stage takes 60% of the mining effort. This stage usually involves dealing with missing bits of information and possibly duplicate data points, smoothing "noisy" data, and identifying and correcting other inconsistencies in the data set. Sometimes, this step is also called "data cleansing."
5. **Data reduction and transformation** involves things such as dropping extra dimensions of data and applying algorithms aimed at making the data more manageable by removing parts of the data set.

6. **Choosing the method** to apply is the next step. Do we want to cluster the data or look for sequences? Do we baseline or uncover associative rules? The method chosen is likely to be driven by the goals, defined several steps above.
7. Are we done yet? No, we need to **choose a specific algorithm** that implements the method chosen. Researchers and tool vendors are constantly working on new algorithms to look for patterns and on the performance of the existing algorithms. The right choice might make a difference between an efficient 10-minute run vs. a multiday database abusing disaster.
8. **Run the mining software** and get the results. That might refer to seeing a picture (when the results are visualized), table, or other textual representation of data.
9. And now, as some estimate, the hard part starts: **figuring out what the results actually mean**. From simple text reports to fancy visualizations, this stage is where we can actually understand whether all the previous steps actually brought the gold.

As one can see, the preceding steps fit closely to a normal log analysis process. That is why in the next section we will start illustrating how one can use DM-like techniques for log analysis.

Let us focus on the last step and discuss a problem of "interestingness."[6] Provided the DM succeeded and the results returned are correct (meaning that the methodology and utilized application do not have flaws), where are the assurances that we actually care to see them?

For example, one of the author's experiments with associative rule discovery on log data brought up the following bit of DM wisdom: If the protocol of the connection is DNS (Domain Name System), then there is a high probability that the port where it was sent is 53. "Duh!" would be the appropriate response here, since the mining algorithm did its job but we didn't really care to see the results. For the analyst, it is fairly obvious that most if not all DNS traffic always occurs on port 53. This shows that DM techniques can discover "hidden" patterns, but why are we so sure that the user will care to see them? "Interestingness" measure is an attempt by the researchers to quantify that. Another useful definition of it is, "A pattern is interesting if it is easily understood by humans, valid on new or test data with some degree of certainty, potentially useful, novel, or validates some hypothesis that a user seeks to confirm." The measure is sometimes classified into objective and subjective interestingness. The former is determined by the computer using whatever "interestingness" algorithm, while the latter is defined by the human expert. This distinction is obviously useful for log analysis, since in many regards, it is "an art, not science" and the human analyst is the ultimate judge of any technique's usefulness.

The main reason we wanted to highlight the "interestingness" at this stage is that when looking into data mining, people often expect miracles. For example, "let me put my logs into the systems and it will tell me everything I need to know at the moment." Such things will hardly every happen, since, even if a system has perfectly tuned data mining capabilities, it will likely have no idea of what you are interested in at the moment. However, the good news is that DM is a technology that allows one to approach the ideal closer than any other method.

After this review, we are ready to see how data mining techniques can be applied for our purposes of analyzing logs.

Log Mining Intro

While log mining is technically a type of analysis, we want to show that it starts where the usual log analysis ends—thus the differentiation. In addition, we hate to say "log anomaly detection" since it is often another way of saying "it doesn't work, but it well might one day if the moons are aligned and the appropriate animal is sacrificed to the appropriate deity."

Knowing a bit about the data mining methods and technologies, let's step back from it and review what we trying to achieve by applying the data mining to log data. In general, we are seeking to:

- Improve the quality of log analysis to provide better answers and predictive power
- Make the advanced and effective methods available without requiring rare and expensive human expertise

Richard Bejtlich in his book *Tao of Security Monitoring* described his view on network monitoring for security. The monitoring obviously covers logs (such as from intrusion detection or prevention systems), and network traffic information, such as netflow[7] and full packet captures. The main tenet of his NSM approach is that highly skilled analysts follow a well-optimized analysis process and run tools to gain insight from the incoming data such as logs, alerts, and packet dumps. A minor problem with this is that such analysts might be simply unavailable or, at the very least, unaffordable for the task at hand. As a result, the entire methodology breaks down ungracefully, since it relies on having trained, intelligent, and motivated human analysts (or even "expert") in front of the console all the time. Thus, this approach will likely remain in the realm of well-funded and security-minded organizations.

By using data mining and other advanced automated analytics, we will try to move as much of the "analysis burden' (or "glory," depending who you ask) to software and automated systems, away from exceptionally skilled—and just as exceptionally hard to find—human analysts. At least, we will prefer that the involvement of such analysis will be critical only at the early stages of the process, when we designed the specific mining methods, as we outlined in the previous section. In this case, the experts might define the specifics of the mining process and then let the less-skilled operations staff run the algorithm and act on the results with no reduction in efficiency.

Let's briefly look at how DM techniques are applied to logs, why do it, and what are the benefits. We coin the term "log mining" to means "application of data mining techniques to advanced log analysis."

We will start by asking, "Why mine the logs?" Ideally, our vision is to reduce the human effort needed and increase the role of the automated system in log analysis. Log mining, in brief, is one of the ways to get there. In fact, it is likely to be the most promising, as we mentioned before. So, log analysis faces challenges such as:

- **Too much data:** A volume of log data floods the log analysis systems and the human analyst, thus destroying any possibility to get the answers out. Indeed, logs can go into gigabytes and then crawl into terabytes, so you need tools to deal with the deluge.
- **Not enough data:** A critical piece of data is missing for various reasons, making log analysis more of a challenge than it should be.
- **Diverse records:** Too many different and dissimilar log sources need to be analyzed to get to the truth. This problem is due to the lack of the universal audit standard; most applications log in whatever formats were developed by their creators, thus leading to the massive analysis challenge. Future standard efforts such as MITRE's Common Event Expression (CEE) will resolve this.
- **False alarms:** Logs are full of messages that do not reflect reality in any measurable way (network IDS "false positives" largely occupy this category).
- **Duplicate data:** Different logs refer to the same events without any indication of that; missing time synchronization between different log sources often further complicates this situation.
- **Hard to get data:** While a device might create perfectly useful log records in a proprietary format, it will not "cooperate" with centralized log collection by lacking "standard"[8] log formats such as syslog or Windows NT event log. Similarly, getting the detailed mainframe audit records may be a challenge.

Let's briefly look at how DM techniques are applied to logs, why we do it, and the benefits thereof. We coin the term "log mining" to means "application of data mining techniques to advanced log analysis."

We will start by asking, "Why mine the logs?" Ideally, our vision is to reduce the human effort needed and increase the role of the automated system in log analysis. Log mining, in brief, is one of the ways to get there. In fact, it is likely to be the most promising, as we mentioned before. So, log analysis faces challenges such as:

- **Too much data:** A volume of log data floods the log analysis systems and the human analyst, thus destroying any possibility to get the answers out. Indeed, logs can go into gigabytes and then crawl into terabytes, so you need tools to deal with the deluge.
- **Not enough data:** A critical piece of data is missing for various reasons, making log analysis more of a challenge than it should be.

- **Diverse records:** Too many different and dissimilar log sources need to be analyzed to get to the truth. This problem is due to the lack of the universal audit standard; most applications log in whatever formats were developed by their creators, thus leading to the massive analysis challenge. Future standard efforts such as MITRE's Common Event Expression (CEE) will resolve this.
- **False alarms:** Logs are full of messages that do not reflect reality in any measurable way (network IDS "false positives" largely occupy this category).
- **Duplicate data:** Different logs refer to the same events without any indication of that; missing time synchronization between different log sources often further complicates this situation.
- **Hard to get data:** While a device might create perfectly useful log records in a proprietary format, it will not "cooperate" with centralized log collection by lacking "standard" log formats such as syslog or Windows NT event log. Similarly, getting the detailed mainframe audit records may be a challenge.

Many techniques have been developed to deal with the challenges. So, why mine the logs, if we have all those other approaches? Here are the top reasons:

- Reduce the reliance on skilled analysts by enabling more human-like pattern recognition and only necessitating such expertise at the early stages of the analysis.
- Deal with sparse data that cannot be effectively analyzed by other, more conventional means. Looking at gigabytes or even terabytes of data is better left to fully automated approaches, such as log mining.
- Detect things that sneak "below the radar" of other methods. Yes, log mining promises to increase the efficiency of detecting the intrusion traces.
- Offload conclusion generation to machines, so that this so far human-only task can also be automated. Humans will still act on the conclusions, but they won't need to wrack their brains trying to figure out what is going on.
- Attempt to predict problems, rather than find ways to deal with things that already occurred. While DM does not provide an easy, guaranteed way to such prediction, it certainly comes closer than any other method.

We should note that even though the trend will likely go toward "replacing" humans, the algorithms will always need to be defined and tuned by experts. However, DM techniques will clearly reduce the skill requirements on the operational staff.

In case of some early implementations seen by the author, the users of DM-based log analysis systems have commented that after a relatively brief tuning period the systems become "better than junior analysts." In this scenario, the system that used DM-like log analysis methods was implemented at a bank to look at the detailed audit data from multiple intrusion detection and firewall devices, deployed across the enterprise. The system developers and senior analysts have utilized the systems during the initial phase; the same people also trained the junior analysts who used to just watch the consoles with log records flowing by and perform the initial alert investigation. Now, with tuned DM-based log analysis system in place, the analysts focus on investigation only since the systems picked the signification alerts and episodes as good as those analysts.

Let's look at what is necessary before we can apply data mining to log data.

Log Mining Requirements

It is important to note up front that many requirements for log mining are the same as those needed for any significant log analysis. However, some added factors either appear to make log data suitable for mining or convert from optional to mandatory requirements:

- **Data centralization**: To look in just one place is nice to have for regular log analysis such as filtering and summarization, but becomes critical for log mining, since mining algorithms can crunch much more data than any single human analyst.
- **Normalized:** to look across the data sources centralized as described above requires a uniform information format. It might not be the real standard, just the uniform way of representing the log data.
- **Relational storage:** relational data storage such as a RDMBS is essential here, but can be left out if only simple analysis and filtering is performed.[9]

Such normalization is accomplished by looking for common fields in logs. Those commonly include:

- Time
- Source
- Destination
- Protocol
- Port(s)
- User name
- Event/attack type
- Bytes exchanged
- Others

Thus, normalized and centralized data can be subjected to the log data mining algorithms. Now, we are ready to review what we will look for by applying the data mining.

What We Mine For?

As we established, DM methods are most useful when we are not sure what we look for (otherwise, we can just filter or search for what we need). How about we find something "interesting," as we hinted in the previous section. As we mentioned earlier, "interesting" likely includes being unexpected to the user and actionable.

- What are some of the common examples a system administrator or a security analyst will find "interesting" and can use some help with finding?
- **Infected system spreading malware**: While obvious in many cases, systems that get infected and then spread the infection enterprise-wide and even Internet-wide are high on the priority list of every security administrator. Despite antivirus and other dedicated solutions, mining logs proves invaluable in tracking that pesky initial system that brought down the house.
- **Compromised system**: Every security pro worth his weight in paper certificates should be interested in knowing that attackers or their minions—"malware"—have taken over a system or systems in his network
- **Successful attack**: If the attacker just succeeded in breaching your system, it will likely be "interesting" to know (to put it mildly). While this actually relates to the previous item, it usually describes the earlier stages of the attack as it develops from an attempt to a full-blown compromise and system utilization by the attackers.
- **Insider abuse and intellectual property theft**: While evil hackers and worms steal all the glory, internal network abuse seems primitive by comparison. However, insiders hold all the keys to the kingdom and have the potential for dealing much more damage. To add insult to injury, detecting their exploits is much harder than average malware. Clear evidence of insider attacks, even failed, will certainly be of interest to administrators and analysts.
- **Covert channel/hidden backdoor communication**: Unless you are "into that sort of thing," covert channels are probably not in regular use on your network; thus, it is highly likely that network security administrators will be interested in knowing this.
- **Increase in probing**: While most sensitive government networks now discount Internet probing activity as mere noise, certain increases in such activity, reflected in logs, are known to serve as precursors to attacks, thus becoming interesting.
- **System crash**: While "denial service detection" always causes a chuckle (by definition, you detect it by noticing that you don't have any service), a system admin might not be monitoring for uptime of all the systems.

Thus, the preceding summary shows some of the universally interesting things we can hope to discovery by mining the logs.

A criterion of what is interesting is very hard to define for a computer, but it is possible with log mining! Let's also look at common examples of *not* interesting, which do not match the aforementioned "interestingness" criteria of unexpected and actionable:

- **Probe (not unexpected):** Network probes and scans happen all the time and people learned to expect them. One should be mindful of those, but will not be likely to spend resources looking for them. At the same time, a change in the number of such probes (per day, week, month, etc.) has a higher chance of being interesting.
- **Common failed attack (not unexpected):** If your security architecture is solid, you can expect to see failed attacks; those occur for various reasons (attacker skill is one). Similar to probes, one should know about them, but not spend resources looking for them.
- **Normal message (not unexpected):** Logs are full of messages indicating completion of some routine process and other perfectly normal events, recorded for audit and other purposes. Those are obviously not unexpected and we do not mine for them. However, changes matter here as well: normal messages that stop coming or the ones that start appearing more/less frequently might well be interesting.
- **Blocked attack (not actionable):** Similar to a failed attack, if your security countermeasures block an attack, even an interesting one you do not expect, no prompt action is truly necessary. Indeed, an investigation might be in order, but this still fails to match the "interestingness" criteria.
- **System status update (not actionable):** Similar to a normal event, those likely invoke no action. At the same time, system status updates happening at some unusual time might well be of high interest.

Let's look at finding interesting things via log mining in more detail.

Deeper into Interesting

Let's look back at our data-mining preview and review some of the methods to see how they apply to the task at hand. Here are the things we can mine for and have a reasonable hope of finding interesting things:

- **Rare things:** Maybe it doesn't happen frequently for a reason! If something just hasn't happened before, it might be malicious. Thus, rare events are prime candidates for our mining. Rare attacks, rare system messages, and users who almost never log in are all fun to detect!
- **Different things:** While we do not advocate total "log xenophobia," one should be on the lookout for things differing from what they were. This is where the baselining methods of data mining come into play.

- **"Out of character" things:** While being closely related to the preceding category, log records that appear "out of character" need to be mined for, since they are more likely to be interesting.
- **Weird-looking things:** If something just looks weird, it might be a sign of trouble. There is a subtle difference here between the preceding two types that we look for. To see something weird, such as your DNS system going to packetstorm.com and downloading exploit tools all by itself, does not require any baseline or prior data collection.
- **Things going in the unusual direction:** Some log records completely change their relevance to analysts and administrators depending on the communication direction. As in the preceding example, a connection to your server is perfectly legitimate, while the server going out and connecting (even on an innocent port such as TCP port 80) will likely raise some eyebrows, at the very least.
- **Top things:** While sitting in the realm of summarization and reporting and not strictly data mining, "Top X of Anything" remains useful for finding interesting log records and their patterns. After all, if it climbed up there to be (for example, "top use by bandwidth transferred"), it well might be interesting for that.
- **Bottom things:** Similar to rare things (which is simply, "bottom by occurrence"), this "evil sister" to "Top X of Anything" is even more useful to look at. It is well known that systems that attract the smallest amount of attention become the stepping-stones to future attacks and losses.
- **Strange combinations of uninteresting things:** This roughly follows a formula of "good" + "good" = "evil." Yes, even a bunch of perfectly normal log records might form something malignant in aggregate. The simplest example is a port scan, which is simply a set (often, a very large one) of benign connection requests.
- **Counts of an otherwise uninteresting things:** Counts of something uninteresting might well generate some interest. Moreover, a change in such count will often be even more significant. A sudden surge in a number of "ping" ICMP packets even outside the firewall might well mean a denial of service, especially if an ICMP flood came suddenly without warning.

Let's look at an example that illustrates this. In this example, a hacking incident involving unauthorized use of a vulnerability scanner is discovered. As we all know, network IDSs (also referred to as "NIDS") are deployed by a large percentage of companies, but many have failed to realize value from such purchases. Some reasons for such misfortune include high volumes of false alarms in their logs, undermining trust people have in such systems. That especially applies to signature-based systems that are supposed to flag packets and connections having specific patterns in them. To realize value from a NIDS, we can use log mining methods, aimed at flagging real attacks over routine noise and false alarms. Note that in this case we might not learn about the attack success, but just the persistence and focus of the attacker and distinguish attacks from benign and erroneous triggering of the NIDS.

When a legitimate connection is recorded by network infrastructure components or whatever misuse detection systems (such as IDS), they usually produce a small number of unique event types in the logs. For example, a connection through a firewall generates one connection message. Even a scan of a firewall will likely generate one event per connecting session and likely one event type (*connection_denied*) for the whole scan (this event will be repeated many times, but will be of the same type). Similarly, a "false positive" will *not* commonly be associated with other suspicious activity between the same hosts, such as recon scanning or other exploits. On the opposite, false alarms are more likely to happen in complete isolation or in large numbers of the same log record type with no other "related" records. Here, by "session" we mean a **unique combination** of:

- Source
- Destination
- Protocol
- Source port
- Destination port

Thus, if we organize events collected in the database by session and record the number of unique events (often the same as the number of attack types) in each session, we will have a way to distinguish real attacks from legit traffic and false alarms. This log mining approach uses a generic pattern to arrive at a specific and interesting outcome of a potentially damaging attack. Again, we give no indication of the attack's success, but just qualify it as real or false.

Conclusion

This appendix briefly looked at using data mining methods for practical log analysis. We illustrated that log mining and knowledge discovery in logs is a novel way to look at log data, which actually works in real life! Many types of logs can be subjected to such mining with useful results. While data mining is indeed a truly esoteric area, log mining (at least some of its methods) is not that difficult and can be implemented in many environments. Moreover, log mining can help where common analysis methods that require skilled analysts working long hours fail.

Finally, active research in the area—including mining of unstructured log via text mining—is likely to bring more useful methods people can use.

Endnotes

1 W. Frawley, G. Piatetsky-Shapiro, and C. Matheus. "Knowledge Discovery in Databases: An Overview." AI Magazine, Fall 1992, pages 213–228.

2 D. Hand, H. Mannila, and P. Smyth. *Principles of Data Mining*. MIT Press, Cambridge, MA, 2001. ISBN 0-262-08290-X.

3 MSN EnCarta searched on December 27, 2005.

4 Data mining on unstructured data is called "text mining." Many logs nowadays are more similar to unstructured, text data and thus text-mining techniques will be useful. Even though the author is conducting active research in this area, this appendix focuses on structure data mining, not text mining.

5 This "limitation" killed many worthwhile data mining projects.

6 Yes, that is a data mining term. Specifically, it is defined at ftp://ftp.gte.com/pub/kdd/kdd-terms.html#Interest as "a pattern instance measures its quality and has several dimensions. The main dimensions are the validation on the sample set, the reliability on the universe, the degree of redundancy with respect to other already known pattern instances, the generality, the simplicity, and the usefulness."

7 Cisco netflow format is used to collect network traffic information from the infrastructure devices (see more at "Cisco IOS NetFlow," www.cisco.com/en/US/products/ps6601/products_ios_protocol_group_home.html).

8 From reading this book, you already know that these standards are not real, but just common formats used by many systems.

9 Text mining we mentioned earlier certainly does not need two of the mentioned requirements. Text mining methods will work on mere piles of log data.

Appendix B

Implementing a Successful OSSEC Policy

Solutions in this chapter:

- The Purpose of Policy
- Step 1: Pilot Your Policy
- Step 2: Assess Your Current Policy Framework
- Step 3: Build and Implement Your Policies
- About Michael Santarcangelo

The Purpose of Policy

Policy Guides

To be successful when implementing OSSEC in your organization, you must have an effective policy to guide and support your actions. This section explains the steps you must take to quickly and successfully develop, and implement, your policy.

Policy, in a broad sense, demonstrates the business value OSSEC brings and guides the technical implementation. Breaking it down, policy is planning—if you can articulate your needs and efforts in *policy*, you will be effective.

Your Policy Comes Before Implementation

If you are like most people, you have a love–hate relationship with policy. Instead of taking the time to figure things out, you would like to just get the solution implemented and write the policy later, when you have more time.

There are two problems with this approach: policy is your guide, but that does not mean you must create your policy in a vacuum, and you will rarely go back and make the time.

While some schools of thought suggest that the policy must be developed first, we do not agree. Before you can write an effective policy, you must understand the information and environment you are protecting. In the case of OSSEC, you must also have a clear understanding of the power of the tool and how you intend to deploy and operate it as part of your strategy.

Policy Drives the Process

As you begin on the three-step plan outlined in this appendix, remember that policy drives your process. Thinking about and framing an effective policy, even an outline, is a good step for setting requirements.

Solutions Follow Requirements

The bulk of the project failures we have been called on to save share a common trait—a failure to create and document requirements before selecting the solutions. You are learning the power of OSSEC, and have therefore already decided to deploy it or are strongly considering it. It might seem odd, then, to suggest that before you select your solution you need requirements.

Even as a one-man band, you work with others, and others depend on your actions. Proper requirements gathering and setting involve:

- Focusing on challenges and opportunities to document the true needs instead of the "wants" for the organization
- Painting a picture of what success looks like
- Focusing on people, and they do their jobs

It is perfectly acceptable to get the experience you need by piloting the program. As you continue to read, we'll explain precisely how to maximize your pilot effort.

Let's be clear: writing policies and requirements is not an exercise that should happen in a vacuum. The closer to reality, and the more experience and insight you have to the problem, the environment, and the constraints, the more effective you will be.

We encourage you to embark on a parallel process to assess and understand your environment. Focus on the challenges of how people do their jobs, and whether your solution will make their jobs easier or harder, while building your policies and requirements.

At the same time, conduct a pilot and learn the language of the solutions, but resist the urge to be swept up in the features. Instead, share your learning with those around you and distill to what you really need.

Complexity kills. Simplify and succeed.

Step 1: Pilot Your Policy

As you seek to learn the power of OSSEC, establishing a pilot program with some planning will allow you the benefit of evaluating OSSEC in the context of your organizational needs. If done properly, you will conclude the pilot with the information you need to ease the implementation and adoption of this tool into your protection strategy.

This section focuses on three things:

- Assessing your environment
- Learning about the tool
- Building effective requirements

Assessing Your Environment

While assessment is typically not a traditional component of a pilot program, we think it is important. In our experience, most assessments are limited to technology assessments and are further restricted to network scans and possibly code reviews. No question that these are important, but they do not reveal the entire picture necessary to construct proper policy, requirements, or yield the information you need to build a concise and persuasive business case.

When considering this sort of assessment, broaden your perspective and consider assessing the following four focus areas.

Information

Information is the lifeblood of your organization, and your goal is to protect that information across confidentiality, integrity, and availability. When assessing information, focus on who is using the information and how they are using it. Without issuing judgment, it is important to understand the different formats used to process information, such as electronic, physical, and verbal. You also must understand how the information is being used and protected at rest and in transit. Try to find the top five information assets to narrow your focus.

Environment

The environment includes the nature of your operations; specifically, how large your environment is in terms of people and machines and in how many locations and countries. Seek to understand more about the people using the information and the natural rhythm of operations.

Risk

Assess risk to the information and the environment to the best of your ability.

Risk Tolerance

The organizational tolerance for risk will help you understand what measures are going to be acceptable.

Learning about the Tool

Each of these focus areas is a discipline and might be more complicated than the pilot program you are planning. Our suggestion is that this can be used informally—focus on gaining information across those four focus areas and broaden your perspective. Look at things as a user and as an executive to gain a sense of where and how the OSSEC solution fits. The likeliness is that OSSEC is a tool that will not be directly used or even noticed by many, but the power and importance are not diminished. Being able to explain the role it plays in protecting the organization will aid in your efforts.

Developing a clearer understanding of your environment will also position you to quickly develop your policy and requirements. In the next section, we're going to explain a quick-and-dirty approach to developing an OSSEC policy that will work in conjunction with your pilot evaluation.

At this point, you should have a basic understanding of what you must do, and can therefore outline (at least at a high level) your policy needs and some considerations for standards, guidelines, and procedures.

Building Effective Requirements

The ability to implement solutions and write policy is heavily dependent on the success of the requirements. Sadly, most efforts bypass the requirement and policy stages in the name of efficiency. When writing your requirements, focus on these three concepts and you will increase your chances of success.

Broad Focus on Availability, Integrity, and Confidentiality

These are the three fundamental concepts in security. Your requirements must address all three. The biggest challenge you will face is drafting a requirement instead of the solution. Requirements are broad. For example, "The confidentiality of information needs to be protected during rest and transit," *not* "information must be encrypted." Encryption is a solution; the requirement is that information must be protected from disclosure. The more practice you have writing requirements, the more powerful and clearer this will be.

Involve Others

It is important to involve other people in your requirement and policy process. Experiences and opinions of others will help improve your efforts. Select people who have a direct stake in the outcome, whether they are directly involved or benefit indirectly. A diverse team will afford you the opportunity to teach, share, and learn.

Solve the Business Problem

Requirements and policy are not justifications for toys. Protecting information is about meeting the needs of the business. Focus on what is needed to make it easier for people to do their jobs, while protecting information. Outline the business and functional needs and the solution will be able to be built on that.

You will revisit these requirements when it is time to draft your policy components.

Pilot Your Way to Success

A pilot program is a great opportunity to learn the elements of OSSEC, especially in a live or near-live environment. As you work through your pilot, take an iterative approach and consider:

- Features needed to meet requirements
- Features not needed (simple is generally more powerful)
- Additional concepts you did not consider in the requirements that have a clear business impact or value
- Information protection with OSSEC

The pilot is another excellent opportunity to involve others—those who might be using OSSEC and those who will benefit from it. When you explain the system so others can see it in action:

- Seek to understand their questions because they might yield valuable insights.
- Listen to their descriptions because these will help when writing policy.
- Consider if you can you enhance value to them. (Perhaps they see uses of the information OSSEC generates.)
- Find out what they need and what they want to see.
- Seek to gain support.

Step 2: Assess Your Current Policy Framework

It takes an entire book to focus on the elements of effective policy. From a tactical perspective, you must focus on three steps:

- Understand the elements of effective policies
- Assess your current policy architecture
- Assess the elements you need to build, not augment

This is meant to be a quick and tactical approach. We do not have the time to assess the efficiency of your current policy program and efforts. Regardless of the policies currently in place, you have to embrace this simple, but powerful concept:

Policy is planning. If you want to be successful, you need a blueprint.

Policy Primer

The word *Policy* is often used incorrectly. The result is a recipe for failure. Let's take a brief look at the four basic elements you might use to implement your successful policy:

Policy

Policy is a simple and brief statement of intent, value, and justification. More importantly, policies are not specific and do not document solutions. Policies communicate the expectations of management and the needs of the business. Given the general nature, policies are often approved once and enforced for years without major, or any, changes.

Standard

Standards are specific and detailed solutions, including key configuration or software revision numbers. Standards define the acceptable solutions to meet the policy needs of the organization and dictate the development and implementation of solutions. Standards are written in a way that yields a *yes* or *no* answer. There should be no question whether a system complies with the standard. Because standards are more specific, they must be reviewed and updated on a regular basis, sometimes as often as quarterly.

Procedure

Procedures are optional. When created and issued, procedures are the step-by-step mandatory actions to take when operating the system. Procedures are developed to be clear to follow and maintain compliance with the standard and policy. Procedures are favored in operational environments because they remove ambiguity.

Guideline

Guidelines are optional. When created and issued, guidelines are nonbinding suggestions of actions to follow. Guidelines and procedures are generally not issued in conjunction with each other. Guidelines tend to be issued with newer solutions, where the procedures have yet to be developed, or when multiple methods of operations are used and acceptable. The guidelines will provide insights to maintain compliance with the standards and policies.

Assessing What You Already Have

You must assess the policies, standards, procedures, and guidelines already in use. In most organizations, policy changes require a lot of time and effort. However, adding to a policy with an addendum, or incorporating a new standard, takes far less effort.

When you conduct this assessment, you must consider the compliance regulations of your industry. Specifically, does your solution meet a requirement or is it subject to specific standards? This is sometimes a bit complicated and might require some assistance from your legal counsel or resident policy experts.

Ideally, a properly constructed policy is already in place that determines the need or justification for OSSEC in a way that meets compliance and regulation guidance.

Step 3: Build and Implement Your Policies

At this point, you should have completed an assessment of your environment, built requirements, possibly created a high-level policy outline, and conducted your pilot. The information, experience, and review of your current policy elements will ease your ability to develop and deploy your OSSEC policy.

The minimum elements you need are a policy statement and a standard. In the event a suitable policy exists, then you will only need to focus on crafting an appropriate standard. We recommend building a guideline or procedure, but that decision rests on your assessment of the environment.

Build Your Policy

You have three basic choices, from easiest to most difficult:

- Integrate into current policy without changes
- Amend the language of a current policy
- Create a new policy

If you integrate into a current policy, the process and decision should be reviewed and documented to ensure future compliance. When you amend or create a new policy, strive for a simple and clear language. You might find a policy template already exists, and you must draft your policy to meet those requirements. Unless your template requires more, a policy for OSSEC should fit on one piece of paper.

Your policy review process must be followed. We recommend engaging with the policy team early in the process and using their guidance as your develop your policy. In our experience, the most successful policies are brief, clear, and focused on the business. If anyone can read the policy and immediately understand the value of OSSEC, you have done well.

Build Your Standard

Because you are deploying OSSEC for the first time, we doubt an OSSEC standard exists. Standards are generally kept short and specific. When building your OSSEC standard, focus on the specifics of OSSEC—which version, configuration, and other specific elements.

Test your standard by having someone review the pilot or planned implementation. After the review, he should be able to answer the question, "Is the system in compliance with the standard?" with a *yes* or *no* answer. There is no *maybe* or *I am not sure* when it comes to a standard.

You must set a process in place to review and update this standard on a regular basis. Initially, you might find frequent updates. As you develop a clear operational tempo, however, the changes will come only with OSSEC upgrades or configuration changes.

Implementation and Adoption

Most policy elements require a few revisions before being approved. Focusing on the process and business value and using clear language free of jargon will ease that process. Take the time to explain the elements and learn from the process how to improve the policy and standard to ensure success.

Keep in Mind

OSSEC is a tool that can be used to aid in your efforts to protect information. If you want to be effective, you must make it easier for others to do their jobs and to protect information. Following a process that includes others, educates people, while documenting expected operations makes it easier for everyone involved.

About Michael Santarcangelo

Michael Santarcangelo is a human catalyst. As an expert who speaks on information protection, including compliance, privacy, and awareness, Michael energizes and inspires his audiences to change how they protect information. His passion and approach gets results that change behaviors.

As a full member of the National Speakers Association, Michael is known for delivering substantial content in a way that is energetic and entertaining. Michael connects with those he works with, and helps them engage in natural and comfortable ways. He literally makes security relevant and simple to understand!

His unique insights, innovative concepts, and effective strategies are informed by extensive experience and continued research. His first book, *Into the Breach* (early 2008; www.intothebreach.com), is the answer business executives have been looking for to defend their organization against breaches, while discovering how to increase revenue, protect the bottom line, and manage people, information, and risk efficiently.

Appendix C

Rootkit Detection Using Host-based IDS

Solutions in this chapter:

- Introduction
- History
- Types of Rootkits
- Host-based IDS as a Solution...
- HIDS Advantages
- HIDS Disadvantages
- Future Developments

Introduction

Rootkits are covert applications that alter the operating system in which they are installed. The purpose of a rootkit, once installed, is to hide files, network connections, memory, and other targeted data from your operating system, deployed anti-malware applications, and users. Rootkits alter the behavior of the operating system to conceal files, running processes, and services.

An attacker who successfully compromises a computer system wants to maintain access for future use. Considering anti-malware programs are more sophisticated today than in the past, simply launching an application on a system would trigger the anti-malware software to remove the backdoor from the host system quite easily. Attackers must now conceal the backdoor application from the host system anti-malware applications and the end user for the backdoor application to stay open. Using rootkits to hide the backdoor application provides the attacker a very good shield against applications looking for backdoors. Users must first find and defeat the protections the rootkit provides, and then find and disable the backdoor application, which could prove to be much more difficult.

History

Rootkits have been in existence for Unix systems for over a decade. It was actually the year 1990 when, we believe, the first rootkit was written by Lane Davis and Riley Dake for the Sun operating system. The term *rootkits* derives from the capability to gain *root* access to a Unix operating system.

Fast-forward to today and Microsoft Windows rootkits are more commonplace. Windows rootkits have been in existence much longer than most people realize. NT Rootkit, written by Greg Hoglund, was the original and first public Windows rootkit. It hasn't been updated in years, and Windows rootkits such as Hacker Defender and HE4Hook are now some of the more popular options for attackers and researchers alike.

Types of Rootkits

In essence, rootkits are programs that are concealed from the host operating system by replacing local programs on a computer system. A few different types of rootkits have been introduced in the last few years, but the following are most well known:

Kernel-Level Rootkits

Kernel-level rootkits modify key areas of the kernel to conceal the rootkit's location and running process. Kernel level rootkits are hard to detect considering that every process that asks the kernel for information about the rootkit will be told that the rootkit does not exist.

Discovering this type of rootkit often requires accessing the infected drive from another operating system (such as a live CD) and then performing the system checks.

Application or File-Level

Application or file-level rootkits replace key operating system or application files with fake files that do not reveal information about the rootkits. A simple example would be replacing the *dir* command on a Windows system with a fake, so that when the command is run, it will not present all the files from a specific directory. Application level rootkits are easier to install than kernel level rootkits, but are also much easier to discover.

Host-based IDS as a Solution...

Given the severity of the security risk a rootkit poses, every precaution must be taken to prevent a system from being infected in the first place. Prevention is ideal, but detection is a must. One precautionary method companies are taking is the implementation of corporate-wide host-based intrusion detection (HIDS). HIDS can protect the host it is installed on, and watch other systems on the network for signs of infection.

A HIDS can help defend against rootkits on initial installation by checking for the following conditions.

Unauthorized Listening Ports and Processes

Rootkits can hide Trojan programs attackers install on a system to maintain access for future use. Well-known Trojans have a common port they listen on, which anti-virus software will detect. Attackers can alter the Trojan to use other ports, but anti-virus software can still discover the Trojan unless the service is concealed by the rootkit; to the anti-virus software, the listening port simply disappears.

A HIDS can detect ports concealed by rootkits by trying to connect to the host on all available ports and comparing the results of the HIDS connections to the operating system report of open ports. If there are discrepancies between the HIDS connect scan and the operating system, further investigation is needed for that host to determine if it has been compromised.

Files with Permissions that Are Uncommon for the File Type

A HIDS can be extremely beneficial in detecting file types with abnormal file permissions. Configuration files, for example, do not require executable permissions. A rule could be imposed that if a file in the /etc directory has the executable bit set, the host should be checked for possible infections. Common files should not have the sticky bits (setuid or setgid) configured; these file settings are reserved for special files, such as installers and directories.

Files that Match a Predefined List of Rootkit "Fingerprints"

Certain rootkits modify key files on a system are detectable by commercial anti-virus software, which is typical of a file-level rootkit. Adding a concealed directory such as "..." or ".puta" will help identify these types of rootkits. Installers often signal the initiator of the rootkit to indicate a successful infection. These signals can be used as part of the signature against that particular file.

Modification of Key Files

Key configuration files do not often change. When a HIDS is installed, it can take a cryptographic snapshot of these key files and alert users when those files change. Files that control the host's DNS settings, lists of users, and user groups are common targets.

Watch for Network Cards that Are Listening to Network Traffic

Many attackers who compromise systems want to capture confidential traffic on the network. Setting the network card on the compromised system to promiscuous mode allows the passive collection of network traffic originating from, destined for, or passing by the compromised host. A HIDS can effectively discover systems that are running in promiscuous mode by monitoring the interface settings.

Users Who Have UID 0

Unix/Linux super users or administrators have the UserID 0. A HIDS can be configured to monitor new users created with the UserID 0 and alert on such findings.

Network Anomaly Detection

A HIDS can be programmed to have profiles that define the type of host it is installed on. If the HIDS notices that a workstation is receiving connections to strange ports or making strange outbound connections, it can block those ports and notify the user that something interesting is going on.

HIDS Advantages

The obvious advantage of implementing a HIDS is the ability to detect an attack to a system within your perimeter. A network-based IDS (NIDS) and carefully implemented firewalls cannot always give you insight into every end system. When you are past the perimeter, you must rely on other tools. A HIDS gives security operators the ability to spot and stop an attack on any host early, which can potentially save lots of effort down the road on cleanup and damage recovery.

A HIDS also has the capability to detect attacks outside your network perimeter. HIDS installed on corporate laptops can protect those systems while they are on the road at customer locations, Internet cafes, and other public access points. If someone attempts to compromise the machine external to your network, a HIDS will be able to notify you before internal resources damage occurs.

Because a HIDS has the capability to see what is happening on the host operating system, it can be used to detect breaches in software policy. If a HIDS sees installed software that is not part of the corporate standard, it can notify an administrator. This notification can prevent users from installing unlicensed software, and stop developers from installing tools in production servers that could weaken the security posture of the host.

A HIDS agent has the capability to monitor all network traffic destined for it on all interfaces on the system. For example, most laptops now include a NIC card, wireless card, and a modem. A HIDS agent has the capability to protect your laptop from network traffic that may try to compromise your system through a wireless card.

To optimize the benefit of a HIDS, a central server is deployed for reporting. The central server acts as the eyes and ears for security officers when it comes to internal hosts on the network. Having multiple IDS sensors in an environment will give greater insight on systems that do not have IDS installed. The more systems with a HIDS installed increases the resolution of the overall security picture.

HIDS Disadvantages

A large-scale HIDS deployment is not an easy thing to successfully manage. Having the logs of thousands of HIDS agents running on traveling users' laptops and your server farm reporting to your central management server will result in a data overload. To effectively use a HIDS in a large-scale deployment, a well thought-out implementation plan must be in effect to help ensure that HIDS policies do not fire off a large amount of false positives, which would leave the HIDS administrator overloaded with data. Rules on the central management server that could combine multiple low-level HIDS events to create alerts would also be complicated to develop, but the decrease in staff alerts is worth the effort.

It's beneficial to ensure that the systems implemented with HIDS protection are not prone to wide-scale configuration changes. Frequently modified systems may force you to alter your HIDS policies often. In addition, if like-systems are not updated at the same time, you may be forced to define host-specific policies, which will lead to additional administrative overhead.

A HIDS installed on a local system is just another piece of software that can affect overall system performance. Busy servers already have a lot to do without having another traffic cop utilizing system resources.

Future Developments

A HIDS is definitely beneficial in detecting rootkits, but newer developments in this area are becoming slightly more attractive. Host-based intrusion prevention (HIPS) technology is becoming more commonplace because it has the capability to prevent an attack from happening versus detecting the event with a HIDS and having a minimal amount of time to respond. If a HIPS is more attractive, but not in the budget, remember there are open source HIDS options you can use. Prevention is ideal, but detection is a must.

Appendix D

The OSSEC VMware Guest Image

Solutions in this chapter:

- Introduction
- Using the OSSEC VMware Guest
- Creating Your Own OSSEC VMware Image
- Conclusion

Introduction

The accompanying DVD contains an Ubuntu 7.10 VMware Guest image with the OSSEC HIDS pre-configured as a local installation. This allows you to try the OSSEC HIDS in a virtual environment so you can fully understand how it works before deploying on a production system.

Using the OSSEC VMware Guest

The OSSEC VMware Guest image was created with VMware Server, the free server virtualization product from VMware, and it has been tested on both VMware Server and VMware Player 2.0.

VMware Server is a free virtualization product for Windows and Linux servers. It enables companies to partition a physical server into multiple virtual machines and to experience the benefits of virtualization. For more information on VMware Server, or to download a copy, see www.vmware.com.

VMware Player is free software that enables users to easily run any virtual machine on a Windows or Linux computer. VMware Player runs virtual machines created by VMware Workstation, VMware Server, or VMware ESX Server. It also supports Microsoft virtual machines and Symantec LiveState Recovery disk formats. For more information on VMware Player, or to download a copy, see www.vmware.com.

You can use whichever VMware product you want on the operating system of your choice, because the OSSEC VMware Guest runs on any VMware supported operating system.

OSSEC VMware Image Minimum Requirements

The only requirements of the OSSEC VMware Guest is that your system must have at least one network interface card (NIC), a minimum 2 GB of free disk space, and 512 MB of free memory for the VMware Guest to operate efficiently. Please note, however, the virtual disk for the VMware Guest is configured to grow to 8 GB as needed by the OSSEC HIDS and Ubuntu operating system.

VMware Server and VMware Player each have specific minimum system requirements that can be found at www.vmware.com.

VMware Guest Information

The VMware image included on the DVD was created using the *New Virtual Machine* wizard included with VMware Server. Table D.1 shows the options chosen during the creation of the OSSEC VMware Guest image.

Table D.1 VMware Options

VMware Option	Value Chosen
Virtual Machine Configuration	*Typical*
Guest Operating System	Linux, Ubuntu
Name	OSSEC_HIDS
Network Connection	NAT
Disk Size	8GB, not allocated, split into 2GB files
User	*marty*
Password	*ossec*
MySQL User	*root*
MySQL Password	*ossec*

Creating Your Own OSSEC VMware Image

To create you own OSSEC HIDS VMware Guest image, you must download and install your own copy of VMware server. Instructions on how to download, install, and configure VMware server can be found at www.vmware.com.

Because VMware can create guest images from multiple operating systems, you can choose to install any of the supported installation types (*local*, *server*, and *agent*) for the OSSEC HIDS on any supported operating system. If, however, you want to duplicate the steps taken to create the provided OSSEC HIDS VMware Guest, you can use the following steps to create your own image.

Downloading the Ubuntu 7.10 ISO

Ubuntu is one of the most popular Linux software distributions currently available. It is well known for its ease of installation and use, which has made it very popular for desktop use. Ubuntu is also available as a server installation image that is also easy to install and use.

To create the OSSEC HIDS VMware Guest image, use the server version of Ubuntu because it requires less disk space than the desktop version. The server installation also requires less RAM than the desktop version, allowing you to create a VMware Guest that runs on lower end systems.

Ubuntu CDs can be downloaded from the Ubuntu Web site at www.ubuntu.com/getubuntu / download where you are asked to select your preferred release. Select the **Server Edition,** called **Ubuntu 7.10 - Supported to 2009**. When asked what type of computer you have, select the **Standard personal computer** option. Finally, select a location near you from the drop-down list and download the file.

Preparing the VMware Guest Image

The VMware Guest image should be created using the VMware Server Console application, as shown in Figure D.1.

Figure D.1 Start Wizard from Console

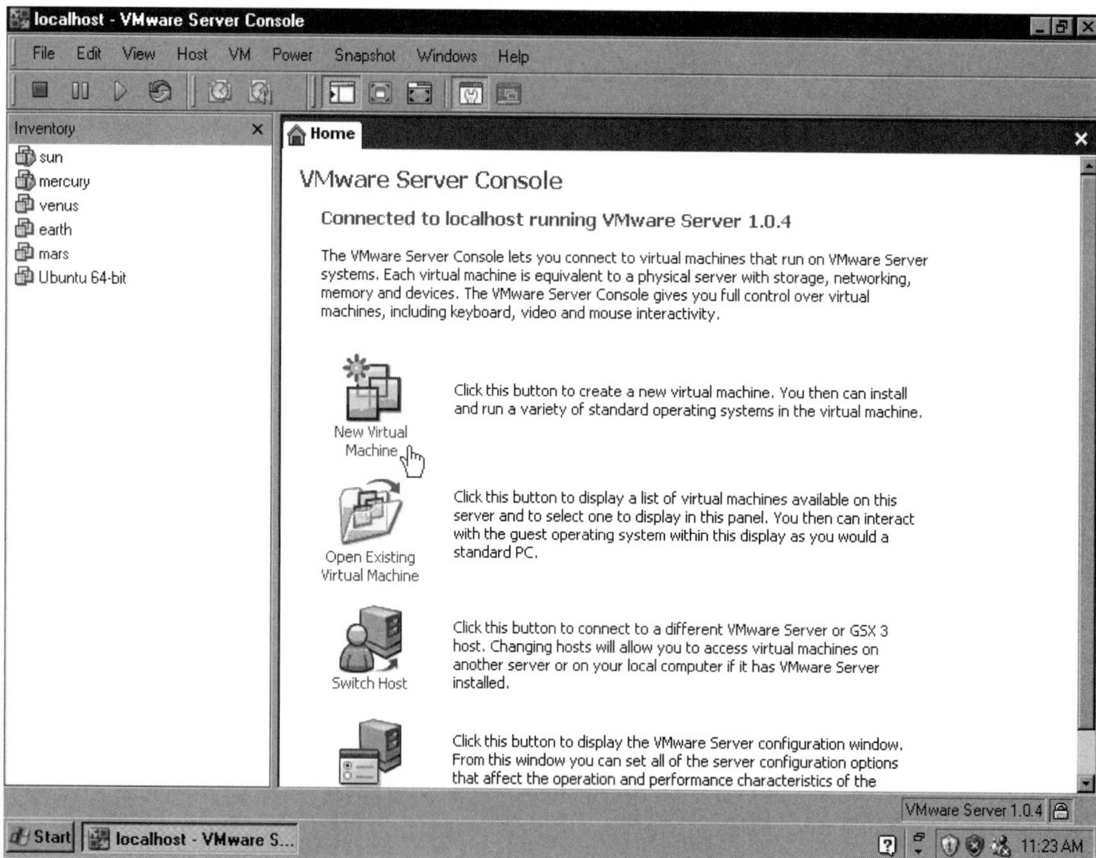

Click **New Virtual Machine** to launch the *New Virtual Machine* Wizard. You can also click the **File** | **New** menu or press **CTRL** + **N**. Figure D.2 shows the first page of the *New Virtual Machine Wizard.*

Figure D.2 New Virtual Machine Wizard

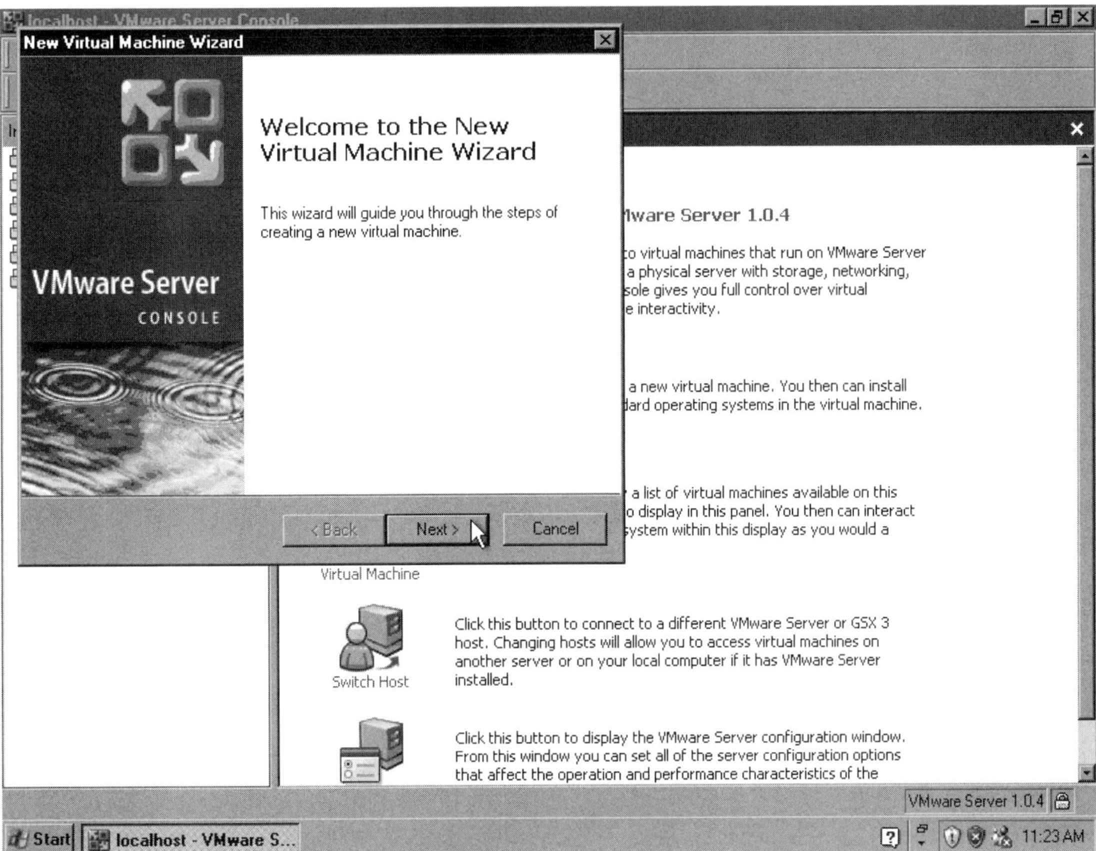

Click **Next** to proceed to the *Select the Appropriate Configuration* section, as shown in Figure D.3.

The *Select the Appropriate Configuration* section prompts you to select a virtual machine configuration. Select **Typical** to ensure the virtual machine is compatible with both VMware Server and VMware. Click **Next** to proceed to the *Select a Guest Operating System* section, as shown in Figure D.4.

Figure D.3 Virtual Machine Configuration

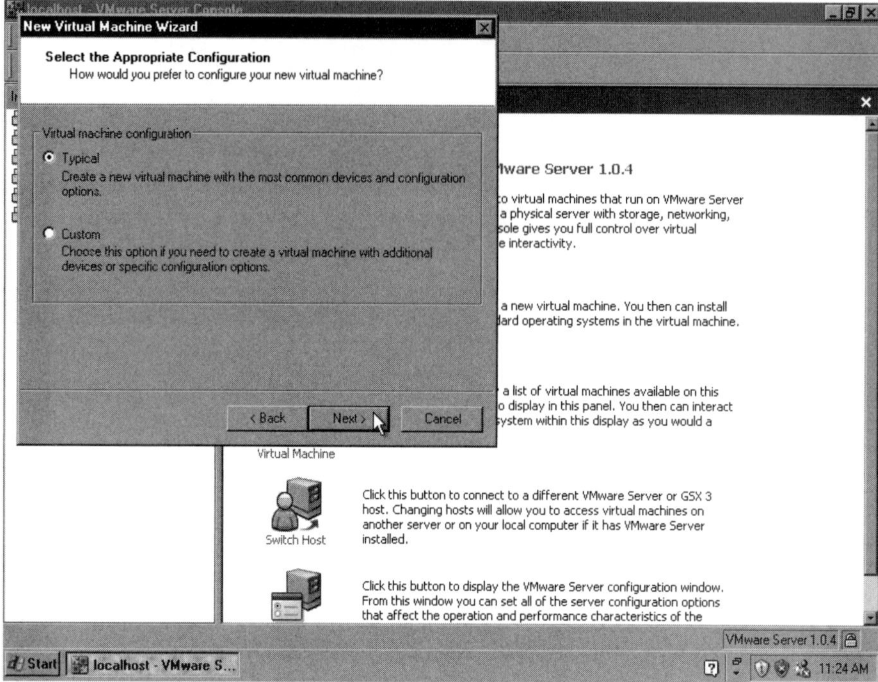

Figure D.4 Select a Guest Operating System

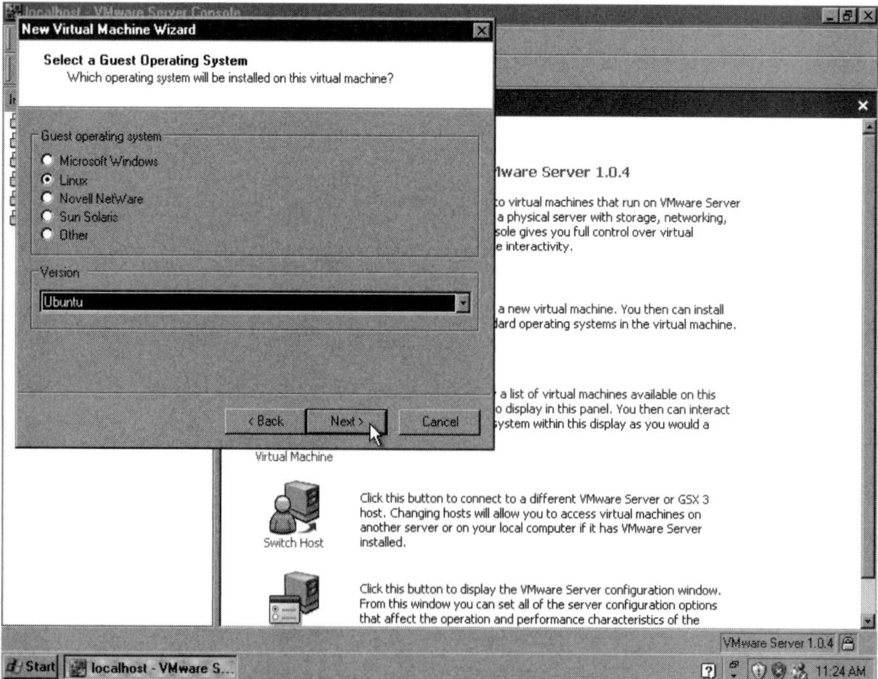

The *Select a Guest Operating System* section allows you to choose the operating system that will be installed on this VMware Guest. Select **Linux** and then select **Ubuntu** from the Version drop-down. Click **Next** to proceed to the *Network Type* section, as shown in Figure D.5.

Figure D.5 Network Type

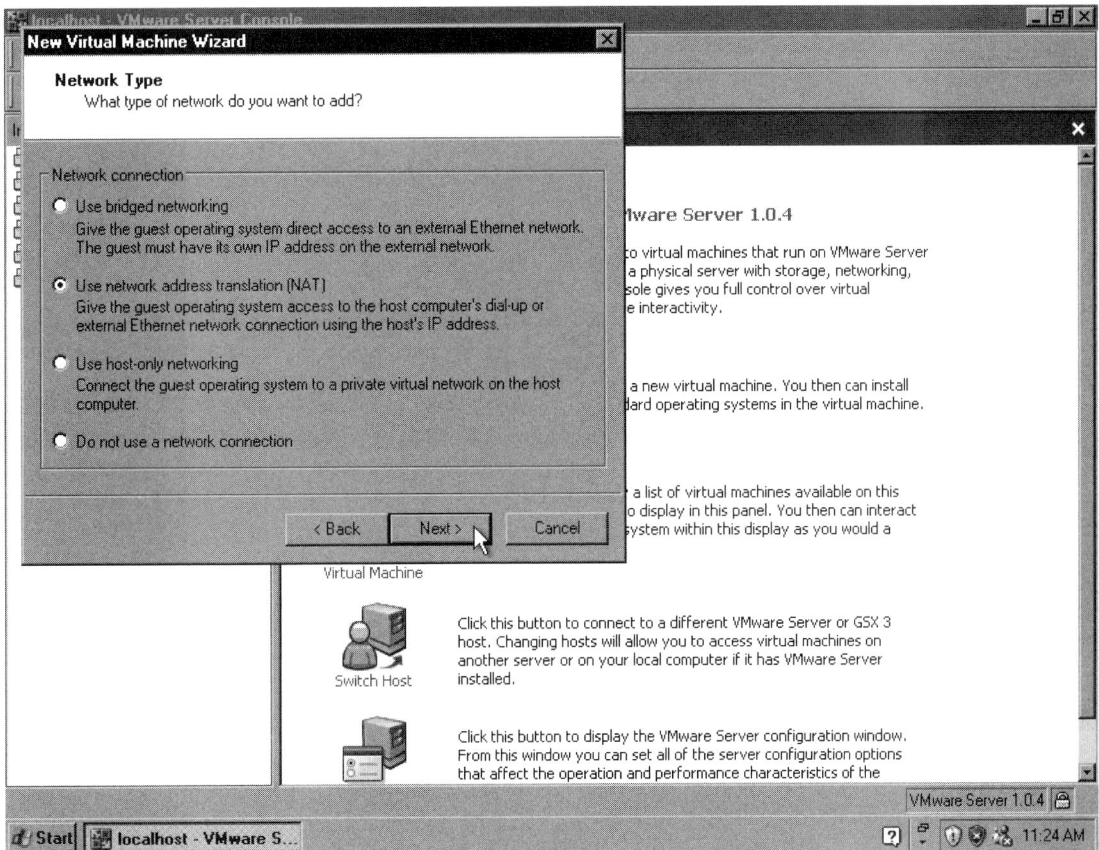

The *Network Type* section allows you to configure how your VMware Guests NIC interacts with your VMware Host. You can configure your OSSEC HIDS VMware Guest using any of the available options. Following the provided DVD image configuration, select **Use network address translation (NAT)** so that your OSSEC HIDS VMware guest can access the network by hiding behind the physical network card of your VMware host.

Click **Next** to proceed to the *Name the Virtual Machine* section, as shown in Figure D.6.

Figure D.6 Name the Virtual Machine

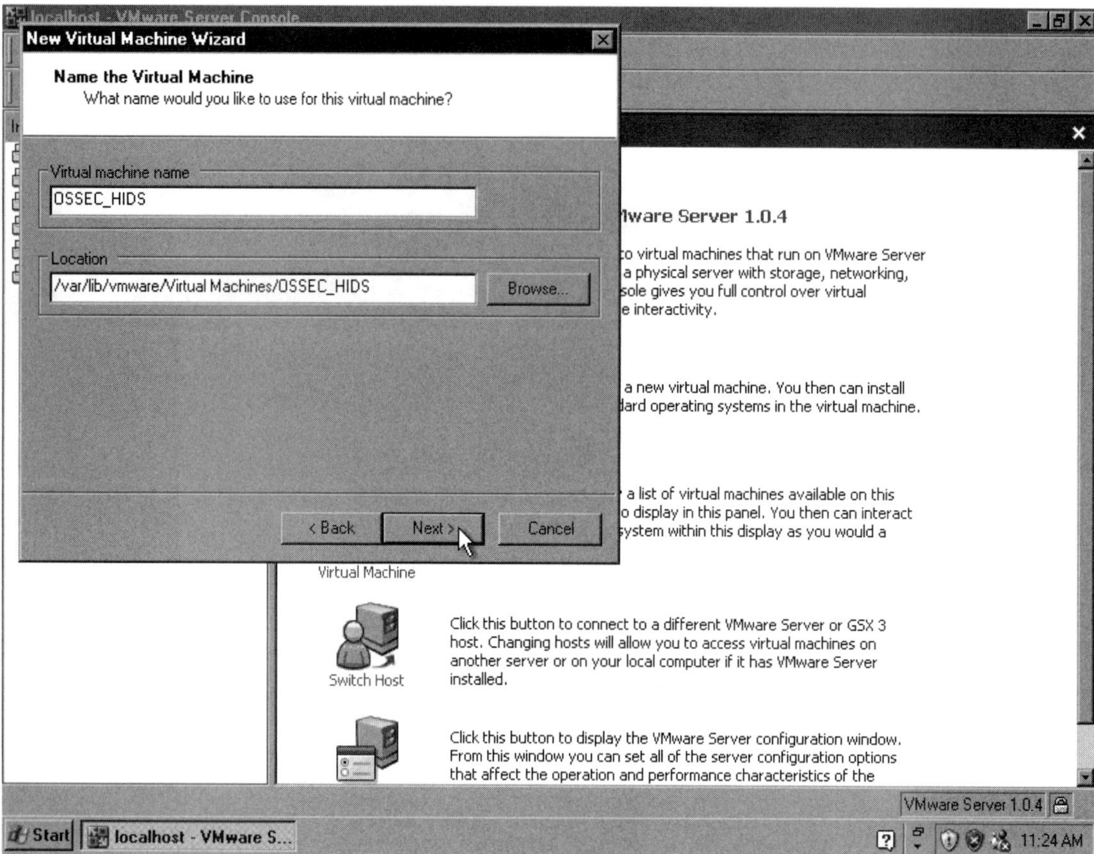

The *Name the Virtual Machine* section allows you to name your VMware Guest machine and specify a location to create the VMware Guest image. Type **OSSEC_HIDS** in the Virtual machine name field. For the Location, specify the same VMware Virtual Machine directory you specified when you installed VMware server. In our case, this is the **/var/lib/vmware/Virtual Machines/OSSEC_HIDS** directory.

Click **Next** to proceed to the *Specify Disk Capacity* section, as shown in Figure D.7.

Figure D.7 Specify Disk Capacity

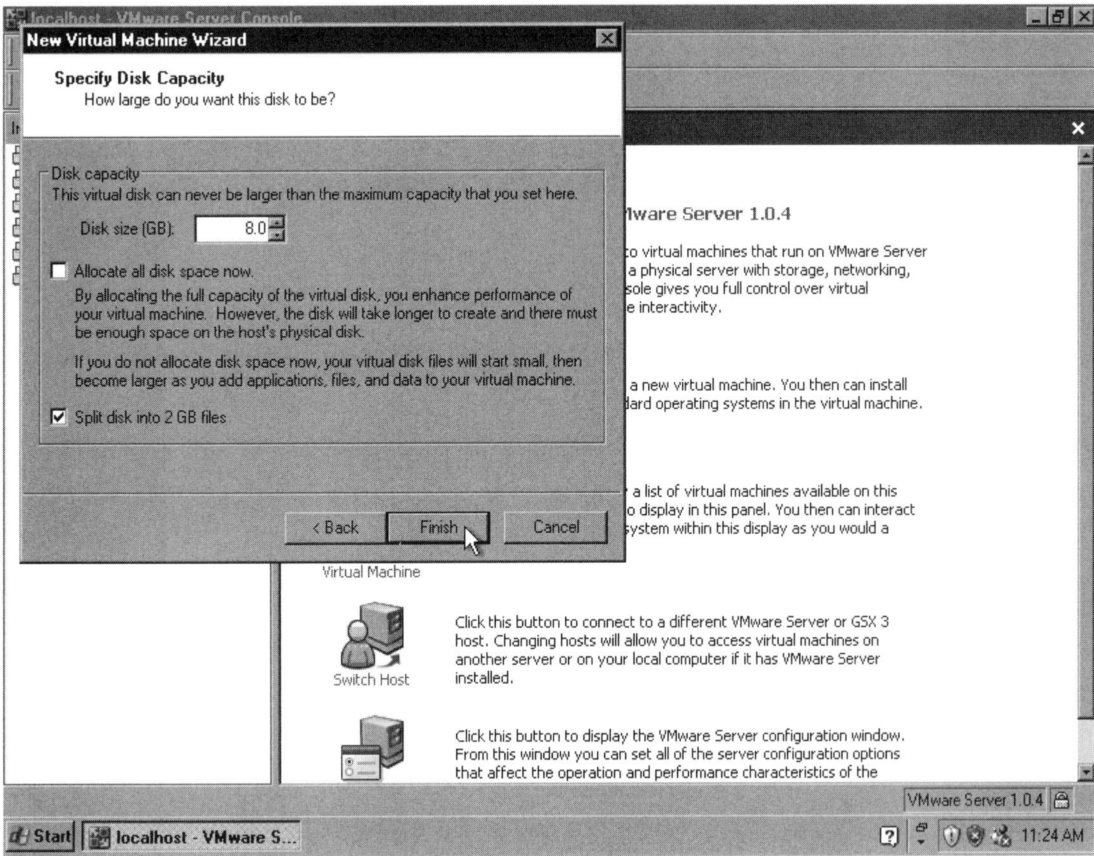

The *Specify Disk Capacity* section allows you to specify the maximum capacity of the VMware Guest. Ubuntu server does not require a lot of space to install (about 700 MB). The default 8.0 GB disk size is sufficient, but deselect **Allocate all disk space now** so unnecessary space is not consumed. As the Ubuntu server requires more space, it will grow up to a maximum of 8.0 GB. Click **Finish** to complete your VMware Guest configuration.

The newly created VMware Guest image is shown in the VMware inventory. The VMware Guest remains powered off and can now be used to install the Ubuntu operating system. Figure D.8 shows the completed VMware Guest installation.

Figure D.8 Completed VMware Guest Configuration

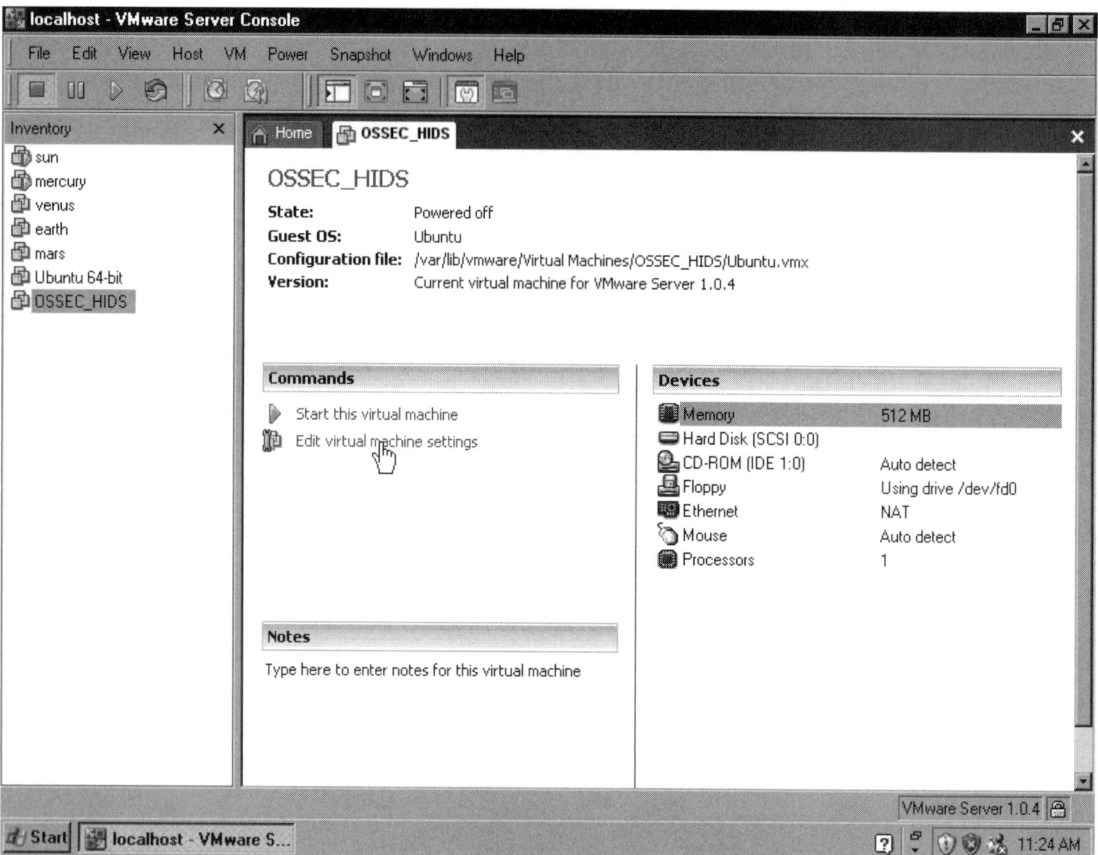

We are now ready to install the Ubuntu operating system on our newly created VMware Guest image. The first step is to select the location of our installation media by clicking **Edit virtual machine settings**. Click the CD-ROM device in the Devices list, as shown in Figure D.9.

Figure D.9 Virtual Machine Settings

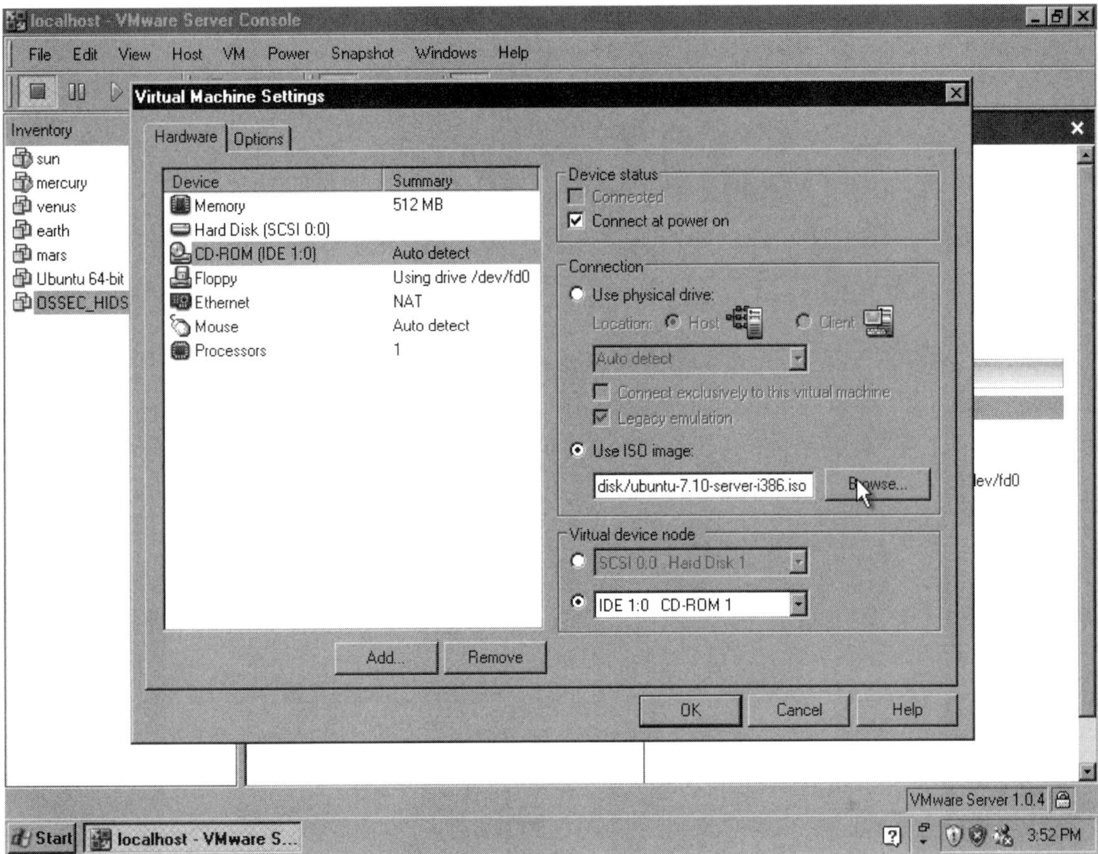

Instead of using the CD-ROM drive from the system running your VMware server, we want to use the downloaded ISO. On the right pane of the settings window, verify that **Connect at power on** is selected so the VMware Guest will start properly. Select **Use ISO image** under Connection. Click **Browse** and locate your downloaded Ubuntu ISO image. Once selected, the full path to the ISO image is displayed within the text box as shown in Figure D.9.

The virtual machine is ready for operating system installation. Click **OK** to close the *Virtual Machine Settings* for your VMware Guest. Now, all you must do is start the virtual machine using *Start this virtual machine*.

Configuring the Base Operating System

The Ubuntu server installation uses simple, text-based screens to guide you through the installation. Figure D.10 shows the installation procedure for the VMware image.

Figure D.10 Boot Selection

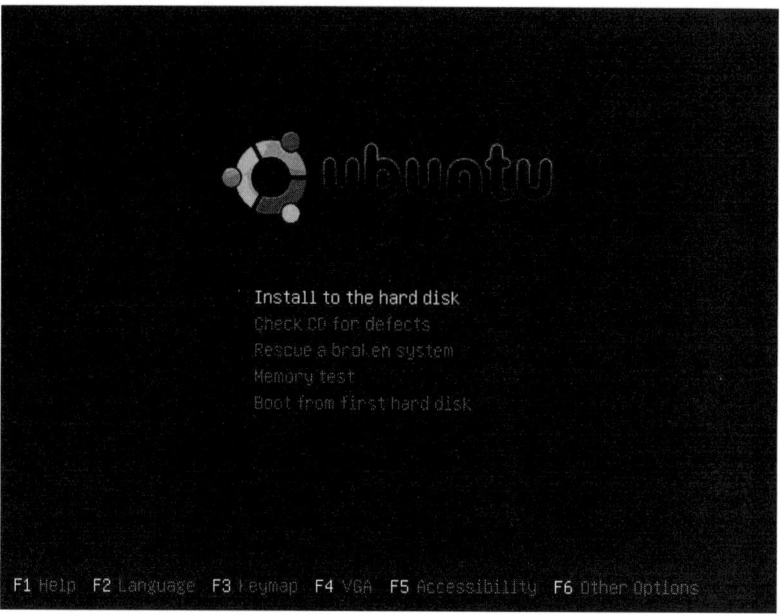

When the system boots from the DVD, choose **Install to the hard disk** and press **Enter**. This brings you to the *Choose language* section, as shown in Figure D.11.

Figure D.11 Choose a Language

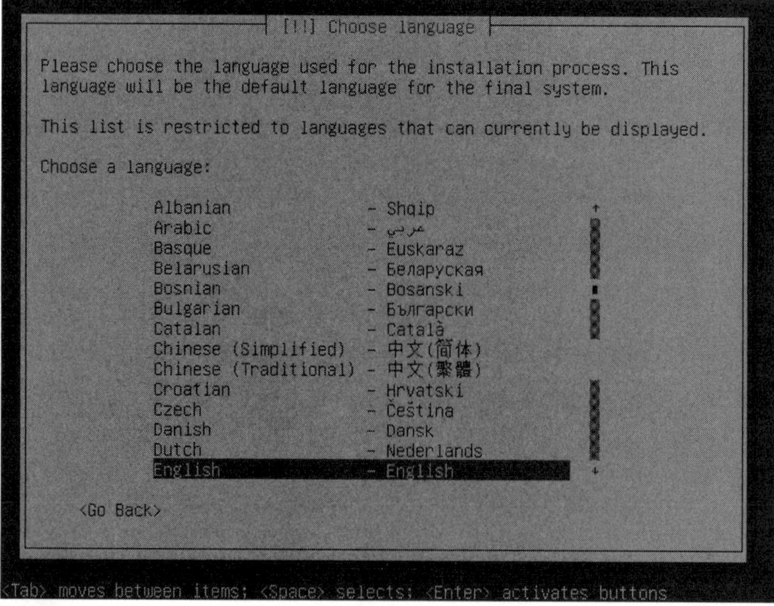

Choose whichever language suits your environment and press **Enter**. This brings you to the *Choose a country, territory or area:* section of the *Choose language* screen, as shown in Figure D.12.

Figure D.12 Choose a Country, Territory or Area

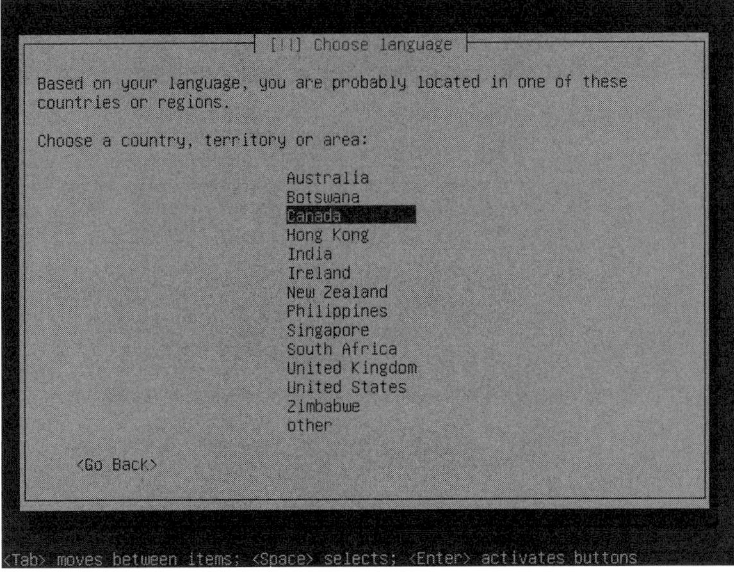

Choose your country and press **Enter**. This brings you to the *Detect keyboard layout* section, as shown in Figure D.13.

Figure D.13 Detect Keyboard Layout

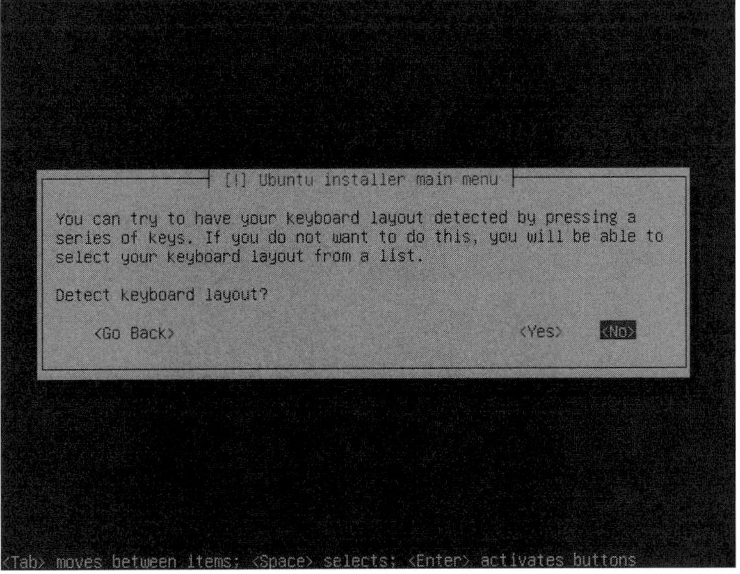

If you are using a standard U.S. keyboard, skip the detection by selecting **No**. Press **Enter** to proceed to the keyboard origin, as shown in Figure D.14.

Figure D.14 Keyboard Origin

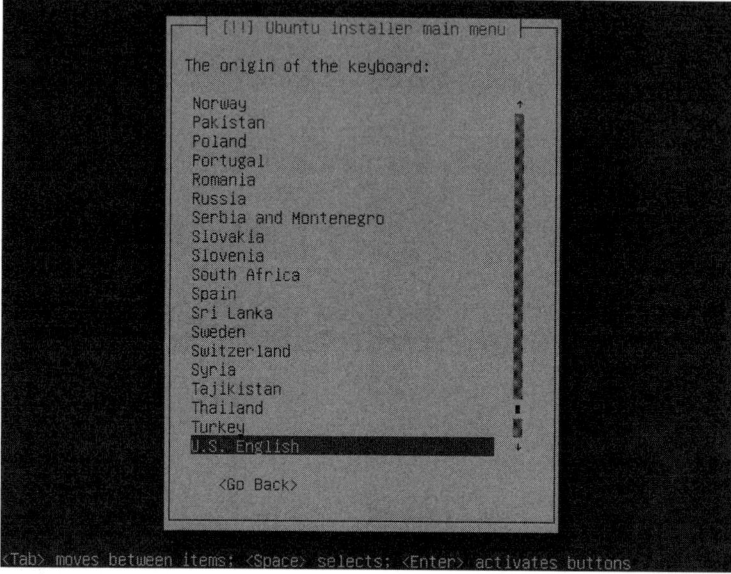

Select the origin of your keyboard and press **Enter** to proceed to the *Keyboard layout* selection, as shown in Figure D.15.

Figure D.15 Keyboard Layout

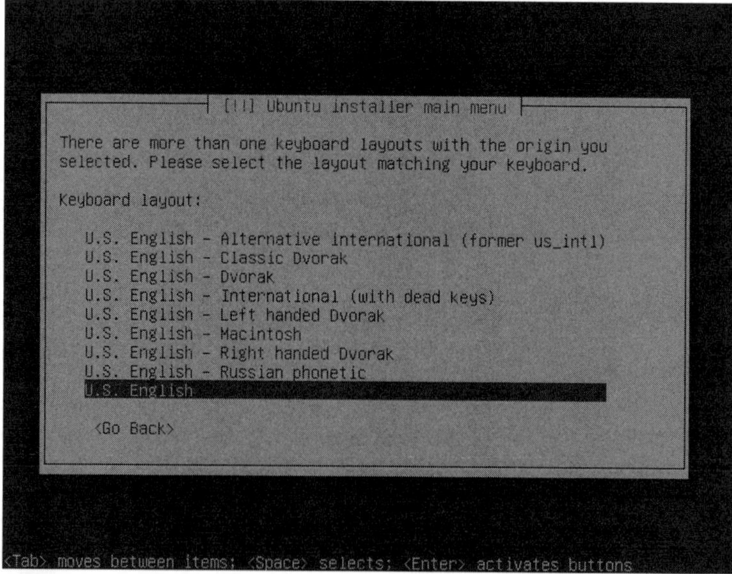

Chose your keyboard layout and press **Enter** to proceed to the *Configure network* portion of the installation, as shown in Figure D.16.

Figure D.16 Hostname

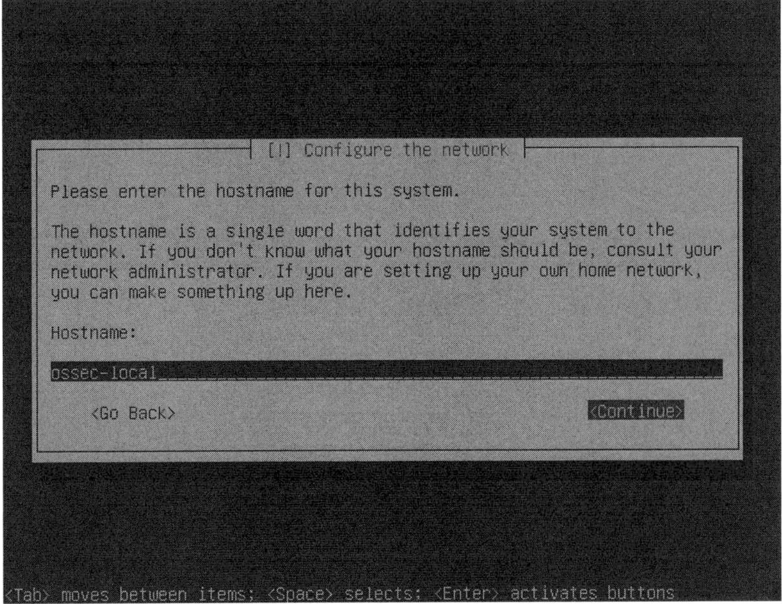

Select a host name appropriate for the intended use of this virtual machine. Select **Continue** and press **Enter** to proceed to the *Partition disks* screen, as shown in Figure D.17.

Figure D.17 Partitioning

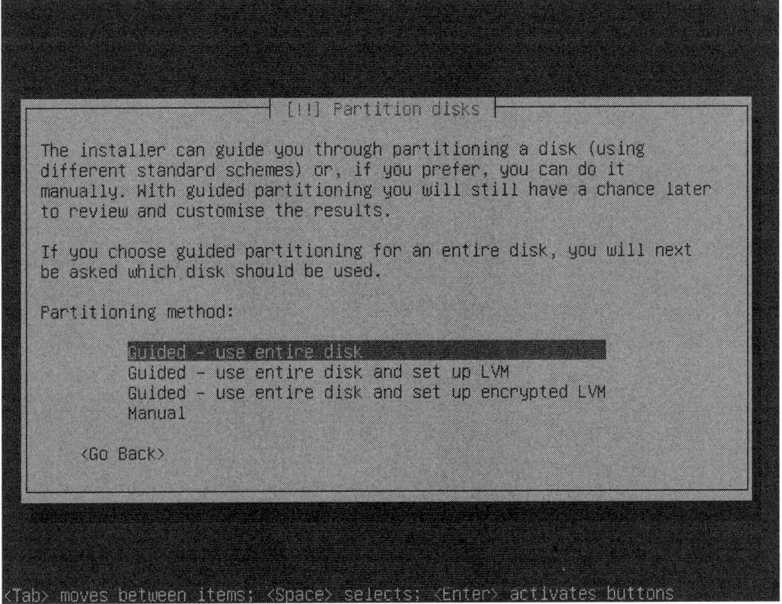

The **Guided - use entire disk** option is sufficient for the disk partitioning requirements of the OSSEC HIDS VMware Guest. If you want to create specific partition sizes, select the **Manual** option. Press **Enter** to select your installation disk, as shown in Figure D.18.

Figure D.18 Selecting a Disk

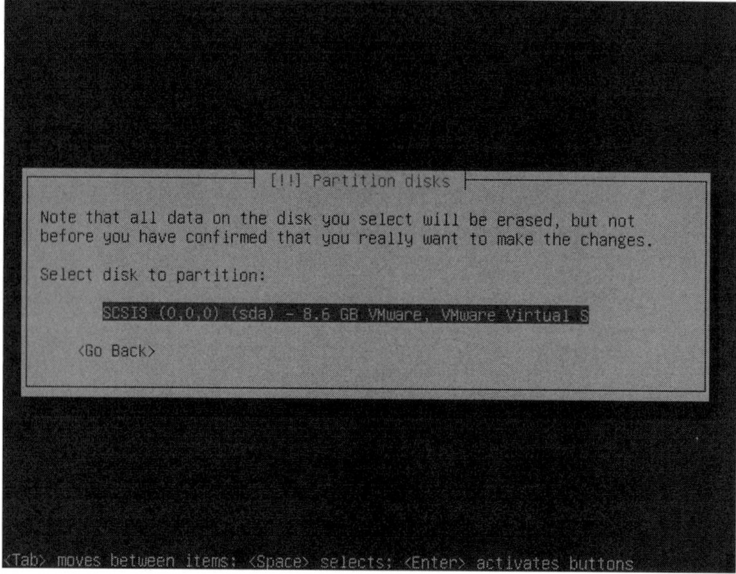

Select the disk you want to format and press **Enter**. A summary screen shows you how the Ubuntu installer plans to configure your disk partitions, as shown in Figure D.19.

Figure D.19 Writing Partition Changes

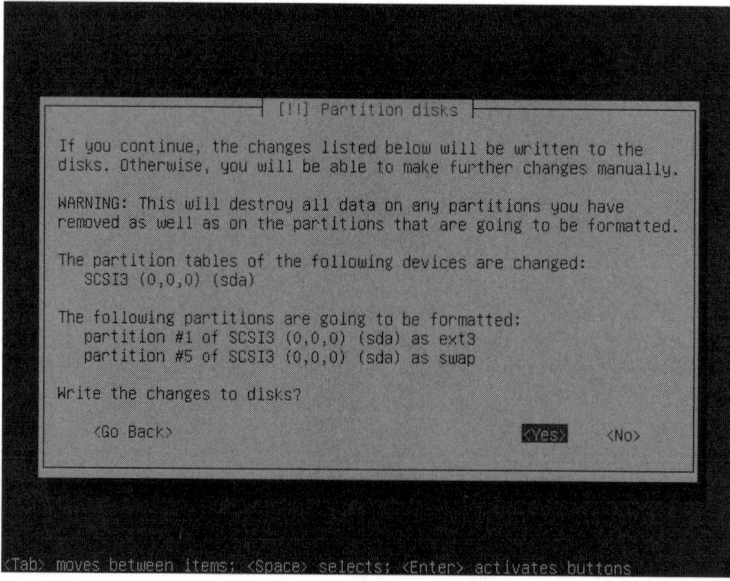

The list of partitions to be created appears. If no further customization is required, select **Yes** and press **Enter**. This brings you to the time zone screen, as shown in Figure D.20.

Figure D.20 Selecting a Time Zone

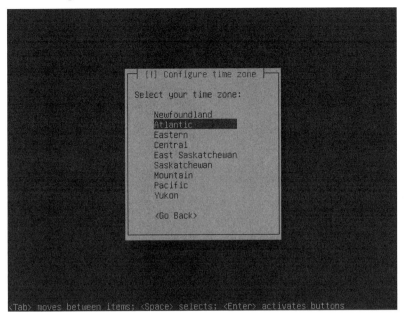

Select your time zone location and press **Enter**. This brings you to the UTC option screen, as shown in Figure D.21.

Figure D.21 System Clock

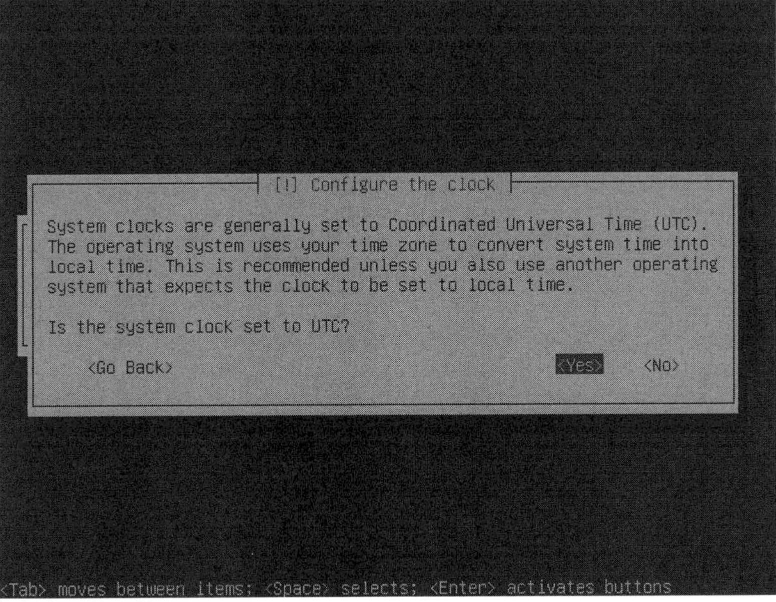

If you are running VMware under Windows, you should select **No**. If you are unsure whether you should set the clock to UTC, select**Yes** and press**Enter**. This brings you to the *Set up users and passwords* screen, as shown in Figure D.22.

Figure D.22 New User

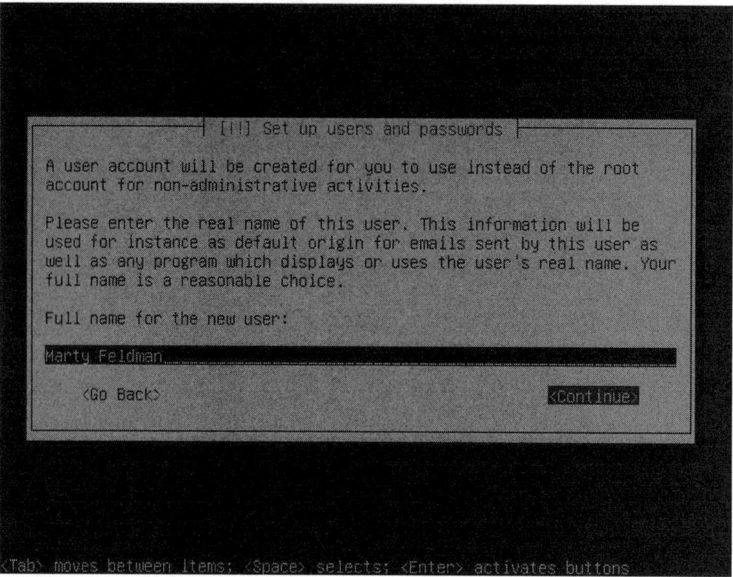

From the VMware image included with the book, we can use Marty Feldman as the primary user. If you are creating your own image, you will probably want to choose another name. Select **Continue** and press **Enter** to define a username for your account, as shown in Figure D.23.

Figure D.23 Username

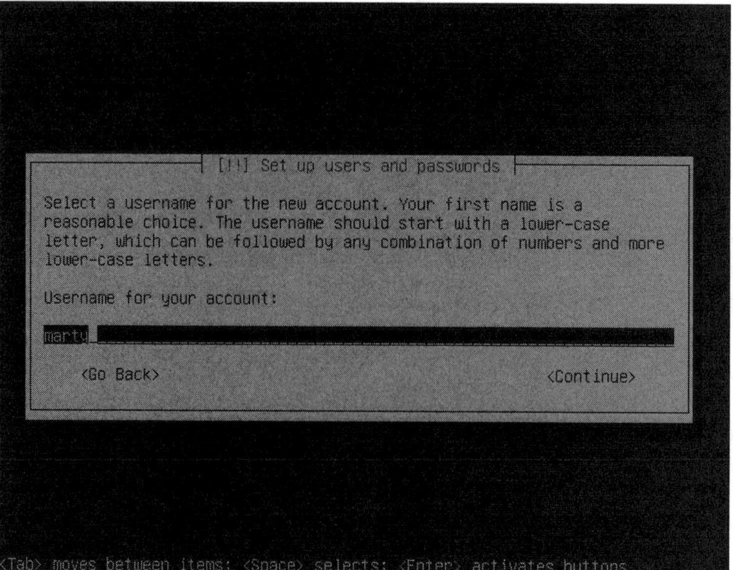

Type your user name and select **Continue**. Press **Enter** and you are prompted to specify a password for the newly created user, as shown in Figure D.24.

Figure D.24 Password

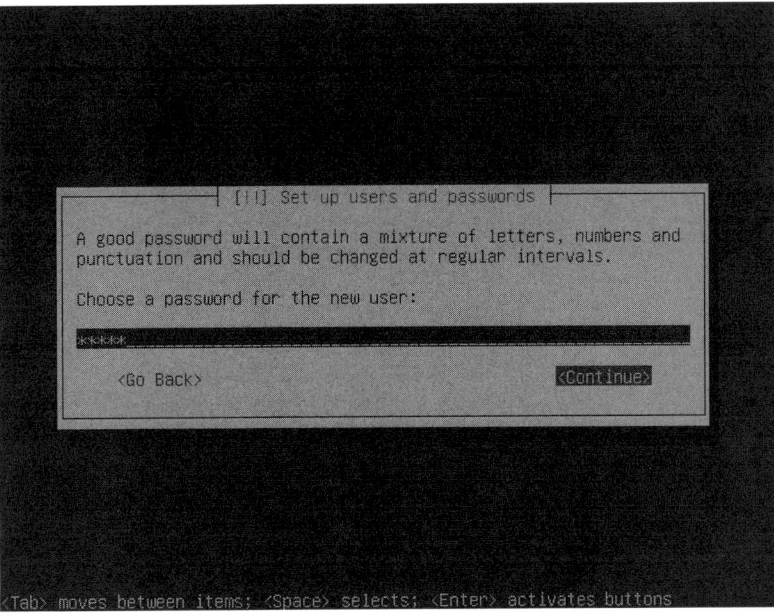

Specify the password and select **Continue**. Press **Enter** and you are prompted to validate the password by re-entering it, as shown in Figure D.25.

Figure D.25 Confirm Password

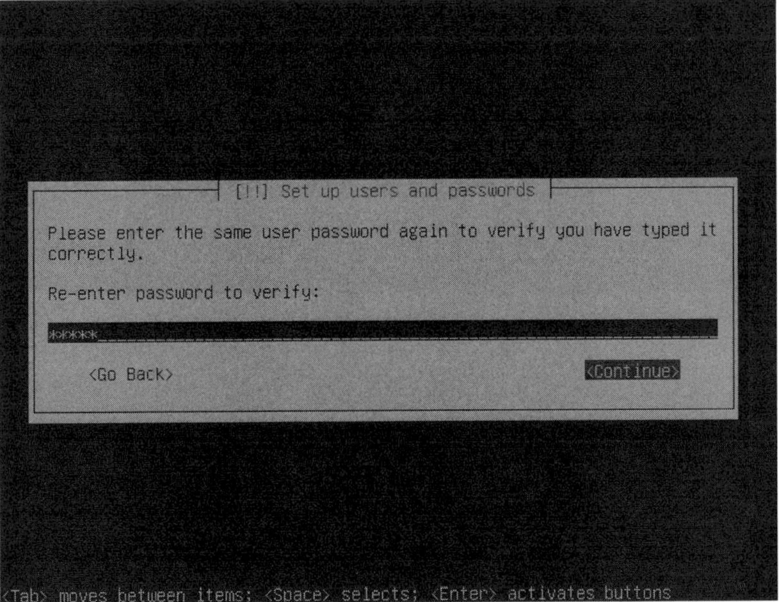

After you verify your password, select **Continue**. Press **Enter** to begin the installation, as shown in Figure D.26.

Figure D.26 Base Installation

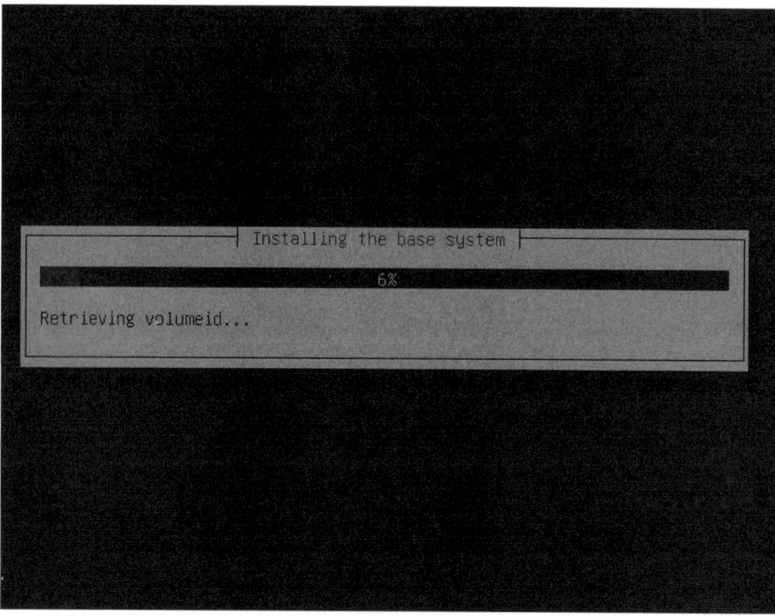

The installer now has all the information required to install the base system. This takes a few minutes to process, after which there is additional customization, as shown in Figure D.27.

Figure D.27 Software Selection

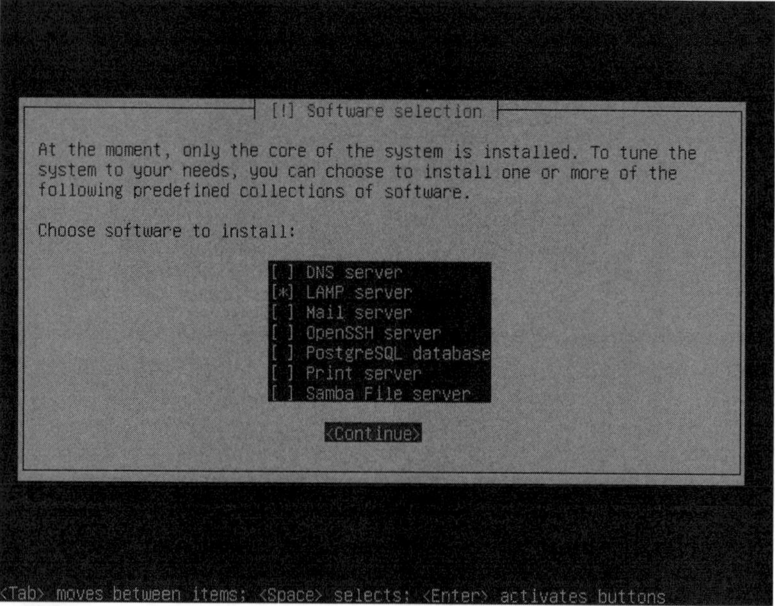

The software selection screen allows you to select the major services the Ubuntu server might provide. Because we are interested in setting up the WUI for the OSSEC HIDS, selecting **LAMP server** now is a good idea. *LAMP* is short for Linux, Apache, MySQL, and PHP. The OSSEC HIDS WUI requires Apache and PHP to operate properly. Select **Continue** and press **Enter** to proceed to the MySQL root user password screen, as shown in Figure D.28.

Figure D.28 MySQL Root Password

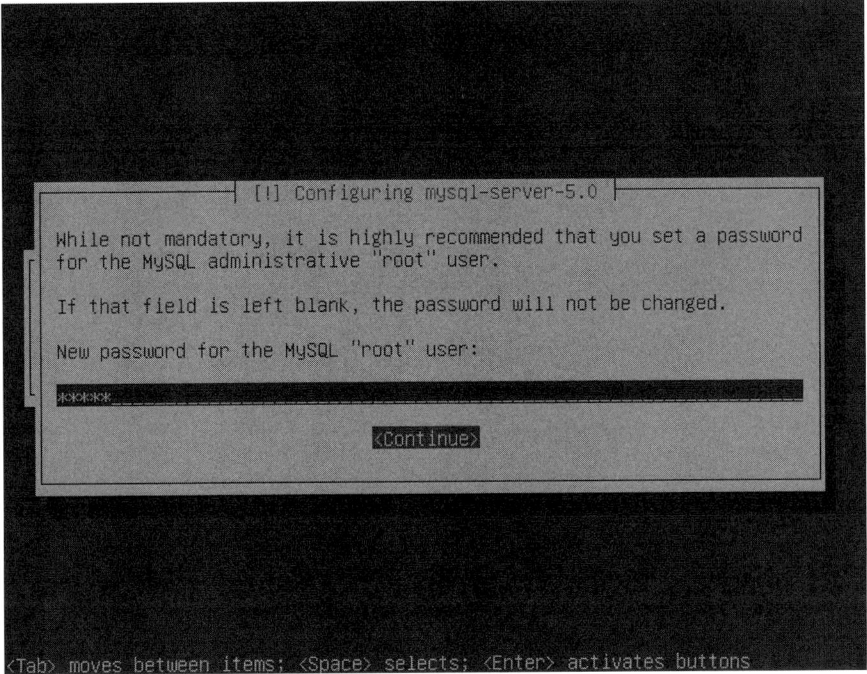

You are prompted to specify a MySQL password for the root user. The OSSEC HIDS VMware Guest used the *ossec* password as the MySQL root user, but you may use any password you like. Select **Continue** and press **Enter** to proceed to the *Finish the installation* screen, as shown in Figure D.29.

Figure D.29 Installation Complete

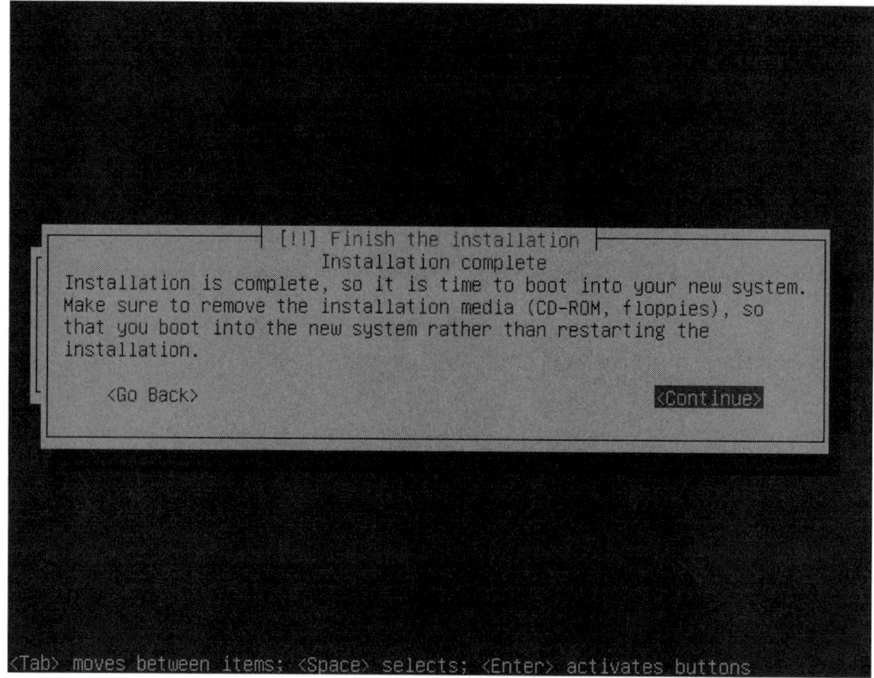

Select **Continue** and press **Enter** to finish the installation. Your newly created Ubuntu VMware Guest reboots when finished and allows you to log in to continue the OSSEC HIDS installation.

Installing the OSSEC HIDS

Installing the OSSEC HIDS in the VMware image is as simple as following the instructions in this book for a *local* installation. Let's quickly go through the installation with some points specific to installation on Ubuntu server. Log in to the virtual machine as *marty* (or the username you specified during Ubuntu installation). Use the *sudo* command to switch to the *root* user. Use the same password you use for your regular user account.

```
# sudo -i
```

To build and install the OSSEC HIDS local installation and the WUI, you have to add some more packages. Install the build tools and the OpenSSL libraries and utilities using the command:

```
# apt-get install build-essential openssl
```

Next, download and extract the OSSEC HIDS source and then run the installer. Choose the *local* installation type and accept all defaults. Use your login name for the email address using *localhost* as the domain (for example, *marty@localhost*). When prompted to specify an SMTP server, use the default *127.0.0.1* value and press **Enter**.

```
# wget http://www.ossec.net/files/ossec-hids-1.4.tar.gz
# tar -xzvf ossec-hids-1.4.tar.gz
# cd ossec-hids-1.4
# ./install.sh
```

After the installation is complete, use the following command to start the OSSEC HIDS service so it is ready for use:

```
# /var/ossec/bin/ossec-control start
```

Installing the OSSEC HIDS WUI

The WUI can be downloaded from www.ossec.net. Unlike the main OSSEC HIDS package, there is no building or compiling involved for the WUI. The WUI files must be copied to your Web server directory, and your Apache HTTP server requires some minor modifications.

Begin by downloading, extracting, and then copying the WUI software to the documents directory on the Web server:

```
# wget http://www.ossec.net/files/ui/ossec-wui-0.3.tar.gz
# tar -xzvf ossec-wui-0.3.tar.gz
# mv ossec-wui/ /var/www/
# cd /var/www/ossec-wui
```

The WUI requires its own authentication mechanisms to prevent unauthorized access. To do this, we use the Apache HTTP server authentication capabilities. The WUI comes with a utility, *setup.sh*, to simplify some of the configuration steps. Execute the setup.sh file and then provide a username and password. The password does not appear when typed:

```
# ./setup.sh
Setting up ossec ui…
Username: marty
New Password:
Re-type new password:
```

Now that the WUI files are all in place and authentication files are created, we must configure the Apache HTTP server to use those files. Edit the /etc/apache2/sites-available/default file and add the following text near the end of the file, just before the closing *</VirtualHost>* tag:

```
<Directory "/var/www/ossec-wui">
  AllowOverride AuthConfig Limit
  Order allow,deny
  Allow from all
</Directory>
```

Because the WUI now runs with the same user credentials as the Apache HTTP server, you must make sure the Apache HTTP server can read the OSSEC HIDS files. Add the Apache HTTP server user, known as *www-data* on Ubuntu, to the *ossec* group using the command:

```
# usermod -G ossec www-data
```

Finally, activate all your changes by restarting the Apache HTTP server using the command:

```
# /etc/init.d/apache2 restart
```

Conclusion

Using the provided OSSEC HIDS VMware Guest image, or your own recently created VMware image, you can learn the installation process without having to find a server on which to install the OSSEC HIDS. You can create decoders, rules, and active responses, tune your OSSEC or WUI settings, add additional WUI users, and so on, in a controlled environment. Perhaps you would like to use it to show a colleague, your superior, or your students just how powerful the OSSEC HIDS is. We leave this entirely up to you.

Index

P

R

S

T

U

V

W

X